Advancing Into Temp, Contract, And Consulting Jobs

Advancing Into Temp, Contract, And Consulting Jobs

A complete guide to starting and promoting your own consulting business

Jimmy Moore

Writers Club Press
San Jose New York Lincoln Shanghai

Advancing Into Temp, Contract, And Consulting Jobs
A complete guide to starting and promoting your own consulting business

All Rights Reserved © 2001 by James Moore

Writers Club Press
an imprint of iUniverse.com, Inc.

For information address:
iUniverse.com, Inc.
5220 S 16th, Ste. 200
Lincoln, NE 68512
www.iuniverse.com

ISBN: 0-595-13005-4

Printed in the United States of America

Warning—Disclaimer

The author and publisher claim that the information contained herein is based on currently accepted practices and was discerned through research and personal experience. No claim is made that these techniques will work for any reader. How this information is used is up to the individual.

This book was written for the purpose of providing information in regard to the subject matter covered. It is sold with the understanding that the author and the publisher are not engaged in the rendering of legal, accounting, tax planning, career, salary, business management, or other professional services. The reader must consult professionals in each field before applying the principles in this book.

The purpose of this book is to educate the reader on possible career and lifestyle improvements, particularly in the way they make their living. The author or the publisher cannot be held responsible or liable, to any person or entity, that has suffered any loss or damage, caused or alleged to be caused, directly or indirectly, by the information contained in this book.

This book is dedicated to all employees who are not being appreciated or who are stuck in a dead-end job, day in and day out. May this book lift up your spirit and get you out of that terrible situation. May it bring to you and your family, peace of mind, variety, and the just rewards that you deserve for all of your hard work.

"Knowledge is power."

Sir Francis Bacon, Religious Meditations, Of Heresies, 1597

Contents

Chapter 1: Ways Of Being Employed 1
  Types Of Employment—The IRS Point Of View 1
  Types Of Employment—Industry's Point Of View 5
  Agencies That Hire On A 1099 7
  Type Of Employment For The Consultant 8
  The Temp, Contractor, And Consultant Name Confusion 9
  Advantage Of 1099 Employment 10
  Summary Of Chapter 1: 10

Chapter 2: Getting Started In Consulting 12
  Here is a list of possible ways to get started: 12
  Summary Of Chapter 2: 16

Chapter 3: Temporary Employment 101 17
  What Job Agencies Do 17
  What Job Agencies Charge 18
  Why Clients Pay Agency Fees 19
  Converting Yearly Pay To Hourly Pay 21
  Overhead And Burdened Labor Rates 21
  What Is A Temp Worth? 22
  Clients Expect Temps To Charge More 23
  How Much Do Temps Charge? 24
  What Does The Temp Actually Cost? 24
  A Win-Win-Win Situation 24

Required Experience For Temping 25
Maintaining Your Worth As A Temp 25
How Could A Temp's Worth Decrease? 28
Advantages For The Temping Employee 29
Perceived Disadvantages To Temping 31
Another Perceived Disadvantage To Temping 33
One Real Disadvantage of Temping 34
Secret To Becoming A Consultant Through Temping 34
Trends In Temping 35
Summary Of Temping 37
Summary Of Pay Increase Due To Temping, After Taxes: 38
Summary Of Chapter 3: 38

Chapter 4: The Consulting Personality 39
Winning Personalities 39
Winner Concepts In Simple Terms: 41
The Story Of The Freelance Knight 41
The Freelance Personality 45
Personality Traits Of An Advanced Consultant 46
Requirements For The Beginning Consultant 47
Summary Of Chapter 4: 48

Chapter 5: Skills Needed By The Consultant 49
Why Consultants Are Needed 50
Timely Opportunities 55
Needs Of The Client 56
Skills Required By The Client 57
What Skills Do You Really Have? 58
Skills Used By Consultants 59
Skills Needed By The Beginning Consultant 63
The Market For The Consultant's Skills 64
Nurturing Good References 65
Summary Of Chapter 5 67

Chapter 6: Look, Before You Leap... 69
Warning About Quitting Your Present Job 69

Starting Your Own Company 70
Setting Up Your Office For Temping 74
Start Up Your Database Of Job Agencies 85
Temporary And Contracting Jobs On The Internet 88
More Resources On The Internet 89
Completely Scouring The Internet 90
Setting Up Your Office For Contracting And Consulting 91
Premeditated Preparedness 97

Chapter 7: Your Portfolio On Paper 99
Writing A Resume For Consulting 99
The Skill Bullet Resume 108
The Personal Reference Sheet 116
Prepare Your Business Card 121
Preparing a Blurb Sheet 123
The Client Reference Sheet 125
Summary Of Chapter 7 127

Chapter 8: What's It Worth To Ya? 128
How Much Do We Need To Break Even? 129
How Much Can You Get? 139
Rules Of Thumb For Pay 144
Calculating Your Extra Profit 145
Budget Planning For Non-Captive Work 146
Consultants May Be Starving 150
!Downtime Warning! 150
The Dream Rate 151
Personalize The Math 156
Summary Of Chapter 8 157

Chapter 9: Basic "Negotiating" Principles 158
General Negotiation Principles 158
The Four Rules Of Negotiating Pay 160
Keeping A Proper Frame Of Mind During Negotiation 166
Summary Of Chapter 9: 168

Chapter 10: Negotiating For Temp Jobs 169
  Never Fill Out An Application 169
  Never Discuss Rates With The Client 170
  Never Get Submitted By Multiple Agencies 171
  Always Have Your Squeeze Factors Ready 171
  Summary Of Chapter 10 172

Chapter 11: Picture Perfect Interviews 173
  The Main Interviewing Principle 173
  Interview Sequence 174
  Purpose Of The Interview 175
  Keep Quiet On The Interview 176
  Presenting Your Skills 176
  Putting The Samples Together 179
  Preparing For Different Types Of Questions 180
  Summary Of Presenting Skills 187
  Appearing Normal On An Interview 187
  Interviewing The Company 191
  Summary Of Chapter 11 192

Chapter 12: Adrift On A New Job 193
  The Law Of Perpetual Consulting: 193
  The First Few Days Are Really Confusing 194
  The First Few Weeks Are Critical 195
  One New Beginning 197
  Summary Of Chapter 12 199

Chapter 13: Beginning By Temping 200

Chapter 14: Contracting: Running Your Own Company 203
  Moving Into Contracting 203
  Contractor's Additional Tax Deductions 204
  Contractor's Additional Taxes 206
  Is Contracting Worth It? 206
  Advantages To Contracting 207
  Incorporating 207

Requirements For Contracting 208
Begin Contracting 209
Summary Of Chapter 14 209

Chapter 15: Advancing Into Consulting 211
The Problems Of Consulting 211

Chapter 16: Financial Principles Of Consulting 213
Financial Principle #1: 213
Financial Principle #2: 214
Financial Principle #3: 216
Financial Principle #4: 218
Financial Principle #5: 219
Summary Of Chapter 16 220

Chapter 17: Billing Methods For Consulting 222
Fixed-Price Bidding 222
Charging By The Hour 224
Using Up-Front Retainer Fees 226
Mixing And Matching Billing Methods 227
Summary Of Chapter 17 228

Chapter 18: Negotiating As A Consultant 229
Consulting Differences 229
Interviewing As A Consultant 230
Presenting Your Hourly Pay Rate 230
Get Your Rate In Writing 233
Get It Witnessed 235
Getting Raises 236
Summary Of Chapter 18 237

Chapter 19: Recognizing Dead-Beat Clients 238
Does The Client Have Enough Money? 238
Indicators Of Dead-Beat Clients: 242
Some Poor Clients Mean Well 243
Going To Court 244
Summary Of Chapter 19 246

Chapter 20: Safeguards For Consulting Prosperity 247

Chapter 21: Getting Consulting Work 250
  Ways Of Getting Consulting Work 250
  Getting Referrals From Industry Friends 251
  Finding Jobs On Your Own 257
  Helping Others Find You 263
  All Of The Above 272
  Continuously Keep Networking 274
  Keep Your "Toolbox" Up To Date 274
  Many Other Ways 275
  Summary Of Chapter 21 276

Appendix A: Recommended Reading 279

Appendix B: General Self-Advancement 281
  Creative Problem Solving 281
  Effective Time Management 282
  Variety Time Management 282
  Speed Learning 282
  Stay Well Rounded 283
  Start Writing About Something 283
  Practice Predicting The Future 284
  Make Better Decisions 284
  Balancing The Mind, Body, And Soul 285
  Tribal Connections 291
  Being Happy 291
  What's left after Consulting? 292
  Final Thoughts 293

Preface

After being let down by job after job, I began a quest for job satisfaction back in the seventies. I was tired of companies laying me off, moving, selling themselves, or just treating me like a number. I kept on moving around, searching for a happy way to make a living. By accident, I started getting involved with job agencies. Soon I was making double the pay for doing the same work. I tolerated a lot more at the higher pay, but that wasn't enough. I kept searching for happiness but really didn't get much further. I stayed at the Temp level for quite sometime, gathering large amounts of experience and exposure to new situations. This new variety I was experiencing started making me happy. I became so excited about the variety and the higher pay that I needed to tell others about it. But, I didn't get a chance. By another twist of fate, I had turned myself into a very busy Consultant. After consulting for several more years, I still felt sorry for all of the people I had met that were miserable about their jobs. Finally, in 1993, I decided that writing this book would be my Noble Cause. This book would be my contribution to the happiness and well-being of others in the workplace.

By 1995 the first version was done, but it was highly disorganized. I realized that I had included, in a scattered-brained fashion, discussions about three different types of employment: Temping, Contracting, and Consulting. So, I spent another year reorganizing it into the sequence of events that I had actually followed.

The book at that time had many horror stories of situations and events that happened to me. Even my spreadsheet calculations sent me into shock for six months because they showed that I could not make a profit at the rate I was at. My friends said it was too scary to try non-captive jobs. So, I decided to rewrite it again and make it fail-safe so that readers would not have to suffer any of the bad situations that I had to endure. After analyzing, testing, and restructuring for two more years, the need for the horror stories vanished. So, I took them out. This made the book easy to follow and well-organized.

Meanwhile, during this whole time, the Internet and computing were changing the ways that I was getting work offered to me. The third time I rewrote the book with the Internet as the key ingredient. I had to reaffirm every aspect of my theories and procedures, but now using the Internet. It was a lot of work, and took a lot of perseverance, but I learned alot. By applying the Internet and using online banking all of the procedures became streamlined.

Finally, I wanted everyone to realize that this is actually a chrono-logical, gradual technique. So I rewrote it once more and put in the action items in step-by-step fashion. It is best read from cover to cover, without skipping around.

So, here it is, seven years in the making. It is safe, highly-tested, sequential, step-by-step, rooted in the Internet, and based on 20 years of know-how.

I am really happy that I got this chance to help other workers by sharing this knowledge with them. I have upheld my Noble Cause. I hope you enjoy it.

Acknowledgements

Special thanks to all of my co-workers and industry friends for sharing the trials and tribulations of their careers. Thanks for brainstorming new employment concepts with me. We sure had fun experimenting, didn't we?

I would especially like to thank my wife Cathi and daughter Amy for all of their encouragement and hard work in helping me get this book together and out there. Without their help, this book would still be an idea.

I would like to express my appreciation to my sisters Bonnie, Sue, and Patty and to my brother Michael for letting me practice my techniques on their careers, over and over. Thanks to you all.

My highest esteem goes out to my parents, Bill and Mary Moore, for raising us kids on a solid foundation of hard work, giving us the freedom to do what is right and good, and making sure we knew the difference.

Introduction

People are business-minded these days, looking for a way to become self-reliant and self-employed. They want a wider range of diversity in their job. Most are trying to harness the Internet. A few want to work out of their house. What would be the easiest way to develop this new lifestyle? How could someone become self-employed, and remain in demand, without having to master a whole bunch of new subjects? Simple: by becoming a Consultant for the industry they are in right now, of course!

The Conference Board, a business research group, surveyed several companies in 1997. Their study predicts that, by the year 2000, 35% of these companies will be using Temps and Independent Contractors to make up greater than 10% of their staff. Furthermore, according to the National Association of Temporary Staffing Services (NATSS), Temporary Job Placement has doubled, from 1993 to 1997! In 1998, 2% of the 136 million workers in the U.S. were Temps. That's 2.7 million Temps filling more than 2.5 million jobs daily. Thus, Temp, Contractor, and Consultant opportunities are growing at an astounding rate!

Consulting has really taken off thanks to the rapid growth in technology, information, the Internet, and the Stock Market. There is a major shortage of talent in rapidly growing, new occupations. Because of this, companies are becoming more flexible in recruiting the talent that they need. Rapid changes in tools, software, data delivery, databases, and the way that businesses buy and sell, is fueling an expanding need for Temps, Contractors, and Consultants.

Until now, launching a consulting career was a complete mystery, to the average person. Consulting full-time requires a huge network of industry friends. It requires a wide variety of experiences gained by working at many companies. Preparing for a consulting career can take a while!

Consulting is also a business. Even the smallest of businesses is not born in a day. Beginning and promoting such a business takes a plan of action. This plan must include a minimum risk in the beginning. The plan must have a built-in potential for growth and expansion.

Look up the word "consult" at a large, online bookstore like Amazon, at *www.amazon.com*. There are so many books on this subject! For years, I kept reading and reading them, looking for a way in. Nothing clicked. There was no logical, step-by-step, method for beginning a consulting career. Isn't there a way to keep working in the same field, get a big pay raise now, and then slowly build up a profitable consulting business?

Yes, there is such a way! **"Advancing Into Temp, Contract, And Consulting Jobs"** documents, at last, the easiest, no-risk, step-by-step, process for beginning and advancing into a consulting career. This technique harnesses the power found in a natural progression: moving from Temp to Contractor to Consultant. This natural progression eliminates all of the risks and fears normally found in these fields.

How can this be true? How can you start a new business, by yourself, and have no additional risk beyond getting a regular job? That's simple. The first few years, other people are paid to help you. Who pays them? Not you!

Starting out as a beginning consultant is quick and easy. Most people with a few years of experience are already qualified. The easiest and safest way to start is by becoming a Temporary Employee (Temp) for a

Job Agency. Job Agencies are companies that get paid to find you work. They send you to work at client companies. There you will meet more Temps, more employees, more vendors, more factory representatives, more salespeople, more marketing people, and more managers. So, you are meeting more industry contacts. You are exposed to a wider variety of projects and tools. Thus, you are gaining more experience at more companies. Meanwhile, at your leisure, you can begin setting up the consulting business.

Temp work has one more added benefit: they pay more! If I told you that it is possible, in one month, to be making almost double your present wages, doing the same work that you do now, would you believe it? How would you feel about asking for that amount right now? Yes, even Temporary work requires a little studying and preparation.

Although Temping by itself is very gratifying, Contracting is even more rewarding. As a Contractor, you will be hired as a company, not as a person. Being your own company gives you added financial advantages in the area of tax deductions, and therefore, extra spending money (did he say extra money?). Because you will still be working for agencies, Contracting will give you the practice of running a company, without the hassle of looking for jobs! Being a self-employed Contractor also gives you clout socially. It indicates to other people that you are serious about your business. This is important when trying to build up a network of industry contacts.

After completing many successful jobs as a Temp and a Contractor, you will be wondering how to move up and out into the more independent part of consulting. Here you will be making even more money, based on all of the contacts, good references, and the reputation you have established along the way. Advancing to this stage as a Consultant will be automatic. After establishing a gigantic network of clients and industry contacts, you will be able to consult, in a relaxed fashion.

My recipe for launching a consulting business is based on my genuine experiences. Starting out by doing moonlight jobs in 1979, I have worked as a Temp, Contractor, and Consultant for over 20 years. In that time, I have designed electronic products for more than 37 companies. I have written many technical manuals, prepared training curriculum, presented technical training courses, managed companies, and motivated personnel. My technique harnesses the full power found in the natural progression: moving from Temp to Contract to Consultant occupations. I have refined this technique to eliminate all of the risks and fears normally found in these fields.

I was so amazed how easy it was to get double, or even triple the pay for doing the same kind of work. Not only is the pay great, but the variety is even better! I decided to write this book to share this excitement with others.

"Advancing Into Temp, Contract, And Consulting Jobs" is organized as a 21 chapter, step-by-step workbook. About midway through the book, you should be officially working on a new job as a Temp. After that, the book explains how to set up your own company, preferably in your home. With your own company, you can take on work as a self-employed, Independent Contractor. Still working through agencies, you can get the benefits of owning your own business, without the hassle of trying to find work. In this phase, you will learn how to run the business, by keeping records, balancing the books, and doing online banking. Eventually, this Contracting Business will blossom into a full-time consulting business. This will occur gradually as you establish a huge network of industry contacts and website links. At this stage, you will no longer need the help of agencies to find work for you. Instead, you will be finding your own work, and others will be finding you, by verbal and electronic referrals. You will see that setting up and promoting a consulting business is easy if you follow the recipe in this book.

For starters, the book contains a powerful new kind of resume called the Skill Bullet Resume. With this resume and the techniques used to get it onto a hiring manager's desk, finding new jobs at higher pay, will be easy.

Want to learn how to win a job interview? Ask someone that has won many…a Consultant, of course. After you get the knowledge, then you will have the power.

Knowing your overhead costs is going to be a key issue when it comes to figuring out how much to charge. You must also determine how much others, in your field, are charging as consultants. Furthermore, even a consulting business is required to be profitable. Financial calculations are rigorously covered in this book.

Negotiating wages seems to be an area that potential Consultants feel that they will have trouble with. Yes, it is tricky and uncomfortable at times, but it is, obviously, very important to master. Come to think of it, negotiating wages is important to master for any kind of occupation. This section of the book is worth thousands of dollars to you. Your pay compensation is one of thee most important subjects! Soon, you will soon be wondering why these good people are paying you twice as much, to do the same thing that you did on your last job!

Surviving your first year is crucial to enjoying your new career. You are going to be working hard on your job and you won't be able to concentrate on seeking your next job, paying taxes, etc. With the recipe in this book, you'll have everything all set up before you need it. You will have semi-automatic systems set up to announce your availability for work, find work, keep records, pay bills, and pay taxes. Furthermore, you'll be very experienced in all of these matters before going completely solo!

You've been working hard for other companies, making them better and richer. Aren't you ready to have positive results on your own life?

Now, with the Internet, it's even easier!

Chapter 1:
Ways Of Being Employed

Working as a Consultant requires, not only specialized skills, but also a sound business sense. This chapter starts at the beginning and compares the different ways of being employed. It also explains the type of employment used by the Consultant. It is important to understand the different ways of being employed from many different angles. Also, some of the slang terminology used in the business is introduced.

Types Of Employment—The IRS Point Of View

The Internal Revenue Service (IRS) has several types of employee definitions. Only the two main categories are important to understand. These two categories are referred to as "Employee" and "Independent Contractor." Other names for these two types are "W2 Employee" and "1099 Employee." Let's investigate these further.

W2 Employee Status

Normal employment involves working for company as a Permanent Employee. This is known as W2 employment, because the form that the employee has to fill out, is called "Form W2" by the Internal Revenue Service, IRS. The W2 terminology is commonly used on the street.

A W2 employee is hired as an "Employee" for a company. The company is required to take out taxes from the paycheck before it gives it to the employee. The W2 tax form tells the company the amount of tax to withhold. In addition, the company is required to pay half of the employee's Social Security and Medicare taxes. The total Social Security tax is 12.4% and the Medicare portion is 2.9% of the paycheck. Together these add up to 15.3%. The company pays for half, or approximately 7.5% of the paycheck. This process is invisible to the employee. It is part of the overhead cost of having an employee. The company also withholds the other half (another 7.5%) from the employee, as part of the taxes that are taken out. Also, State Disability (0.5%), State Unemployment (3.4%) and Federal Unemployment (0.8%) taxes are taken out. These numbers vary a little, from state to state.

The IRS has "20 Factors" that distinguish between an Employee and an Independent Contractor. These are also referred to as the "20 Rules" or "20 Questions." These rules are left up to the interpretation of each and every IRS agent as they apply to each taxpayer's situation.

Workers are usually considered to be employees and not Contractors if they:

1. Must follow the employer's instructions about performing the actual work.
2. Receive training from or at the direction of the employer.
3. Provide services that are integrated into the business.
4. Provide services that must be rendered personally.
5. Hire, supervise, and pay assistants for the employer.
6. Have a continuing relationship with the employer.
7. Must follow the employers set hours.
8. Work full-time for the employer.
9. Must do their work on the employer's premises.

10. Must do their work in a sequence set by the employer.
11. Must submit regular reports to the employer.
12. Receive payments of regular amounts at set intervals.
13. Receive payments for business or travel expenses.
14. Rely on the employer to furnish tools and material.
15. Have not made a major investment in facilities used to perform the service.
16. Cannot make an employer suffer a loss from the services.
17. Work for one employer at a time.
18. Do not offer their services to the general public.
19. Can be fired by the employer.
20. May quit work any time without incurring liability.

An advantage to the IRS is that there is a big undefined overlap or "gray area" in the definition of these 20 factors. For example, in the real world, a Contractor would still have to:

- Follow some instructions by the client.
- Work some hours that the client has set.
- Keep up some kind of continuing relationship with the client.
- Submit some regular status reports.
- Be paid regularly, hopefully.
- Depend on the client to supply some of the tools and software.
- Work only for the one client sometimes.

So, it is humanly impossible to follow the IRS guidelines 100%, in my opinion.

Independent Contractor Status

There is an alternative to working on a W2 basis. It is referred to as "Working on a 1099." That's because of the associated IRS tax form that the client must fill out. Working on a 1099 means that the client has hired an Independent Contractor (IC), who is acting as a company.

An IC can either be a company that uses the individual's name or it can be a company operating under a fictitious company name statement. Of course, the IC is the only person in that company, so that IC still has to do all of the work, in addition to taking care of the accounting and taxes. The "Estimated" taxes for this business should be paid every three months, or the IRS will add a fine of about $1000 at the end of the year. The IC also has to get his own benefits: medical, dental, sick leave, vacation, retirement, and unemployment. Furthermore, the IC has to pay what is called "Self Employment Tax." This is really the other half of the Social Security Tax plus Medicare, the 7.5% of your paycheck that the employer used to pay.

The Independent Contractor must be able to answer "No" to most of the 20 Factors, to satisfy the IRS requirements. The main things the IRS checks for are:

- The IC is supplying some of his own tools.
- The IC is not reporting to the company at specific hours.
- The IC is working mainly unsupervised.
- The IC owns some of his own equipment.
- The IC advertises his services to the public
- The IC has worked for more than one company at a time.
- The IC works for more than one company every year.

The last three items mentioned are probably the most important for achieving IC status. Since I prefer to work out of my home, I like the IRS rules!

The Client, Agencies, and the IRS treat an Independent Contractor as a company. There are three types of companies: Sole-proprietor, Partnership, and Corporation. As an individual Consultant, the need for a partnership would be pretty rare, so that limits the choices to two. A sole-proprietor can actually use his name and Social Security number, to work on a 1099 basis. However, as shown later, there are advantages to filing a "Doing Business As" (DBA) fictitious company name statement. Eventually, the sole-proprietorship can be converted to a corporation. This provides more tax advantages as well as financial dangers, and so must be carefully planned for. For a corporation, an Employer Federal Tax I.D. Number (EIN) will have to be used for tax I.D. purposes, regardless of the number of employees.

Types Of Employment—Industry's Point Of View

Captive Employment

The IRS refers to a "Permanent Employee" of a company as an "Employee". Companies try to "capture" these types of employees and lock them into their company's stock option and retirement plans. For example, it usually takes 5 years to get the full worth of the stock, or become "fully vested" in the stock plan. Because of this, these plans are referred to as the "Golden Handcuffs." That is why regular employees are referred to as "Captive" employees, on the street.

A Captive is employed directly by the company. He is working on a W2 basis. He is expected to work 40 hours a week, for a fixed salary, and usually doesn't get paid overtime. The company takes money out of his paycheck for his taxes. The company supplies benefits in the form of medical and dental insurance, retirement plans, paid vacation, sick leave, and sometimes profit sharing, bonuses, and/or stock options. The Captive gets Unemployment Benefits if he gets laid-off. In addition, it is harder for a company to fire a Captive employee. The Captive employee must get three written warnings, or two weeks of sovereigns pay, before being fired, usually. If the Captive employee quits or gets fired, he looses most of his stock options! Usually, Captive employees sell their stock options just before quitting. Captive, W2 employees end up paying about 50% of their paycheck in taxes.

Temporary Employment

A Temporary Employee works for a Job Agency. This employee type is referred to as a "Temp." Most Temps work for their job agencies as W2 employees. Since they are W2 employees, the agency must withhold taxes out of their paychecks. However, the agencies usually do not offer many other benefits to the Temp, such as medical and dental. These days, that is all changing, however. Some agencies offer a wide variety of benefits, but we will assume this is not the norm. Agencies ALWAYS do pay the Temp for overtime work, beyond a 40 hour a week! However, overtime pay is usually NOT time-and-a-half.

A "Job Agency" is a company that finds employees for a Client Company. Job Agencies are also referred to as People Brokers or Body Shops in other textbooks. Several recruiters may work for one job agency. Most of us, on the street, respectfully call these recruiters "Head-Hunters." Each agency specializes in finding Temps for certain occupations.

The "Client" company is the job site where the work is actually performed. The client may need Temps from many job categories all at once. Usually the client company hires Temps from a few agencies that they have dealt with in the past. Temps work only for the time that the client company needs them. They perform the same job tasks as the Captive employees at the client's company. When the client company no longer needs the Temp, the client, and usually the job agency, lay him off the same day. The client is not obligated to give notice, sovereigns pay, or pay unemployment benefits. The agency is not obligated to give notice or sovereigns pay, either, but does have to pay for unemployment benefits.

Everyone assumes that the Temp is only employed part of the year, and spends a lot of his time looking for a new job. This is not nesscessarily true, in many occupations, as you will realize later! Since the agencies are good at finding jobs, the Temp is rarely laid-off or unemployed for long. However, it is great that everyone thinks the Temp is unemployed alot. Because of that, Temp's get to charge much more money, per hour!

W2 Temp employees have a few more, limited, tax write-offs. They get to deduct mileage to drive to the client's place of work and recover some of the expenses they paid for medical and dental benefits. Basically, a W2 Temp pays about 45% of his income in taxes.

Agencies That Hire On A 1099

To distinguish 1099 Temps from W2 Temps, the term "Contractor" is used. This leads to a great confusion in the industry, as we shall see later. Contractors can also find work through job agencies. A Contractor can set up a home-based office, claim the car as a company car, and so forth. This often leads to a greater tax advantage than W2 employment.

Many large job agencies, that hire individuals on a 1099 basis, will require that the Contractor be "Incorporated." Some agencies further require that the client hire the Contractor and the agency, at the same time as two separate corporations. This is referred to as hiring on a "Corp-to-Corp" basis. Many of these agencies also stipulate that the Contractor carry his own liability and disability insurances. All of this is done because of many agency fears of the IRS and it's unusual record for abusing power. The IRS is changing these days after being heavily scrutinized by the U.S. Congress.

Type Of Employment For The Consultant

Independent, Job-Shopper, Freelance, etc., are all titles for what is, effectively, a Consultant. A Consultant finds his own work without the use of agencies, but is referred to as an Independent Contractor by the IRS.

Not commonly known is the fact that most beginning Consultants start out as W2 Temporary employee of a job agency. Then, they work their way up to 1099 Contractors that still find occasional work through agencies. But, as their years of experience and the number of industry contacts increases, they no longer need the assistance of agencies to find work. It is at this point, that the individual starts finding his own jobs, that he is considered a Consultant.

Thus, a Consultant finds his own jobs by networking mostly with clients and individuals he has worked for, or with, in the past. Networking is a new age term for keeping in touch with all of the past managers, friends, cohorts, and acquaintances met on previous jobs. Finding jobs this way is also referred to as working by "Word-of-Mouth" referrals. As you will see later, this is another big misconception in the consulting world.

This all implies that to be a real Consultant, where agencies are never used to find work, two things must be in place. First, the Consultant must build up and maintain a good reputation. Second, the Consultant must know enough people that need his services, or that recommend his services.

To establish this reputation, the Consultant must have been exposed to many companies and have done good work for them. They must regard his work highly. They must also feel that the Consultant can always contribute a positive, winning force to their projects.

Notice that, in these discussions above, we can begin to see a natural progression developing. Starting out as a Temp, achieving Contractor status, and then progressing to Consultant. This is a natural progression! The technique used to accomplish this, is the fundamental basis of this book. We will discuss, step-by-step, how this career path works, in the remainder of this book.

The Temp, Contractor, And Consultant Name Confusion

Since agencies refer to W2 Temps and 1099 Temps wrongfully as "Contractors," and since the IRS calls all 1099 individuals "Independent Contractors," there is a big mis-use of the word "Contractor," going on. What's worse, is that Temps of all kinds are frequently referred to as "Consultants" at the job-site. So, everyone that is not an employee of the client is also frequently called a "Consultant."

As the population becomes more business savvy, they are honoring more the official IRS terminology. Thus, the latest trend is more towards calling everyone "Contractors" in the IRS sense. This has now progressed to the point where Consultants, Contractors, and Temps are all called "Contractors," by agencies, clients, websites, books, and trade magazines. So, now everyone is becoming a Contractor.

It is impossible to treat this nomenclature subject, in a clean manner, without setting down some rules that this book will follow. So, to prevent confusion, this book distinguishes between individuals that get jobs through agencies and those that do not.

This book will use the following terminology:

"Temp" = anyone that finds W2 jobs through agencies.
"Contractor" = anyone that finds 1099 jobs through agencies.
"Consultant" = anyone that finds 1099 jobs without going through agencies.

Remember though, you will more likely be called a "**Contractor**" everywhere you go.

Advantage Of 1099 Employment

Why would so many people want to be on a 1099, if it takes so much extra work and bookkeeping then? Doesn't it seem like a lot of trouble and worry? The main advantage to working 1099 is that you get more tax deductions and write-offs. The level of these tax deductions depends on the type of company established, and where the office is located. Some of the things that can be deducted are office supplies, postage, computer equipment, software, seminars, college courses, books, tools, car maintenance, car fuel, advertising, internet fees, blank CD's, and many others. As a result, a 1099 employee pays much less, about 35%, of the paycheck in taxes.

Additional tax deductions can be realized if one of the family cars is claimed as a company car, the office is located in the home, and the company is incorporated. We will discuss these aspects in another chapter. A Consultant that is incorporated, with the office in the home, pays about 25% of his paycheck in taxes. That's half of the amount that a Captive employee has to pay!

Summary Of Chapter 1:

This chapter introduces the concept of working either on a W2 or a 1099. The different distinctions used for the different categories of employment: Temp, Contractor, and Consultant were covered. The tax advantages of working on a 1099 was also compared with W2 employment.

Some advanced ideas of saving money on taxes was also introduced, including 1099 self-employment, company car deductions, office in the home, and being incorporated. These are popular business deductions. They help save approximately 25% more of the paycheck instead of loosing it to taxes.

This chapter also hints at a very powerful career concept. There seems to be a natural progression, moving from Temp to Contractor to Consulting occupations! As the book continues, we will see the power and safety in this concept. Can you tell how easy this is going to be yet?

Chapter 2:
Getting Started In Consulting

Getting started in consulting can be quick and easy, depending on the method you choose. There are a limited number of ways to do it. Naturally, it would help if you have a Ph.D. degree, are a professor at a university, and know somebody at Bell Labs. But if you are like most of us, you'll have to find some easier method of getting started.

Here is a list of possible ways to get started:

1. Become a Consultant for the company you are working for now.
2. Wait for all your friends to be promoted to the Board Of Directors, and then become a Consultant for them.
3. Become a Consultant for a company where a friend has recommended you.
4. Start a company, sell it, and then become a consultant to that company.
5. Retire, then Consult for the company you retired from.
6. Quit your job and start calling yourself a Consultant.
7. Become a Temporary Employee for a Job Agency.

Method number 1: *"Become a Consultant for the company you are working for now,"* is the most thought of method. To this day not many people have been able to do just that. However, if it appears that you are a successful Consultant for others, and if you didn't "burn your bridges", you will probably be consulting for the company you are working for today, someday. But, you may have to leave first. Sometimes, the day that you resign, is the day that you are offered your first consulting position with that company.

Method number 2: *"Wait for all your friends to be promoted to the Board Of Directors, and then become a Consultant for them,"* on the other hand, always works. All you have to do is wait about twenty years to start your consulting career.

Method number 3: *"Become a Consultant for a company where a friend has recommended you,"* is a feasible concept. This method involves a lot of risk, however. First off, it assumes you have an inside associate pushing your talents for you. For a first time consulting job, you better have a good idea what you are doing, because both your reputation and your friend's reputation are at stake. If you know what to expect, then this is an okay way to start out. You can reduce the risks by keeping your present job and moonlighting on this new job. You can insist that you do most of the work off-site (at your house at midnight). Of course, you will end up working nearly 80 hours a week.

Method number 4: *"Start a company, sell it, and then become a consultant to that company,"* is unrealistic for most people, because it takes money and time, first. If you already have the money, go for it. Just make sure you don't play too much golf instead of doing actual work.

Method number 5: *"Retire and then Consult for the company you retired from,"* makes me tired thinking of it. Don't actually plan to work during retirement. Let it be your choice at that time. Save some money so that you won't have to. You may realize that you don't wish to work your entire life. But, if you still want to work, you are not alone. The American Association of Retired Persons (AARP) estimates that 25% of all retired persons work full or part time! Many of these old-timers are making a great living as Consultants.

Method Number 6: *"Quit your job and Start Calling Yourself a Consultant,"* is the craziest way to become a Consultant! You will be risking more than you think. You will be running out of work because you did not develop a big enough network of industry con-tacts. You may not be charging enough because you don't understand the costs of self-employment. You may end up working for cut-throat businessmen that know how to rip off Consultants. In general, you will be risking your livelihood because of your lack of experience in all of these matters.

Building a consulting business should be a gradual step-by-step process. It takes time to learn about self-employment. It takes time to experience different job situations. It takes time to develop a big list of contacts and referrals. It takes practice negotiating for high wages. It takes money to set up an office, a computer, and an accounting system. Remember that it's not just a matter of intellectual freedom becoming a Consultant, it also has to be a profitable business.

This technique, referred to as "jumping in with both feet," is really impractical. Let's suppose you take the plunge. Are you going to feel comfortable asking someone for 3 times your current rate of pay? Or maybe you were planning on working for far less than everyone else works? Do you think people will hire you at $35/hr. when all the other Consultants are bidding $75/hr to do the same job? No, it doesn't work that way in consulting! Maybe with gardeners it works that way, but not with Consultants. Only clients that are poor will hire you at that low rate, and you probably won't get all of your paychecks.

This technique also runs against human nature. Let's suppose your first job is a great success, but you can't find a second job right away. Do you think you will feel like going back to work as a Captive employee at that point? I doubt that. Once you taste the variety found in consulting, you will make a miserable Captive employee!

Unfortunately, this technique of "jumping in with both feet" is the very technique emphasized in most other consulting books. Most describe this technique as the ONLY WAY to get into consulting. Just Dive In, they say! Then they try to cover every possible way to get a consulting job; covering hundreds of techniques to remain employed. That's why those books are so thick and so hard to understand.

The techniques for finding consulting work, described in other books, include presenting seminars, giving speeches, teaching courses, starting a newsletter, writing magazine articles, giving expert quote to newspapers, starting a Web Page on the Internet, and so on. These are all good techniques for expanding a consulting business, not starting one!

This book considers those techniques mentioned above as "Advanced Consulting Techniques." Obviously, Advanced Consulting Techniques should only be used AFTER you've been consulting for some time. Right now you just want a safe way to start a consulting business and make more money without risking your home or your family's welfare.

If you still insist on "jumping in with both feet," go ahead and try it. Theoretically, with good references, and enough contacts, you can Consult anytime. This technique tends to work better for people with high credentials such as advanced college degrees, special licenses, and so on.

However, there is a much easier, safer way to get started, described below.

Method number 7: *"Become a Temporary Employee for a job agency,"* is the least risky, most comfortable, and quickest way of beginning a consulting career. It is also the least known method of getting started in consulting. That is the reason this book was written. The power of this technique is simple and amazing! Because of the importance of this Temping Technique, we need to investigate it in great detail, in the next chapter.

Summary Of Chapter 2:

There aren't that many ways to start up a career in consulting. In addition, very few of them are safe ways. Some techniques are too risky to try for someone that is married, has to support a family, and make house and car payments. Even if we took a risk for one job, we may not get more jobs after that. So, the argument for becoming a Temporary Employee for a job agency seems to be the most promising. Let's investigate how and why Temping works in the next chapter.

Chapter 3:
Temporary Employment 101

Becoming a Temporary Employee of a job agency is a great way to get started in consulting. By doing Temp jobs for a couple of years, a person can gain the skills and the contacts needed to sustain a living as a Consultant. Being a Temp eliminates the problem of staying employed in the beginning phase of consulting. Because of this, Temping is thee only, no-risk way of getting started as a Consultant. Temping also offers several advantages over captive employment.

Temporary employment is an easy subject to understand. Most people that don't know anything about Temping are afraid or confused by it. Well, fear not. This chapter covers all of the aspects of Temping.

What Job Agencies Do

Job Agencies specialize in hiring out Temps, or Contractors, on a W2 or 1099 basis, respectively. Their business is to connect you with a client company that needs your talent. They are similar to the Talent Agencies used in the Hollywood TV and movie industries. They advertise, collect databases of resumes, call potential clients, match jobs with resumes, send resumes to clients for review, negotiate pay-rates, send potential Temps to interviews, and float the payroll until they get paid by the client.

There are agencies for almost every type of skilled laborer. Thousands of agencies, all over the world are specializing in placing mostly professional and technical people. These are people with some trade school or college education. They place a variety of skilled people including secretaries, accountants, technical writers, publicists, technicians, engineers, scientists, and many others. The technical fields have recently been subdivided into "IS" and "IT" groups. These stand for "Information Systems" and "Industrial Technologist" groups. The IS group is mainly for all types of computer database programmers and system analysts. The IT group is for all other technical and scientific categories. Agencies even place top company executives these days, including CEO's, Human Resources, Marketing and Sales personnel.

There is an interesting article in the August 1998 issue of **"Contract Professional"** called "The Untouchable Topic: Agency Fees." It explains what most people don't notice is that, "an agency may have to make 500 telephone calls to get 100 contacts, to get 10 [job] requirements, to get 4 interviews, to get 1 actual start." Agencies do have to do quite a bit of work to find job openings and match candidates.

What Job Agencies Charge

Job agencies usually get paid by the hour, for every hour that their Temp employee works. The hourly rate agencies charge is based on a percentage of what the Temp gets. This agency fee varies from 12% to as much as 50% of the Temps' hourly rate. The average rate is somewhere between 26% and 33% for IT placements. *Who Cares? The Temp doesn't have to pay it, the client does!*

In the Engineering fields that I'm involved in, $45/hour is a standard beginning, rate. Let's say you charge $50/hr. When you make $50/hr, the job agency could add 50% more on top of that, or $25/hr. That means the client company must pay $75/hr. total, $50 for you and $25 for the agency, per hour. Some Temps in Engineering are charging $75/hr. Just think how much the agencies are billing for them. These are some lucrative numbers! You can now see why Headhunters do so well for themselves.

Why Clients Pay Agency Fees

By hiring Temps, the client has several financial and scheduling advantages. Most people think that the client doesn't like to pay agency fees. But, the opposite is true. The client wants the agency to intervene in the search and hiring processes. The client depends on the agency to weed through the myriad of resumes. The agency can provide 3 candidates that are a close match in a few days. This saves a lot of time for the client.

According to the National Association Of Temporary Staffing Services (NATSS), it takes, on average, 6 weeks to hire a captive employee, the normal way. The client can save time and keep up the project momentum by hiring a Temp instead. The client's personnel department doesn't have to get involved in hiring the Temp employee. This saves money in a few different ways. First, lengthy, long-term, staffing studies do not have to be presented to upper management. Advertising the job opening is not necessary. The client does not have to wait for the ad to go into print. Sifting through resumes is not necessary because the job agencies sorts them for key words before the client gets to see them. References have already been checked by the agency to save time for their clients. The client does not pay for the expenses of relocating the prospective employee. Telephone interviews become adequate for hiring a seasoned Temp. Once hired, the Temp does not have to be presented the standard employee benefit package. The Temp employee is not required to go to indoctrination meetings. The Temp is ready to work the first day. Hiring a Temp instead of a captive employee can save the company up to 8 weeks!

In addition to speeding up the hiring process, hiring a Temp allows the client to have finer control over his manpower budget. He can stop the work whenever he wishes, without any further obligation to the Temp employee.

If the Temp employee has too many flaws, the client can fire him immediately without any repercussions, that day. Firing a captive employee is much more difficult. The client would have to give him 3 written warnings before firing him. This process could take up to 3 weeks or more, depending on how soon the employee could make 2 more mistakes. So, if the wrong, captive employee was hired, a company could loose up to 12 weeks before they fired him. Furthermore, the company would have to pay for ½ of that person's unemployment benefits. The company would also be back at square one, and have to start the hiring process over again. This, again, could take 8 more weeks. It, therefore, requires much less overhead to hire or fire a Temp.

The Temp is usually hired because of his particular skills. This saves the client large amounts of money, since he doesn't have to train someone, and wait for them to come up to speed. These skills could be in software, such as using a particular word-processor, spreadsheet, CAD, or publishing program. Other savings are brought to the client when the Temp makes recommendations for equipment or software, that the client should be using. The expense for investigating new software systems and equipment can be significant. The expense for training can be even larger in certain subjects. In many IS and IT technical fields, for example, 95% of the skills required must be learned on the job. You must learn the latest CAD software, the computer Operating System, and the state-of-the-art technology being used. The technology changes rapidly, also. These training costs are hidden in each project. They usually are not considered part of the overhead rate, like they should be.

So, one of the biggest savings, in highering a Temp, comes into play when you consider how much it costs to train an employee. A Temp doesn't have to be trained because he already has the proper experience. This saves enormous amounts of time and money.

Finally, and probably the most important reason of all, a Temp can save time getting a product into the "marketing window". This "window" of opportunity is the expected life cycle of a product. The first company to get a product into the marketplace has the potential of capturing up to 60% of the market's potential customers. The rest of the competing companies have to fight over the remaining 40%. Getting into the marketing window first could literally be worth millions of dollars of profit. Having the proper personnel ready to design this product and produce it quickly, puts the company into a much higher profit-making stance. Now, you can see that the actual worth of the Temp, or team of Temps, can go ballistic.

Converting Yearly Pay To Hourly Pay

We will frequently be using a formula for converting yearly salaries to hourly rates throughout this book. Here it is. First, there is 40 hours in a workweek. There is 52 weeks in a year. So, there are $40*52 = 2,080$ work hours per year. Now, if we take the yearly salary and divide it by 2080, we will get the hourly rate. But, that's too hard to do without a calculator. So, lets approximate by using 2000 instead of 2080. Now we can easily convert. For example, $40K per year/2000 = $20 per hour.

Overhead And Burdened Labor Rates

Surprising as it may seem, it is actually cost effective for commercial companies to employ Temps, compared to Captive employees. One reason for this is that companies suffer from overhead expenses.

In most commercial companies, it costs the company about 1.5 times the employee's pay, for the "burdened labor rate". For military, aerospace, and unionized companies, it even becomes more feasible to use Temps because of the company's extremely high burdened labor rates in the range of 2.25.

Let's say a person is employed at a commercial company making a salary of $40K/year. This is equivalent to $20/hour. At a burdened labor rate of 1.5, it would cost the company about $30/hr. in actual expenses, to keep this employee around. At a military or aerospace company, with a burdened labor rate of 2.25, it would cost the company about $45/hr. These "burdened labor" rates are the actual costs that the company has to pay to employ their captive workers. These rates include basic salary, one-half of the Social Security and Medicare taxes, benefits, plus the company's "overhead".

Overhead costs include advertising job openings, employee relocation, medical and dental plans, education reimbursement, retirement, stock options, stationary, computers, software, tools, lighting, furniture, water, coffee, travel, rent, utilities, etc. Note that overhead rates do not account for personnel training or product failures.

Temps and Contractors, on the other hand, do not have overhead associated with their pay. Instead, the client must pay agency fees. The agency is, however, incurring some overhead. So, from the client's point of view, there is an overhead savings in hiring Temporary employee. At a commercial company, with a 1.50 burdened labor rate, the savings is 50% of a captive employees' salary. But that's not the entire picture.

What Is A Temp Worth?

A Temporary employee could easily save 6 months of time getting a product to market sooner. Let's see how this adds up.

Temps save, on average, 2 months during the hiring-firing processes. Temps then save training time because they have experience from previous companies. Temps save more time by making less mistakes, again because they have experience from previous companies. Temps, furthermore, add more value by recommending equipment, software, and processes already in use at other companies. And, finally, most important of all, Temps get the product into the marketing window of opportunity sooner. This is a tremendous advantage, in that it usually pays for the full employment cost of the Temp. These savings easily add up to at least 6 months of savings of equivalent captive employee's salaries.

In addition, as mentioned earlier, the Temp is saving 50% of a captive employee's salary in burdened labor rate savings. That 50% savings plus the 6/12ths of a year's time saved by hiring the Temp, comes out to a 100% savings in a captive employee's salary!

However, there is a catch. Temps charge more, as we shall see later. It is justifiable, though, that a Temp could charge double the rate of an equivalent captive employee, since he is saving 100%.

So what is a Temp actually worth? The actual worth of a Temp is somewhat hard to pinpoint. That's because his worth starts out high and then decreases. A good estimate, when first getting hired, is that a Temp is worth twice that of a captive employee, mostly because of experience. Since a Temp can easily save 6 months of time getting a product to market sooner, he must be worth 2X of a captive, at least for the first year.

Clients Expect Temps To Charge More

Clients and Job Agencies assume that Temps are employed about half of the time. Furthermore, it is also known that the Temp has to pay for his own benefits, training, holidays, and vacation time. So, clients and agencies expect Temps to charge much more than captive employees! In fact, they expect that a Temp needs to charge about 2 times more than a captive employee does!

How Much Do Temps Charge?

Temping can provide a substantial increase in pay. Professionals that go the Temp route can usually get double their captive, hourly pay! Technical and Clerical personnel can get about 1.75 times their captive hourly pay. Note that these are only averages though. If you are good, you can get much more. These are some healthy raises, aren't they?

What Does The Temp Actually Cost?

We have already shown that the Temp, alone, costs the same amount as a captive employee because of saving 50% on overhead and 6 man-months of time. However, that doesn't account for agency fees. Since most agencies charge about 30%, it will cost the client 30% more to pay for a Temp. But don't forget that because of experience, the Temp is worth 2 times more than a captive employee is, for at least the first year.

Now, you can begin to grasp, why it is cost-effective to employ a Temp rather than a Captive employee, in terms of actual worth. The Temp is worth twice the pay of a captive employee to the company, but is only going to cost 1.3 times that, with agency fees. This is like getting 2 employees for the price of 1.3 of them.

A Win-Win-Win Situation

In actuality, it usually doesn't matter how much the Temp costs. Most savvy clients realize that getting to market as fast as possible will always out-weigh the costs involved in hiring Temps. Being first in a new marketplace is literally worth thousands or even millions of dollars, in most cases.

By hiring Temps, the client saves time, gets expert skills, and gets to market sooner. The agency makes a healthy amount of money, by the hour, for the placement. And the Temp gets about twice the pay of a full-time, captive employee. *That's a Win-Win-Win situation!*

Required Experience For Temping

When we talk about the Temp's required experience, we are talking about work experience that is second nature to the Temp. Companies can be too overloaded or have quite a few very under-skilled employees. When they find the Temp's resume, they think they have found a genius. The Temp may not even realize what skill they were looking for when they hired him. They may not even mention it for quite some time after he has been employed there. Sometimes, they just wanted a more positive, friendlier person on the project. Hence, the experience required for Temping is experience that you already have. It, also, just happens to be the same expertise that the client company is lacking!

Maintaining Your Worth As A Temp

When a Temp or Contractor keeps up his competitive edge, he can be employed at a job site for many years! In effect, he can stay worth his hire-in rate. There are several things Temps must do in order to accomplish this.

1. ***Long Term Temps must keep bringing new expertise to the job.*** They have to keep learning new subjects *before* the client needs them.

2. ***Long Term Temps must continuously point out that lower-paid personnel can do the mundane jobs more effectively.*** This makes middle managers look more efficient to upper management because they have to get several departments involved in borrowing a lower paid employee (known respectfully as a gopher).

3. ***Long Term Temps must become important to their fellow co-workers.*** When they help others learn and enjoy free transfer of knowledge, then the captive employees become grateful and push management into keeping the Temp on staff.

4. ***Long Term Temps must become important to Upper Management.*** This takes a little luck. The best way to become important is to have a company-wide crisis occur. After all the other experts try to resolve it, the Long Term Temp comes up with an elegant solution. Of course, they don't realize that he has been researching the problem all night at his house.

In general, what it all amounts to is that Long Term Temps have to stay immune to the company's systematic way of creating disasters. They cannot get involved in politics or personality conflicts. They cannot break the surface tension and sink into the swamp, so to speak. If the Long Term Temp keeps up his competitive edge, he can remain at his hire-in rate, forever.

In my career, I have worked at well over 35 companies as a Temp, Contractor, or a Consultant. At all but 3 of those jobs, I resigned on my own account. Usually, I leave in order to keep from going stagnate or just to learn something new. Of course, I never quit in the middle of a project.

One of the 3 jobs where I was actually laid off, was the first time I was laid-off by surprise. That was one year when Congress "forgot" to renew the fiscal government budgets in time. At that time, I was Temping on a military project. Surprise! All government projects went broke overnight and we all were laid off the next day.

The second time I was laid-off, it wasn't a surprise. I worked for that client for 6.5 years as a Contractor. Now that's Long Term Temping! Yes, on that one, I just stayed too long. To overcome stagnation on that job, I would take on jobs from other clients at the same time. I worked for 4 other companies, as a Consultant, during that same 6.5 years.

The third time I was laid off, it was a big surprise that resulted in a lesson I'll never forget. On that one, the client was in an unfamiliar field and I was an expert. When I saw all of the misconceptions going on, I wrote a report to the project director and tried to clarify that the project he wanted to do would take more than 6 months with 4 engineers. In addition, there was going to be a tooling fee of $250,000 that for some reason management thought they were going to get for free. Furthermore, I tried to convince them that a working prototype would have to be developed first before they could make their own microchip. So, my report went over like a lead balloon. Basically my report was interpreted as: a) They underestimated the manpower required, b) they underestimated the budget required, and c) they did not understand the proper procedure to develop such a product. That interpretation was exactly correct! My reward for caring and publishing my concerns was that I was laid off the next day. Bamm, that was it. So it goes to show you, you cannot tell the client the truth, directly. All a consultant can do is help the client stumble across the truth by himself. That company 1.5 years later, after spending more than a $500K more, and firing several more people, has just started to look at the procedures and technologies that I had originally proposed. How do I know this? I monitor their activity through all of my industry contacts, of course. Hey, but I get to say, "I told you so," with email, as often as I want!

How Could A Temp's Worth Decrease?

There are several reasons that the Temp's worth could eventually decrease. One reason is that he looses his competitive edge. He is swallowed up by the corporate ways of doing things, a little bit each day. Another reason is that he begins to stagnate. He stops learning new things. For example, many times Middle Management tries to keep him on the job at all costs. Middle Management recognizes that the Temp is a great asset and easy to manage. So, when things get slow, they give the Temp endless lists of mundane tasks to do. These tasks could have been done by the lowest paid employee on the project. So, the Temps' skills as an expert professional begin to stagnate.

The most important reason a Temp's value decreases, is because some of his expertise has rubbed off onto the captive employees! In actuality, the Temp has increased the worth of the captive employees on the project! So, relatively speaking, the Temp "appears" to be worth a lesser amount.

At some point in time, the Temp's worth will begin to be questioned by Upper Management. The beginning sign to watch for is when Middle Management starts arguing with Upper Management about the need for the Temp. From my experience, and from responses received from other Temps, this phenomenon occurs in about 1.5 years of time, on the average. The Temp crosses back under the threshold where his worth, plus agency fees, have "apparently" become more than the cost to train and maintain a full-time employee. If you are a Consultant instead of a Temp, then you have a little longer. Two years is the average amount of time that a Consultant can last on the job before his worth will be questioned. His time is extended because there are no agency fees involved. If all companies could do long range planning, then they could hire captive employees and spend the money training them. However, they would still loose about a years worth of productivity waiting for this to happen.

Advantages For The Temping Employee

There are several advantages to becoming a Temp employee. One is that all of a sudden your resume looks better. All those crummy jobs you've had, 1 year here, 8 months there, etc., make it look like you have a wider range of experience. It's true! You do. You always did. It's just that no one has ever acknowledged that. If you apply for full-time work with a resume like that, they view you as someone who is unstable and not worth spending their overhead or training dollars on. So, this advantage will actually help you find more work as a Temp than as a Captive employee.

Another advantage of becoming a Temp is the Overtime pay situation. This will just blow your mind when you think of it! How many times have you worked for a company that didn't pay you for every hour that you were there? As a Temp, those days are over! You will get paid, for every single minute you are at the job site. How does that sound?

Let's see how much that is worth. In a special Supplemental Issue of Electronic Design News, Volume 38-3A of February 1993, they report from a survey of Engineers and Managers across the nation, that an average of 9 hours a week are worked in unpaid overtime. This comes out to 56 days worth of work per year (WOW)! As a captive employee, at $50K/yr., you would be loosing $11,700. As a Temp, at $100K/yr., you would be gaining $23,400. So, if your pay is similar to this example, i.e. $50K/yr., and if you are not Temping, but are working 9 hours of overtime per week for free, then you are loosing a whopping total of [$23,400—(-$11,700)]= $35,100. Now that is a 35% raise above and beyond the initial doubling of your hourly-rate! No matter what your occupation, I'm sure you can appreciate this major Temping advantage!

An additional advantage of working for a job agency comes into play when your assignment nears completion. The client usually notifies the agency a week in advance that your work is almost completed.

The agency immediately begins a new job search for you! They do this because they don't want to loose the income they are presently getting for your work. Of course, by then you also heard your assignment was coming to a close. So, you broadcast out your resume to all of the other agencies, and they start looking at the same time. In my case, I could easily have 105 agencies looking for a job for me, in my local area, one week before I got laid off! Now, I know you're not used to thinking about this situation yet, but having a large amount of agencies looking for a job for you is a very secure feeling!

Another, very important advantage, that must be emphasized, is the number of personal and industry contacts you meet while Temping. Remember your goal is to become a full-fledged Consultant someday. You are going to need people to recommend you for work, by word-of-mouth. Serving your internship as a Temp allows you to meet these people and establish your reputation! First off, you are working for two companies, the agency, and the client. So, you are meeting two groups of people already. Then, typically you do about 1 job assignment every 1.5 years. So, you are changing jobs more frequently. Sometimes, you meet other mercenaries (another name for Temps) at the job site. Sometimes they are working for the same agency as you, and other times they are working through a different agency. Usually you become friends and keep in contact. Later on, when one of you moves on to a new assignment, the other may recommend you for a job opening. This is the result of "Networking," or keeping in touch with your industry contacts. This process of meeting people eventually mushrooms. Before you know it, someone that you've worked for, or with, in the past, calls you. But this time they call you directly at your house. They no longer need the services of a job agency to find you. They know your home phone number and your skill level. Now, you come in to the client's workplace on your own, directly. You can give yourself another 33% raise if you want, because now there is no agency fees!

Accidentally (on purpose), you have just become a Consultant. How about that!

Another advantage of Temping is that management respects your opinion more frequently. When you come into a new company as a Temp, many people regard you as a Consultant. In effect, you are, because you have the particular skills they need. That is rewarding in itself. They treat you with respect. What is additionally enjoyable, however, is when you are asked to give your opinion of a process or a tool needed. They actually listen to you and usually decide that you are right!

Don't forget the additional tax advantages to Temping that we touched on in a previous chapter. You will be keeping an additional 5% to 25% depending on what type of company the IRS will allow you to set up. That's another huge raise!

Perceived Disadvantages To Temping

Now I know that you are anxious to learn about the disadvantages of taking Temp work. You think you have already figured them out, right? It goes against the grain of everything we've learned about working from our parents, schooling, and childhood. We were supposed to go to college, become rocket scientists or money moguls. We were supposed to start with a company and stay with them. Don't forget though, that we were also ***supposed to get rewarded*** by these same companies. They weren't supposed to lay us off. They weren't supposed to move to a different state and leave us hanging. They weren't supposed to fire your boss after 17 years of service, the only guy that knew what you did. They weren't supposed to fire you, for being right. And finally, they weren't supposed to act like they were better than we were and treat us like just another number! My career was full of these hardships and many more. I bet it is the same for most of us. In fact, lets point out one thing now: Almost every single person that has started in consulting was fired or laid off before they had the guts to try it! I'm not kidding. Not only that, it was usually the second or third time that they were "down-sized" before they did something about it. Hopefully, this book will change all that by allowing people to plan for a gradual progression into a Contracting and Consulting careers.

So, with that introduction, lets state that the biggest apparent disadvantage of becoming a Temp is that the assignments are Temporary. In reality, however, if you are a good worker, and if you can get along with almost anyone, then the job is yours forever! And that is the honest truth. Why wouldn't it be this way? You are as cost effective as an employee, if you keep your skills up to date. Everyone there likes your work and your attitude. Then, you keep bringing new skills to the job before the client realizes he needs them. You get to stay if you don't goof up, for a long time. Please, place this concept in the front of your mind. Throw away all of those inherited fears about this Temporary subject. In conclusion, the biggest disadvantage of Temping, the thing that stops everyone from trying it, doesn't exist in the real world! If you are Temping and you are getting laid off, then the client is having financial hardships or you are slacking in some way, as they view it.

There are a few other real disadvantages to becoming a Temp. As we will investigate in great detail later, you loose some company paid benefits when you switch to Temping. You will have to carry your own medical insurances. You will loose your holiday pay and sick leave. You will probably have to travel further, on the average, to the job-site. You will have to pay for your own seminars, education, software, computers and so on. Also, you will have to manage your own retirement plan.

Some employees think that the loss of their Stock Options would be a great loss. It's true, many millionaires are created by cashing in their stock options. Of course, most of these people had to wait five years before their stocks were fully vested. This is the "Golden Handcuff" technique corporations use to keep employees from quitting. And it's true that every 11 minutes Silicon Valley produces a new millionaire. However, the success rate for corporations is really quite low, especially for startups. According to the book **"High Tech Start Up"** by John L. Nesheim, only 6 out of 1000 companies that are funded by venture capitalists, do well. In fact, Nesheim says that 60% of all funded startups eventually declare bankruptcy!

I had the experience of working at a large company who's stock had hovered at $50 a share, when it first went IPO. Two years later, the stock sank to $8 a share and stayed there for three years! That's the point where I was hired to consult for them. What I witnessed was some of the most unmotivated, miserable employees ever seen on the face of the earth. The employees had taken low wages for five years, waiting for their stock to become fully vested, only to find that they had made nothing on their stock. They left the company like rats on a sinking ship.

So, on the average, the benefits lost by Temping do not amount to a hill of beans when compared to the huge increase in your salary! You will see this soon, when we do some actual calculations in a later chapter. Most people think their benefits are worth huge amounts of money! Get the word out: *"Benefits" aren't worth all that much.*

Another Perceived Disadvantage To Temping

A second possible disadvantage to Temping is that the client may like you so much, that he will want you to become a captive employee (how rude). There are several ways to weasle out of this, so it really isn't a disadvantage. Normally, on an interview, if they bring this up, I might say "Sure, I will consider becoming an employee, after I see how the company performs for about a year." Then, later on, I say "O.K. I'm willing to hear you're offer. Remember though, I'm making double what others are making and I have more tax write-offs than a captive employee right now." That usually calms them down for a while.

One Real Disadvantage of Temping

When you accept an assignment from an agency you have to sign a contract. In that contract it says that if you get laid off by the client, or quit, then you cannot go to work for them, on your own, for a certain period of time. Usually that period is 90 days. Some agencies get carried away with this concept and specify 90 working days, 6 months, or even a year. This 90-day exclusion clause puts a delay in your ability to come back on your own and consult for the same client. We refer to this as the "leash law." This is not a real big problem, just a slight delay.

Secret To Becoming A Consultant Through Temping

Let's say you perform well for a company as a Temp and the agency has you on a 90-day exclusion. The project is finished and you are laid-off. Many job agencies help you find your new job. You are back to work with more experience and you probably gave yourself a raise, to boot. You're meeting a new group of people and probably working on something completely different than the previous company. Sounds good doesn't it? Sure.

Eventually, though, the previous client may need you to come back. His company may fall back into their old ways of doing things, especially if the organization is running in crisis-management mode. Or perhaps, he may be enjoying so much profit coming from a previous project you helped with, that he wants you to be part of the new project. Whatever the case, they realize that they need your skills again. This time, though, they call you at home. Somebody there has your business card or your home phone number (because you made sure they did before you left). They don't need an agency to find you anymore. This time, they call you up at home and, abracadabra, POOF, you're a Consultant!

How much can you now charge, after returning to the client, as a Consultant instead of a Temp? How about what was being charged before? How about charging the same amount that the client was paying you, plus what the client was paying the agency? Only now, you get to keep the amount that the agency was making!

Unfortunately, this scenario frequently comes up when you are already working as a Temp for another client company. So, sometimes, to accelerate your new career, you may have to work two jobs at the same time, for a short while. Notice, also, that if your assignment ends, and you can't find any more work as a Consultant, then you can call the agencies again. The agencies will be glad to help you find a new job so they can make more money off of your new skills. If this were true, wouldn't other people be using this technique? Well, they are. Let's check out some studies that were done on Temps.

Trends In Temping

If Temping is such a good deal then why aren't more people aware of this? The status of the temporary job market may hold a clue.

The National Association of Temporary And Staffing Services (NATSS) reported in 1993 that there are were more than 1,100 Temporary Staffing Agencies (companies), operating more than 7,400 offices (divisions) in the U.S. alone. NATSS also reported that revenue for Temporary Staffing Services rose 22% in 1992 to a $25 billion dollar industry, in the U.S. The Temp work force at that time was filling more than 1 million job openings per day.

In May of 1993, Cable News Network (CNN) presented a half-hour special on the "Temping of America." They reported that from 1992 to

1993 there was an increase of 27% in temporary employment in America. It was assumed that this dramatic increase was due to the desperate economic recession we were going through in 1993 America.

At the same time, a trade newsletter, "Executive Recruiter News" by David Lord, reported that 12% of the 1 million daily job openings were for executives and professionals! This includes CEO's, Accountants, Attorneys, Marketeers, and Salespeople. Your future boss may be a Temp!

Also, in 1993, a market database company, Omnicomp Group, predicted that the total revenues for Temporary Placement Agencies would hit $47 billion in the next decade.

Looking at the 1997 data that was downloaded from NATSS website at *www.natss.com*, things have really accelerated. It the free article titled "**Temporary Help Reaches Record Levels In Strong Economy**," it states that, "Receipts grew 15.4% [from 1996 to 1997] to $50.3 billion." Wow! The industry has doubled from a $25 billion to $50 billion in 4 years. This indicates that even in a strong economy, Temps are in a bigger demand. The article also states that the Average Daily Employment (ADE), "rose 9.7% to 2,535,220; and payroll expanded 19% to $37.4 billion in 1997 from the previous year." Imagine a 10% increase in the number of Temps with a 19% increase in their payroll, in one year.

The NATSS article goes further to explain that the increase was due to several factors. "These are:

- **Tight Labor Market**—increase in demand for all types of employees.

- **Changing Worker Attitudes**—"workers believe that long term employment with a single company is less certain and that employment security lies in having the right skills and knowing where to get those skills."

- **Expansion of Staffing Services**—staffing services now provide complete staffing service solutions including expertise in labor and employment law compliance."

In 1998, NATSS reports that 2% of the 136 million workers in the U.S. were Temps. That's 2.7 million Temps filling more than 2.5 million jobs daily. Thus, Temp, Contracting, and Consulting opportunities are growing at an astounding rate! If the present trends continue, Temporary Employment will become the norm for mainstream society, in a relatively short time.

Summary Of Temping

So, are you starting to grasp the idea of working for an agency? It really makes sense in terms of beginning a consulting career.

First, it lets you begin an immediate job change. It makes your resume look better. It helps you establish the industry contacts you will need later. It frees you from the fear of looking for a job when the time comes. Management starts honoring your opinions and suggestions. It gets you a big pay raise. You get paid for every minute you work. You get extra tax write-offs. If you do a good job and they like your personality, you are not temporary at all. Finally, the actual work is the same as far as you are concerned, but you make much more money, even after recovering your lost benefits.

That is the real beauty of the Temping first, before Contracting or Consulting. You can get a Temp job almost right away, increase your salary, and just do the same work you have been doing, virtually the next day! Then, if you want to progress further into consulting you can attack that problem at your leisure.

How does this technique sound to you?

Summary Of Pay Increase Due To Temping, After Taxes:

Pay Increase: 175% to 200%
Overtime Increase: 35%
Tax Write-Offs Increase: 5% to 25%
Total Increase: 215% to 260%   ☺

Summary Of Chapter 3:

Starting out as a Temp is a good way to get exposure to new techniques, while meeting more people in the industry. It is a good way to begin developing a reputation for your good work. Temping provides a great financial gain! And finally, Temping doesn't require much more skill than you already have!

Are you looking forward to the new territory you are about to go into?

Chapter 4:
The Consulting Personality

Temping, Contracting, and Consulting may not be for everyone. It takes a certain personality to be a non-captive. Let's see if your personality is just right for beginning down this career path.

Winning Personalities

In any discussion of personalities, we must first consider "winner" personalities. During our lifetime, we will meet only a few people that are true winners. A very advanced Consultant unquestionably has a winner personality. To become a winner, it takes a lot of self-discipline and drive. It is an on-going, life-long process. It takes a while to become a winner. Throughout their lives, winners strive for the best.

From the book, **"Born to Win"** by James & Johnward, we can learn the basics of a winner's personality:

"Winners are authentic. Authentic people actualize their own unprecedented uniqueness and appreciate the uniqueness of others. They do not use their energy putting on a performance, maintaining pretense, and manipulating others. They are aware that there is a difference between being knowledgeable and acting knowledgeable. They do not need to hide behind a mask.

Winners may loose ground occasionally and may even fail. In spite of setbacks, winners maintain a basic self-confidence.

Winners are not afraid to do their own thinking and to use their own knowledge. They can separate facts from opinion and don't pretend to have all of the answers. They listen to others, evaluate what they have to say, but come to their own conclusions.

Winners do not play helpless, nor do they play the blaming game. Instead, they assume the responsibility for their own lives. Winners successfully make the transition from total helplessness to independence, and then to interdependence. Winners are their own bosses and they know it.

A winner's timing is right. Winners respond appropriately to the situation. Winners know that for everything there is a season and for every activity a time.

To winners, time is precious. Winners don't kill it, but live it here and now. Winners know their past, are aware and alive in the present, and look forward to the future.

[Winners] know when they are angry and can listen when others are angry with them. Winners can give and receive affection. Winners are able to love and be loved.

Winners can be spontaneous. They do not respond in predetermined, rigid ways, but can change their plans when the situation calls for it. Winners have a zest for life...

Winners are not afraid to go after what they want, and they do so in appropriate ways. Winners do not get their security by controlling others. They do not set themselves up to loose.

A winner cares about the world and its peoples. A winner is not isolated form the problems of society, but is concerned, compassionate, and committed to improving the quality of life. A winner works to make the world a better place."

Winner Concepts In Simple Terms:

- Winners are unique in how they do things.
- Winners do not put on a show or hide behind a mask.
- Winners are not afraid to do their own thinking.
- Winners listen to others, but reach their own conclusions.
- Winners always question everything said or written.
- Winners have a positive, enthusiastic attitude for everything they try.
- Winners have good timing and know when to change direction.
- Winners never have an excuse for not starting something.
- Winners are always early in everything they do, never late.
- Winners have compassion for, and help others as much as possible.
- Winners strive to make the world a better place.

In addition to being true winners, an advanced Consultant knows how to interact with people in the workplace. He can do this under extreme pressure by upper and middle management, and remain friends with them. Dealing with these pressures takes a strong sense of self-confidence, which can only come from years of experience. To appreciate this and other key aspects of consulting, let's take a look at a situation that could have happened long ago.

The Story Of The Freelance Knight

Back in medieval times, there was a special kind of knight, called the Freelance Knight. The Freelance Knight was a very skilled fighter. He was so good, that the king could not force him to obey his laws. His motto was "All for one, but loyal to none."

Now on occasion, a king would need some extra fighting power. So, he would summons the services of the Freelance Knights in the area.

Normally, these mercenaries were summoned by carrier pigeon. Each Knight would send his prospective employer a pigeon to keep for just such an occasion. That way, the geographical location of the Freelance could be kept secret.

Upon arrival, a lengthy interviewing process would begin. The chosen Freelance would have to kill 10 soldiers in one minute. Now knowing that the king was going to need these 10 men in the upcoming battle, a good Freelance would only knock them out. You see, a good Freelance knows what is best for the king.

After the "interview," the king invites the Freelance into the castle. There the Freelance negotiates what he wants the king to pay him for going into battle. The king eventually agrees to hire him and a contract is drawn up and signed. The Freelance agrees to fight the kings' mortal enemies, for special privileges and a large fee. He would never agree to totally eliminate the enemy because this would be too unrealistic. To the Freelance, money is usually not as important as the special privileges.

Before battle, the Freelance is obliged to show the king's soldiers a few pointers. In the king's mind, these new techniques would make his men so good, that he would not have to hire the Freelance the next time. The Freelance realizes all of this, but still provides his best efforts to teach the soldiers. After all, he has been in their shoes before. Where do you think he learned his basic skills, anyway?

As the real battle breaks out, the Freelance fights hard. He easily outperforms the other soldiers 3 to 1. He provides his best efforts in order to uphold his part of the contract. Shortly into battle, he notices that the king is misdirecting the entire army. After a long debate, the king refuses to relinquish control of the army to the Freelance. After all, the king hasn't known him that long.

In a situation like this, the Freelance knows it is time to take drastic measures. He pulls a carrier pigeon out of his satchel and releases it. A short while later, some of the Freelancer's mercenary friends show up.

The Freelance and his friends agree that the king needs to "step aside" in order for the battle to be won. But they know that the king won't do it voluntarily. So, they secretly sneak up behind the king, and capture him in a burlap sack. They lock him up safely in a closet, somewhere in the castle. You see, behind the scenes, all Freelancers are working together. The Freelance had a feeling he would have to resort to these drastic measures before he accepted this contract. He could tell that this king was a little bit arrogant, during the interview, and may be difficult to work for. The Freelance is still acting in the best interest of the king, of course. He just wants to make sure that the king will allow him to do a good job. Besides, the king will be safe now. He is out of harms way. The risk the Freelance has just taken is great, however. That's okay, though. The Freelance is used to this. He has helped other Freelancers do this in the past.

Now the Freelance takes command over the entire army. During the course of battle, he sees that the men are not trying the new techniques he had shown them. That is natural because these men were not given enough time to become confident in their newly acquired skills. So, the Freelance commands them to try the new methods. He also rearranges the direction of the attack. He encourages the soldiers. He gives some of them command over sub-divisions. Soon the soldiers regain confidence. In a short while, they are victorious.

After battle, the king no longer feels that he needs the services of the Freelance. The king assumes that since so many men died, the Freelance must not have been a very good teacher. But, many of the soldiers died because they did not have time to master the new skills that the Freelance had shown them. The king also assumes that the army will not have to go into battle again for a few years. So, the Freelance is not retained to further train the army. This doesn't hurt the Freelancers' feelings, though, because he knows he did his best. He is still willing to work for this king again, in the future.

As you can tell, the present and future employment of the Freelance is promoted by the kings' own mistakes. The king lets the Freelance train his men for only a few hours. The Freelance has to manage the entire army during battle in order to achieve victory, and the king doesn't realize it. And finally, the king in his short-sightedness does not further retain the services of the Freelance after the battle, to continue training the army.

A few months later, the castle is attacked again. The king has to take his army into battle again. Thinking that his men are in top condition, he is confident to win this battle. Immediately, however, his army suffers heavy casualties. During the course of events, one of the king's most trusted soldiers sees the king misdirecting the attack, again. This loyal soldier explains to the king what really had happened in the last battle. He explains how the Freelancer's leadership and organization actually won the last battle. The king, finally realizing his errors, has the Freelance summoned immediately. The king no longer needs to interview him. The king no longer needs to question his skills. The king even knows that this Freelance will already have new skills to be shown that he has never seen before.

The Freelance immediately knows why he is summoned. Battling was his business. He heard rumors of the upcoming battle long before the king knew about it. The Freelance was already prepared to go. He shows up right away, and takes command. Within a few hours, the king's army is, again, victorious. The king apologizes to the Freelance and promises him that more notice would be given to him the next time. The king takes confidence in this particular Freelance, and decides to himself that he will never hire a different Freelance again.

and they lived happily ever after

This story contains many of the aspects that will be experienced while Freelancing. First, the Consultant has a reputation to uphold, or no one will hire him in the future. He knows he will have to perform well, under pressure. He knows he will have to take high risks and make unorthodox decisions. He does not have to agree with anyone else's philosophy of managing a kingdom, however. But, this cannot get in his way when doing his job. Although we would all like to gag our boss and lock him in a closet for a few hours, the Consultant must continuously figure out how to work around erroneous decisions made by management, or fellow workers. The Consultant must provide a solution that is politically acceptable and polite. Of course, he can call his mercenary friends and brainstorm the situation first. Finally, the Consultant cannot make a king angry by persuading all of the captive knights to become Freelancers (so he writes a book for them, on the side).

The Freelance, not only performs well, but performs better than most. Since his clients and co-workers regard him highly, he is allowed to charge more. Since he charges more, he has to pass a more rigorous interview. Several people may interview him at once. He has to win their confidence by being confident. He has gained this confidence by having many years of experience in this field. In addition, he has to carefully choose whom to work for, and when. Some of his clients may be competing with each other. To be able to do all of these things, the Consultant must have a strong, righteous, yet compassionate, type of personality.

The Freelance Personality

An advanced Consultant must have the same personality traits as those of the Freelance Knight. He has to have above average or even exceptional skill in some area. He is self-motivated and keeps his skills finely tuned. He has developed a reputation of getting a job done quickly and efficiently. He questions everything. He ignores red tape. He has chosen a lifestyle that purposely avoids getting into the politics and philosophies of others. He has good timing when it comes to choosing whose side to be on. He never seems to care what others think of him, because he is constantly measuring himself. He never stays long in an uncomfortable situation. He appears to be working for some kind of a more noble cause, more important than money. He also owns and operates his own tools, which are, of course, state-of-the-art.

Most other books on consulting avoid this "personality" subject, that is one key factor to success as a Consultant. One author, however, did have an interesting view on the subject. In Hubert Bermonts' book titled, **"How To Become A Successful Consultant In Your Own Field,"** he states that "If you are indecisive, dour, fatalistic, deterministic, plodding, or pessimistic, stick to what you are doing and don't consider a consulting profession for yourself." He also explains that, "If you feel you have a need to take assertiveness training…forget consulting." Hubert is emphasizing that an advanced Consultant needs a strong, righteous personality. Let's summarize all of the personality traits that an Advanced Consultant should have.

Personality Traits Of An Advanced Consultant

1. The Consultant is above average or exceptionally good at his work.
2. The Consultant is able to get along with almost anyone.
3. The Consultant likes to teach others everything he knows.
4. The Consultant is self-motivated and perpetually refining his skills daily.
5. The Consultant has a good reputation for getting a job done.
6. The Consultant was born with a drive to question everything.
7. The Consultant is adventurous and willing to take risks.
8. The Consultant is a very good, active listener.
9. The Consultant is confident, optimistic and enthusiastic.

10. The Consultant seems to ignore what others think of him, because he is constantly measuring himself.
11. The Consultant has a high degree of "Common Sense".
12. The Consultant finishes early, almost everything he starts.
13. The Consultant has a knack of predicting how something will turn out.
14. The Consultant must be able to deliver blunt advice and conclusions.
15. The Consultant may have been fired for giving blunt advice, but still continues to do so.
16. The Consultant seems to be working for a noble cause, more important than money.
17. The Consultant owns and operates his own state-of-the-art tools.

These are the main personality traits that an "Advanced Consultant" will eventually acquire. Many of us have some of these traits. It seems, however, that we are usually missing a few of the most important ones. Some of these traits will take practically a lifetime to acquire. We can only conclude, then, that after we have been consulting for quite some time, we will have the above personality traits and skills.

Requirements For The Beginning Consultant

Lucky for us, not all of the personality traits above are required to **begin** consulting. Only a few of them are. The required personality traits and skills needed by a Beginning Consultant are listed below:

1. Your co-workers think that you do good work ("co-workers" does not necessarily include managers).
2. You are confident in your work because you have been doing it for some time, at more than one company.

3. You can, and do, get along with almost anyone.

4. You like to teach others everything that you know.

5. You seem to have more "common sense" than others do in your field.

6. You know how to operate the state-of-the-art tools of your trade.

7. You are not afraid to try Temporary Employment through job agencies.

This is not a trivial list of personality requirements for the Beginning Consultant. These personality traits are a little rare, in actuality. You should know, right away, if you meet these requirements, without giving it too much thought. If you have to really think about this list, then you may not be quite ready to begin a consulting career. If the last item is the only one that you have mixed feelings about, then you probably are ready! Ask others if they think you have these prerequisites. With these minimal personality traits and a willingness to try something new, you will be able to prosper as a Consultant.

Summary Of Chapter 4:

It takes a certain personality to enjoy non-captive work. In the beginning, the personality requirements are minimal. But as a worker moves higher up into consulting, the personality blossoms into a powerful winning and compassionate one.

Chances are, if you meet the minimum prerequisites, you have already decided to try a more adventurous, rewarding career. A career where you can help many more people. A career that will promote exposure to a wider diversity of challenges and solutions. One that is full of countless, new opportunities. Do you have an aggressive yet compassionate personality? Do you have the minimum requirements to be a Freelance? If so, are you ready to take action?

Chapter 5:
Skills Needed By The Consultant

Companies are just starting to realize that utilizing the skills of Temps, Contractors, and Consultants can be much more efficient. Consultants get products to the market place sooner because they have already gone through the learning curves. Their experiences bring forth products that are more desirable in the marketplace. The products they produce are more ingenious and reliable. If used properly, Consultants can be much cheaper to retain, than employees are.

Consultants are very small, flexible entities. They don't get too bogged down with big company politics. Because of this, they can work more than three times faster than an employee can. Consultants bring their experience from many other companies. Consultants require very little overhead to employ. Most of the time they work off-site and usually have more computing power than an entire engineering department. Having a good consultant on the job-site boosts the morale and knowledge pool of all the employees on the project.

However, consulting is not a specific type of job, requiring a specific skill. It is just a new way of being employed, while doing the same old job. The actual job skills that a Consultant uses to perform a particular task are the same ones he used when he was a Captive employee. However, because of the experience gained from working at many companies, a Consultant's skills are vast, and ever expanding. The Consultant is constantly adjusting his skills for every single project he works on, no matter how small. This wide variety of exposure produces a Consultant that is well versed in technical, professional, and, what is termed, "people" skills.

It is the net sum of all the skills, gained at several companies, that makes up the Consultant. The Consultants confidence and attitude develop automatically as years of experience are accumulated. When a Consultant is asked a question, he answers in a matter-of-fact manner, because he already has experienced that situation.

Most people think that Consultants are hired just to give advice and opinions. This isn't at all correct! Consultants are hired to work just like a Captive employee. They have a specific task to accomplish in a specific time frame. Now in the course of working on this task, they are frequently asked for advice and opinions about how to accomplish this task, easily and quickly. So, it is in this context that they do give advice and opinions. These days there are many discussions about which software packages, which materials, which outside vendors, and which machines to use for a particular task. But, first and foremost, a Consultant is hired to be a hard worker just like the rest of us! Because of his vast experience, a Consultant works much faster than a captive employee. Again because of a wide range of experience, he is qualified to give advice on how to work faster. Let's clarify the Consultant's role further, in the next section.

Why Consultants Are Needed

Most Consultants are needed because the client is feeling pressure to get something done in a certain amount of time. We can refer to these needs as "time-pressurized" needs. Rarely will a client not have a time-pressurized need. If this situation does occur, then the client may be entering into a new product area. They are looking to expand. These expansion-needs can be categorized into "growth-pressurized" needs.

Professor Michael Ames Ph.D., taught a course at California State University Fullerton called **"How to Start And Operate Your Own Successful Consulting Practice"**. In that course, he lists ten main reasons why corporations need Consultants.

Ten Reasons Why Corporations Need Consultants:

1. The need to Cope With Overloads.
2. The need to Turn Things Around.
3. The need to Overcome Competition.
4. The need to Learn Something Quickly.
5. The need to React To A Change.
6. The need for Capital.
7. The need to Assist Allies.
8. The need for a Particular Skill.
9. The need to Start New Ventures.
10. The need to Find Something New.

The first 7 needs above are time-pressurized needs. These are good opportunities for consulting. The client has to react quickly. Therefore, the Consultant's billing rate is not much of a concern. Some of these time-pressurized needs are short-lived, however. So, the Consultant is challenged with trying to figure out how to stay employed by the client after his immediate needs are satisfied. The last two needs, in the list, are growth-pressure needs. For some reason the corporation feels that it needs to expand. Perhaps it has too much cash in the bank and wants to spend it. So, it wants to invest in new endeavors. Need number 8, the need for a particular skill, may involve both time and growth pressurized needs. In the next section, Professor Ames discusses these further.

Need #1: The need to cope with overloads:

This is a very common time-pressurized need. The client has either received new work or is behind in backlogged work. This time deadline forces the use of outside help. Nothing new is needed, other than time-effectiveness. A Consultant can certainly crank the work out about 3 times faster than captive employee can.

Need #2: The need to turn things around:

The corporation has reached some sort of stalemate. Maybe a key person has resigned and the rest of the staff does not have the knowledge to proceed. Maybe a vendor or Contractor, hired by the corporation, can't figure out how to complete a project, or make it work up to specification. The need in this case is for both new ideas and new directions, with time-pressure thrown in for the fun of it. It could also be a managerial roadblock, or a political problem. A Consultant, immune to corporate politics, and qualified at "carefully making suggestions," can certainly get the project moving in a proper direction. However, he must be aware that the budget for the project may be quite low by now.

Need #3: The need to overcome the competition:

Usually a corporation that is first in the marketplace with a new product captures 60% of the market. The rest of the corporations fight over the remaining 40%. This is very common. Corporations should be used to dealing with and solving this type of problem: keeping up with the competition. If the problem reaches a high degree of seriousness, the company's actual existence may be in jeopardy. This will cause internal pressures and personality clashes to develop, leading to the need for a Consultant. The Consultant's role in his case is to be a buffer or an arbitrator. This situation is about 85% politics. It could also lead to other factions hiring their own Consultants. In which case, Consultants arguing with Consultants will be inevitable. There is a real good chance that one of the Consultants will end up with all of the blame for the failure to keep up with the competition!

Need #4: The need to learn something quickly:

This need can arise when there is an acquisition of a new product-line from another company. The corporation has to come up to speed on this new product. The Consultant is needed to transfer the technology from one corporation to the other. The Consultant is also needed to train the employees quickly. To land this type of work, the Consultant must sell his personality, not just his technical and teaching skills. Usually a Consultant referred to this type of job has performed teaching before or has given seminars.

Need #5: The need to react to change:

In a broad sense, all corporations are reacting to change all of the time. When they must react quickly or are taken by surprise by an external event, a Consultant is usually brought in. This could be the need to react to a new government regulation, a new technology, a major change in the economy, or a competitor cut his price drastically. The need to react may not even be real but merely perceived. A perceived need is a time-pressurized need that may not have a firm deadline. The Consultant's technical skill level is important for this kind of opportunity.

Need #6: The need for capital:

Raising money is an important need for a Consultant. It makes up about 20% of all consulting business. The Consultant's role is to define the need to Entrepreneurs and Venture Capitalists. How many people need the money and why they need the money, must be documented. The Consultant has to be careful when taking this type of job. Can they afford to pay the Consultant?

Need #7: The need to assist allies:

Corporations form strategic alliances with other corporations in order to help each other sell more products. Sometimes, large corporations even buy portions of smaller allies, to financially boost them. However, sometimes these allies get into trouble and can't deliver. Since the larger corporation is too busy with it's own problems, it may need the aid of a Consultant. The Consultant's job is to represent the corporation in defining the ally's problem, and recommending the solution. Sometimes the Consultant is chosen because he lives close by to the ally. This type of job could end up being a long-term consulting situation. However, there will be a good deal of politics involved. Before taking the job, the Consultant should ask himself, "Would I buy part of this ally company?"

Need #8: The need for a particular skill:

This is a frequent need by client corporations. It could be that they don't have the time to wait for captive employees to come up to speed. It could also be that they want an expert to set up a new system or methodology, correctly, regardless of how long it will take. For example, quite popular these days, is to bring in someone to set up an ISO9000 documentation standard or to develop an Intranet network. Whatever the case, they need a particular skill. The client might not know that the skill they are requiring is really quite common in the industry. This is one of the better opportunities for Consultants, because they can pretty much charge what they want.

Need #9: The need to start a new venture:

This need can arise when a corporation has saturated a marketplace with product. For example, if every airline had 1000 jets, and each jet lasts 50 years, then there is no longer a reason for jet manufacturers to make any more jets. Corporations in this situation have both time and money. What they don't have is new ideas, new directions, new skills, or maybe they just lack confidence. A few Consultants are brought in to give them new ideas. The Consultant must be careful not to give up his ideas for free, during the interview. He must also try to figure out a way to remain essential to the implementation of the new venture. This job requires a high degree of imagination and people skills.

Need #10: The need to find something new:

This is a similar need to the one above, except that it is a need to find something in the same field. This job could be defining a new product of the type that the corporation is already used to dealing with. This job requires using imagination, in a more practical way. The new product must fit in with the old product-line, for example. Corporations requiring this skill probably have money, but are weak in the marketing department.

Timely Opportunities

You can tell that most of the corporations' needs are related to solving time-crunches. Therefore, most of the consulting opportunities, out there, fall into this category. Poor planning, mismanagement, or an overloaded workforce can sometimes cause these time-pressurized needs. Time crunches may also be caused by corporate success. The customers may want new features added to the existing product. The marketing department may have identified a new market for a product that doesn't exist yet. The potential customer may have said they will spend millions on this new product idea if the corporation can deliver it by a certain date. These are all examples of perfect consulting climates. To a Consultant, these time-crunches mean good money and a good opportunity to work for someone that really needs his skills. To a

Consultant, time-pressurized situations are not "negative" situations. Working against time is a perfect opportunity to get consulting work.

Needs Of The Client

Although the corporation has a general need to fulfill, emphasis should not be put on that! Instead, the project manager, your boss, has his own subset of needs. These are more important to achieve. Professor Ames points out the client's most fundamental need:

"The need to be right about you!"

Professor Ames explains that in order to figure out if the right Consultant was selected, the client will ask himself the following series of questions:

1. Will the Consultant make me look bad?

> Do I really understand my problem?
> Do I really need a Consultant?
> What will my colleagues think?

2. Does the Consultant really know how to deal with my problem?

> Does the Consultant understand the problem?
> Has the Consultant dealt with similar problems before?
> Does the Consultant know how to solve my problem, step-by-step?

3. Does the Consultant have the skills to intervene and help me solve my problem in a positive manner?

> Will the Consultant be too bossy?
> Will the Consultant be too opinionated?
> Will the Consultant be unwilling to accept my direction?

Will the Consultant be unwilling to heed to my advice?

Will the Consultant be too eager to please and not tell the truth?

4. Is the Consultant worth his fees?

Are the fees reasonable?

Will the Consultant concentrate on MY problem?

5. Will the Consultant be discrete?

Will the Consultant maintain confidentiality?

Will the Consultant say the wrong things to the wrong people?

6. Will I be sucked in?

Is the Consultant going to recommend work just to build up fees?

Does the Consultant realize that I will be stuck with the outcome?

I can testify, for a fact, that not only does the client think of these questions before he hires you, but also he worries about them everyday! Especially item #6!

Skills Required By The Client

Most of the time, neither a job agency nor a client knows what type of skill is really needed to perform a particular job! In fact, the Consultant may not know what the client likes about him, until he has been on the job for several weeks. What may be common sense to the Consultant, is usually the "special skill" that the client has been looking for.

Several Consultants in the same field can have completely different techniques for accommodating the client's needs. Personality Traits are sometimes more important than actual job skills. People Skills, are even more important. As far as pinpointing the actual job skills required, we could list a few that seem to help, but it would be misleading to say they are always required. When it comes to required skills, all we can say is that the Consultant's skills, in his particular field, must be above average or even exceptional. Beyond that, he must be politically savvy, and treat his boss like he is always right! However, if the Consultant disagrees, he also knows how to get his point across.

What Skills Do You Really Have?

Have you ever tried to write down everything that you have ever learned during your working career? It is amazing how much knowledge each one of us has soaked up into our melon. I recommend that you try to make a list of everything you have done on every job you've ever had, as soon as possible. It is a great way to boost your self-confidence and give you some insight on where you want to go with your new career. All of this talk, about exceptional skills, can be somewhat depressing, for a beginner. Hopefully, while making this list, you will remember a few things you are good at, and maybe even some you want to try to avoid. One of the benefits of consulting is more freedom in choosing what you want to do! Making this list is a great way to start a career change.

Step 5.1: Make A List Of Everything You Know How To Do.

Now, how are your people skills? Do other people think that you're swell? How do you cope with company politics? Write down some of your past political crisisies and the outcome. How well did you survive?

Step 5.2: Write Down Some Of Your Past Political Crisisies And The Outcome.

Skills Used By Consultants

In the story of the Freelance Knight, in the last chapter, what were the actual fighting skills that made him better than a soldier was? He did seem to know what to do, right away. He had his strategy and tools ready, before he needed them. He knew how to deal with bad leadership.

Is bad leadership something that still impedes victory at job sites? Yes, sometimes. Most of the time, however, clients and their departments are usually over-worked or overwhelmed by many things. That doesn't mean they are bad at their job.

Let's look at some more special skills that will be needed while consulting.

Technical Skills

It is assumed that whatever the Freelancer's skills were yesterday, tomorrow they will be more advanced. A Consultant's skills, likewise, are forever expanding. The Consultant is equally free to use older skills anytime he wishes. The Consultant, with his vast experience, can perform the same task, in a number of different ways. He is completely flexible.

Special Skill #1—Understanding What The Client Really Wants And Needs.

One of the important skills learned while consulting is being able to understand what the client really wants and needs. What is the client's problem? Does he want a clone of himself? Does he want us to kick somebody else's butt, for him? Does he want the same thing that the corporation wants? After working on several projects, we will be able to read the minds of clients.

Special Skill #2—Being Honest With Yourself:

Many times the Consultant will break the project down into steps. The Consultant may choose which step would be the most fun to work on. He may find something entertaining in the project, and rationalize that he should be working on that task instead of the others. He may confuse the most important thing to do, with the more entertaining one. It is a constant struggle trying to remain focused on what the client wants done. To do this, you must be honest with yourself. Being honest with oneself is a skill used regularly in consulting.

You must be honest with yourself, first. Only then, can you clearly see what the client wants. Make sure you are doing what the client wants, and not what you want, and not necessarily what the corporation wants. Think of it as a sacrifice. By sacrificing your desires, and sometimes the corporation's desires, and satisfying the client's first, you are overcoming one of the biggest obstacles to success. Keep yourself in check [mate]. It takes a lot of self-discipline to be honest with yourself, continuously.

Special Skill #3—Respect For Authority At All Times

Clients act like they actually know more about your field than you do! You can never fight that problem. It is a fact of consulting life. In addition, if a project is going too slow, the client will bring in more know-it-alls or heavyweights (Consultants). All of this can be very frustrating to an expert in the field. Consultants are frequently faced with this situation. A Consultant must play the role of servant. A Consultant must remain a Humble Servant of Authority, at all times.

Remaining mellow, at all costs, is one of the most powerful concepts in the universe. It is the teachings of Christ, Buddha, and many other important philosophers and leaders, throughout all time. Getting the proper exercise and meditating on positive things will also help make you a mellow person.

I remain humble by cheering myself up with a truism that I learned from a well-known Consultant, Gerald M. Weinburg at *www.geraldmweinburg.com*. Quoting him,

"It's not the beginning of a crisis, it's the end of an illusion."

I say this to myself, whenever I see a crisis situation and I try to help my superiors overcome the loss of their illusion!

Special Skill #4—Ability To Help The Client Discover The Real Truth

A Consultant must never tell the client his real, honest, opinion. It will only cause huge ripple in the space-time continuum. Besides, even if the universe doesn't collapse, you will be fired! Instead, the Consultant is obligated to get the client to arrive at the truth on his own.

The Consultant accomplishes this by bringing up issues in the form of questions:

Instead of: "If we don't test all of this software, it's all going to crash someday."

Say: "Do you think we have time to test the software or should we put it aside for later?"

Note that the actual wording is crucial!

Special Skill #5: Ability To Blurt Out Instant Facts, Anytime

Being able to blurt out instant facts is a required skill for a Consultant. If a "management-type" comes up to ask you a question, you can bet that it will be about **cost** or **schedules**. "How long does such and such take," is a common question. If you are experienced, you should know. These numbers should come pouring right out of your mouth, without hesitation. Start measuring everything that you do, so, you too, can be prepared to regurgitate on your next boss (facts, that is).

Think of a fact that the client might need tomorrow. Go and calculate it out today. Have it ready, on the tip of your tongue, for your next run-in with the big cheese.

Let's say I see my boss eyeing a map of the Red Sea. Now since he has a trucking business over there, I get a gut feeling he'll be asking an important question in the status meeting tomorrow. I get a feeling that he wants to cross the Red Sea, or go around it. Sure enough, the next day in the meeting he asks, "Jimmy, how long will it take you to part the Red Sea?" "About 10 minutes a foot," I blurt out.

Special Skill #6: Ability To Work Under Time-Pressure

A Consultant must be skilled in working under time constraints! Time–pressurized problem solving is the Consultant's normal mode of operation. This skill can only be learned on the job. Usually a beginning Consultant doesn't have it yet. The more you Temp, Contract, or Consult the faster you will get. Speed comes from having done a similar task before. Starting out as a Temp is a good way to build up speed.

Other Skills

A Consultant, in addition to having expert technical skills, must be a marketeer, salesman, manager, trainer, accountant, contract negotiator, inventor, computer operator, a politician, a motivator, and general guru. This book will give you quick and easy insight to pursue and develop all of your own skills in these subjects.

Many of the political and people skills needed have to be learned on the job, however. These can only be learned by being exposed to a variety of situations. It takes practice to have respect for your superiors at all times. This is one of the most important reasons that beginners should start out as Temps.

Skills Needed By The Beginning Consultant

Well, do you think you can cut the mustard as a beginning Consultant? If not, are you afraid of finding out?

Special Skill #7—Seeking The Unknown With Enthusiasm

A Beginning Consultants' main obstacle is getting used to "Seeking the Unknown" with enthusiasm and excitement! You should never be afraid of trying something new (as long as it is legal and moral). You should look forward to it!

A good book on creativity and problem solving is called **"Imagineering—How To Profit From Your Creative Powers,"** by Michael Le Beouf. In it, Michael lists many of the typical excuses that people use for not being creative, quite eloquently. Michael describes them as Traps:

> **"Trap #1.** I'm too old.
> **Trap #2.** I'm too busy.
> **Trap #3.** What will other people think?
> **Trap #4.** I don't have the proper credentials.
> **Trap #5.** I might fail.
> **Trap #6.** I work for a company. I can't be creative [there].
> **Trap #7.** I'm a woman. Men are the ingenious Ones.
> **Trap #8.** I don't have a high I.Q."

He goes on to explain that the majority of these problems are rooted in fears. Fear of Failure, Fear of Ridicule, and Fear of the Unknown are the leading three. Purposely "Seeking the Unknown" is the only way to overcome the "Fear of the Unknown".

According to Le Beouf, "the strength of the human brain is that it seeks the 'new' automatically." He says, "without newness being input on a regular basis, we humans do not live well. This especially applies to the job world where we spend the majority of our waking hours." Our quality of life will decay radically if we don't expose ourselves to new things on a regular basis.

Look forward to going into the newness, and freshness, of the unknown! Don't be afraid. Be glad! Look forward to new things, without fear. It's a great feeling! It occurs frequently in consulting. You are luckier than most people to have that feeling. Most people are stuck doing the same job, over and over. They are too afraid to try something new. They have deprived themselves.

The Market For The Consultant's Skills

There has to be a substantial market for the Consultant's skills, in his local, geographical area. Corporations in your area must frequently experience time-pressurized goals, in your field. My field of electronics is great for that!

If you pick a specialty niche that is too narrow, you may not get enough calls. Diversify! You will be much better off. There is no such thing as having too many skills, especially in consulting. Be well rounded! Be Open-Minded! Stay Flexible! Some Consultants take this concept to the extreme, by having many different resumes and business cards. If you can truly perform the work, why not have several versions?

What the Consultant does today to make a living may not be needed 2 years from now. The Consultant is self-motivated, however, and therefore keeps learning newer skills. Make it a point to read a new book, on a new subject, about every two weeks. These days you can go to the large bookstore chains like Borders or Barnes & Noble, and read a book while you drink coffee.

Now, do you realize that in a captive environment, the company tends to prevent you from being well rounded? Management wants to comprehend your skills so they can track, allocate, and measure your progress and expansion (supposedly so they can give you the proper raises, ha).

For consulting, it is considered an asset to be well versed in many subjects. Don't be like those hardheaded Freelancers, out there, that are starving. Listen to the world. The world will tell you what you are good at and how to fill its needs. In fact, listen to the whole universe!

Many Freelancers, of all types, fail in market selection. They all get locked into the thought that they will tell the world what they are going to do. For example, they might say, "I don't want to Consult for companies that are under a time-constraint." Well, guess what? As a Consultant, you've just wiped out the majority of job opportunities.

Nurturing Good References

Consultants need good references to get hired. While you are in good standing with a company, you can nurture good references. The best technique is to always ask for them. When a project comes to a close, ask your boss if he has the time to write you a letter of recommendation. Most managers will take the time to do it. Don't forget to ask for their home phone numbers and email addresses while you're at it. Make it a habit of collecting these letters, phone numbers, and email addresses throughout your travels. Collect them from fellow workers, as well as managers.

Another technique for insuring that your references are good is to voluntarily write Letters of Recommendation for others. Whenever I work with someone that really tries to help their company, I like to make sure they get recognition for it. Before I leave a project, I will write letters of recommendation for certain employees that I feel did a great job, especially if they helped me out. I give these letters to the personnel office, where they put them in the employees' file. I also ask the personnel manager to keep it a secret. When it comes to review time, the file is pulled and both the employee and department manager are surprised to find this letter in there. Many times, the letter will help them get big raises!

One fellow I worked with was trying to get a company to hire him and move him out to Colorado. That company said they couldn't hire him unless he had the title of Project Engineer. At the time, I didn't know of this. I had worked with him for several years, and wanted to help him get some recognition for his hard work. My assignment there was about to end, also. So, I wrote a Letter Of Recommendation for him. One month later, after I was gone, the company gave him his review. They found the letter in his file and were very pleased. The president of the company wrote me a letter thanking me for telling them about their employees' performance. The president also thanked me for doing a good job and wanted to know if I needed a reference! Anyway, they gave this fellow a big raise and promoted him to Project Engineer. Then, he called the second company and told them about his new title. They immediately wanted to interview him, so he flew out to Colorado. When they got around to discussing about pay, he told them he wanted 10% more than he was presently making. They also agreed to pay to move him out. He received a 25% raise, total, received a new title, and was moved to the place of his choice! They also sold his Condo for him and paid for his family to live in a hotel until he found a new house! Now, I can't accept credit for all of this, because this fellow, after all, was a hard worker and deserved all of this. However, the simple Letter of Recommendation that was found in his personnel file triggered these events. Use them freely and you will always be remembered for it, especially when you need a recommendation.

One thing to notice is that complimenting others is contagious. If you give compliments to someone, they are reminded that you deserve compliments too. Pretty soon it is decided that we really were a good team and did accomplish a major project, after all! Even verbal compliments can provide you with future references. Let other people know that you appreciate them! When a Consultant compliments a beginning employee the effect is magnified. [Of course, a good Consultant knows that a beginning employee is just as important as the president of the company]. Make it a habit to freely give compliments! Shake people's hands and tell them how much they have helped you. Remember when you were a kid playing baseball and someone says to you, "Nice Catch!" Well, keep that rally going!

Summary Of Chapter 5

An Advanced Consultant has to be above average or exceptionally good in a certain field. He has to be able to anticipate how the client expects him to perform his assignment. This requires the he be flexible in the ways that he actually performs his job.

In addition to technical skill, an experienced Consultant must have people and political skills. This means that he has to attain the seven additional Special Skills mentioned in this chapter, which include respect for authority and the ability to work on what the client really needs.

There also has to be a sizable market need for the Consultant's technical skills, in his geographical area. Without enough contacts in the local area, it will be difficult to stay employed as a Consultant.

The Consultant also needs good references. Nurturing good references by complimenting others is the best way to get these.

A beginning Consultant's greatest challenge is to not be afraid of the unknown. He must constantly be looking forward to experience new and unknown job opportunities. Are you ready to seek the unknown with enthusiasm?

Chapter 6:
Look, Before You Leap...

Before you begin Temporary, Contracting, or Consulting work, you need to get a few things prepared. How many times have you had the opportunity to prepare for a new career? If you are planning on Temping, then the preparation should be relatively painless. You will need to carry your own medical insurances. You will also need to set up a database of job agencies and contacts. If you are preparing to Contract or Consult, many more systems need to be in place, including those for Temping. You must be your own company and have a complete electronic accounting system. The company will have to track all of its expenses and profits. Hopefully, most of this will be accomplished with the aid of a personal computer.

Warning About Quitting Your Present Job

Before going into preparation for a new career, I need to make sure that you understand a very important concept. *It is at least 50 times harder to get a job, if you don't have a job! If you have a job right now, don't quit.* It will take time to find a new job using the techniques of this book. If you quit your job, nobody will believe anything that you say. You will have to prove everything. Potential clients will assume that you are one of those lazy, deadbeats that has deserved to be either laid off or fired. This makes it extremely difficult to find a new job. Remember this fundamental concept for finding a job. It applies to any type of employment. People that aren't working have a hard time getting job offers. Ironic, isn't it? If you are unemployed right now, Temping could be your only hope. That is when many people try it, when they are desperate.

Starting Your Own Company

Whether you plan to Temp or Consult, you should set up your own company, first. When you are a Temp, having your own company greatly improves your chances of getting consulting work.

Companies come in three basic categories. These are as follows: sole-proprietorships, partnerships, and corporations. For a first-time operator, you want to be a sole-proprietorship. It can be a single person. The other types of companies require more than one person, or at least a tax advisor. You don't need any help right now mismanaging your money. You should be able to handle that yourself.

A partnership, which is basically a sole-proprietorship with more than one owner, has more problems to deal with. How will the partners decide when to buy and when to save? Will your partner work as hard as you will? These problems are more ethical and social in nature. They are hard to manage and correct. A sole-proprietorship doesn't have the complication of extra partners.

A corporation can be owned and managed by a single person, although on the books there has to be more than one officer. Eventually, all Consultants should be incorporated. Some job offers require that you be incorporated. However, corporations are a little expensive. As you advance into your consulting career, you will need to become incorporated. It will take a taxman and an accountant to track the financials. It will give you the highest tax advantages. But, let's not get sidetracked by this right now.

At this point, starting a new career will be difficult enough without having the extra complexity of a corporation to setup. It's hard enough doing your job. Why complicate the problem with a bunch of other people's personalities? You should gain experience loosing your own money first, then later, you can get other people to help you loose it. First try running a sole-proprietorship. It's hard enough. Besides, a sole-proprietorship can easily be converted to a corporation later on.

Defining The Company's Mission

To keep yourself focused, you need to write down what your company's mission in life is. What will it be doing after it matures? Look into the future three years and write down some goals. Will you be offering a service or a product? Will you be a researcher or a developer? Do you plan to manufacture your own products someday? What skills can you provide to others?

Don't limit your options too much. A three-year plan is not very long range. Besides, if you haven't tried Temping yet, you probably don't realize what clients need. As you perform more and more jobs, your worth to society will become more clearly defined. Clients will soon be telling you what your are good at! Keep re-writing your company's mission as it matures.

Selecting The Company Name

With a mission statement in mind, it is a lot easier to select a company name. Selecting a name can be difficult. Select a name that summarizes what your mission is. Some people select names that begin with the first letters of the alphabet so their name will appear sooner, in the phone book. Consultants don't really depend on the phone book for referrals, though. Try to make your name positive sounding. Avoid the temptation to be too cute or witty. Also, don't make the name complicated to say. Be creative in choosing your name. Steer away from standard phrases like Standard, Advanced, Consultants, Enterprises, Associates and so on, because they lack creativity. Get your family and friends involved with the name creation. Make sure they understand what you are going to do and let them brainstorm with you. Make sure it is easy to spell. Say it to your friends over the phone and see if they automatically know how to spell it.

The name you choose is not really all that important, however, you will be stuck with it for a while. Make sure it makes you happy above all else. Spend some time and have fun with it.

Filing The DBA

After selecting what is called a "fictitious" name, you must file a Fictitious Name Statement with the county clerk. First, you go down to the County Clerks Office. There they have catalogs of other company names. You must look up your name and see if someone is already using that one. If not, you fill out a Fictitious Name Statement and pay about a $20 fee. Three copies of the statement are given to you.

The first copy of the Fictitious Name Statement is taken to a newspaper. You must announce your new company in a newspaper, 1 day a week for 4 weeks straight (in most counties). This announcement is called a DBA announcement. DBA stands for "Doing Business As." The announcement says, "[your name] is Doing Business As [your company name]." There are several business reasons you must announce this. One reason to equate a real person responsible for the company so that: the people at the bank can recognize a face that belongs to the company name, the IRS can hold someone responsible for the companies taxes, and so on. Running of the DBA ad costs around $80. Some large newspapers will file the Fictitious Name and run the DBA announcement for you, at a much cheaper rate.

The second copy of the name statement is taken to the City Clerks Office. You must tell them what type of business you are starting. They check the local zoning laws to see if it is O.K. to have that business at that address. For example, if you are a tool and die consultant, your house will not be zoned to run a 60-ton stamp press in the garage! A normal consulting job, where you do most development at the customers' site, most likely comes under a "secretarial" or "administration" category for your home. The city, once satisfied with your zoning, charges about $35 for a city license. Most cities require you to renew that license every year. It is very helpful to have a city business license when dealing with the IRS, since they may try to come in and call your business a hobby.

The third copy of the Fictitious Name Statement is needed for opening up a bank account. You will need both a saving and a checking account in the company's name. Everything you purchase for your company should be paid for by check or by a company credit card. This leaves a paper trail for the IRS to follow. When you get paid as a Contractor or a Consultant, you need to deposit your checks into the company checking account. The bank makes you wait 5 days for this type of company check to clear, before you can use the money! Usually, only your first check will have this surprising effect.

Make sure your bank accounts can be converted to do Online Bill Paying. This will be required for Contracting or Consulting later. It is also recommended for Temping, now. This is discussed further in this chapter.

Step 6.1: File A Dba And Open Bank Accounts Now.

Congratulations, you are now a company! There are several advantages you have now over those that are not yet a company. First of all, it indicates to the rest of the world that you are serious about succeeding in your chosen field (in case they still weren't sure). Furthermore, people consider it safer to give you work because you are a responsible, self-made, above-the-norm, company manager with some insights into the business and employer side of things (little do they know that you just started your company yesterday). Also, if you are on a Temp job, and your boss (the client) finds out you have your own company, the next time he needs you, he knows he can call you directly without going through the job agency (our biggest goal)!

Setting Up Your Office For Temping

A normal office must have few forms of electronic communications in it. These include telephone and Internet services.

Get A Company Phone Line

Every company must have it's own phone number. Get a company phone number installed in your house. Don't use it for dial-up Modem communications, however. Use your home phone for dial-up web surfing instead. The company phone must be kept clear so you can accept calls, at any time.

Get An Answering Machine

It goes without saying, but every business must have an answering machine. This will allow you to receive offers for work when you are away at other jobs. A good machine will allow you to play back all of your messages, over the phone, to your present location. More important than the machine itself, however, is making sure you listen to the messages daily! A good way to really make people angry is to give them a method of leaving a message for you, and then ignore the messages.

Get A Pager

Most answering machines have an automatic paging mechanism built in. When you receive a message on the machine, it pages you. A few minutes later, you can call your machine and listen to the message. If it is an important message, you can respond immediately and contact the caller. You can return their calls in minutes rather than hours. I personally use a pager that is built into my watch called the BeepWear Pro.

Get A Cell Phone

If you are in your car when you get an important page, you need to be able to call people back. A cell phone is the only choice in this situation. Although expensive, you can get a few calls in while driving, and bill your client for them. Keep your cell phone number a secret. Don't allow anyone to call your cell phone. Only use the cell phone to call others, when it is convenient for you.

Get FAX Capability

Additional hardware should also include a FAX machine. When the proper moment arrives, being able to send, or receive a FAX will be the only difference between getting a job and getting turned down. Most computer systems come complete with a MODEM capable of FAX-ING. For this type of FAX to work, the computer will have to be left on to receive a FAX. Initially though, you will need your FAX peripheral only to send a FAX. The faxes are sent "paperless," directly from the Word processing program into the phone line.

Get Email And Internet

These days, Email and Internet accessibility is a must. You must be able to send and receive email, and search the Internet for jobs, from your home office. This also requires the use of a dial-up MODEM.

Microsoft Network™, at *www.msn.com*, is an adequate dial-up service that comes with Microsoft Windows™. Under Windows, the sign-up is automatic, if you have a credit card. Microsoft Explorer™ is the browser that comes with Windows. There are many other providers, also, such as America On Line™, Netscape™, and Earthlink™ to name a few. Most services are around $20 a month. If your Internet Service Provider (ISP) does not have a local phone number for you to get online with, then your phone bill will go way up. Make sure whomever you sign up with has a local phone number for Internet, and that it is not a toll call. Get connected now!

Get A Personal Digital Assistant

A Personal Digital Assistant (PDA) is great for keeping track of contacts and appointments. The Palm Pilot™ is a popular brand. Remember that since it is a computer, it needs to be backed up just like a regular computer. Daily the PDA should be uploaded to your big computer. Then the big computer should be backed up weekly onto a writable CDROM. Keep all of your appointments in the PDA.

In lieu of a PDA, Microsoft's Outlook™ software, which is usually used for the email, can also be used as an organizer. It has a built in Task List that I use a lot. I can also download my appointments and phone numbers into my watch by holding it up to the computer screen and waiting a few seconds. Outlook is a good program to use for email or appointments, but you must be by your big computer to get them.

Change Your Mailing Address

The next thing to do with your new company is to get all of your occupation-related mail sent to your new company address. This includes trade magazines, parts catalogs, and any new literature you may request from vendors. The point of this is to get the whole world to start recognizing that you are a legitimate company. From time to time, you may need to purchase parts or software, or get free samples for your own company. It will help you later if you are already on their mailing list or in their computer.

Step 6.2: Set Up Your Communication Systems Now.

Start Keeping A Bonded Notebook

Your ideas and consulting work for others will soon become invaluable. So, it is imperative that you keep them in a bonded notebook. Some of your ideas may be patentable. Others ideas may be handy to use on a job 10 years from now. The notebook offers, as a minimum, a place to collect everything. In the notebook, I keep track of the hours I worked, and what I'm working on. I keep a separate notebook for each client I work for. I have an another notebook for all of my own personal ideas. In addition, a third notebook is used to store just names, addresses, and phone numbers of people I meet in my field. Furthermore, the IRS likes you to use the notebook concept. They prefer that you keep a separate notebook for each project, especially if you are working for the same client long-term. Finally, keeping a notebook at all times helps organize your time and your thinking.

A special kind of notebook is required for consulting. It must be a bonded notebook because the pages are numbered, and you can tell if one was torn out. The page numbering also makes it handy for developing a Table of Contents as you progress through a notebook. Besides being bonded, the notebook must have large enough pages to glue in regular 8.5x11 pieces of paper. The only brand of notebook I have found satisfactory for this is the "Computation Notebook", by the Dennison Stationary Products Co. in Framingham, MA. The model number is 43-648. It is a bonded notebook with a sheet size of 11+3/4 "x 9+1/2", and it is quad-ruled. I order mine locally through the office supply company called "Staples". They are about $12 each and last about 3 months.

It is also recommend that you also purchase several glue sticks for gluing things into your notebooks. In my notebooks, I glue in computer printouts, photographs, oscilloscope waveforms, data sheets, purchase order copies, vendor quotes, and basically any xeroxes, faxes, or important emails that other people send to me. I also glue in everyone's business card, in the back few pages of the notebook. I then make little notes next to them as to what they sell and how it affects the project I'm working on. I have found the notebook invaluable as a storage tool. I rarely loose track of any piece of paper, and if I do, it's because I forgot to glue it into my notebook. Keeping track of things impresses everyone working around you.

Carrying a notebook around at a clients office also shows that you are ready to record the latest changes in the clients thinking and his new ideas and strategies. It makes people think you are ready to do some serious analysis.

It will take some time getting used to the notebook concept. It is very awkward at first. If you hired a Consultant wouldn't you expect him to write down everything into a notebook? Start up this good habit as soon as possible!

Step 6.3: Start Your Notebook Now.

The Furniture

The most important part of the office is the desk. You've got to have a dedicated desk for any kind of serious work. The bigger the desk the better. My desk is 11 feet long! It holds my computer, mouse, keyboard, monitor, scanner, FAX, printer, answering machine, PDA cradle, and cell phone charger.

In addition to the desk, you will need a filing cabinet and some bookshelves. The filing cabinet will be used to store all of your receipts and IRS records. The bookshelves will be used to hold all of your notebooks.

Don't forget to get a very expensive comfortable chair. You will be spending 1000's of hours in this chair.

Step 6.4: Buy Office Furniture Now.

Choose Your Insurance Companies

After you land your first Temp job, you will need a few types of health insurances. The time to begin finding out about their cost is now. Don't buy any until you actually start non-captive work, however.

The first type of insurance we need to consider is Medical Insurance. Medical insurance is required for you and your family. It is needed due to the high cost of hospitalization, if someone in your family gets ill. A Health Maintenance Organization, or HMO, offers a full coverage of categories for your whole family, including preventative measures. You must go to their facilities, most of the time, however. Examples of these are Kaiser Permenente, Pacificare, Maxicare, FHP, Blue Cross, Blue Sheild and Healtnet. Many others exist, and more are being started all of the time. These organizations have a reputation of being non-personal, and treat people like herds of cattle. Most of them are trying to overcome this reputation by offering more versatile benefits, and letting you go to the doctors of your choice. Start asking them questions. Visit their waiting rooms and see how many people are in there. Get their current prices. Blue Shield has a good plan where you can go to your own doctor on an 80/20 plan, but if things get serious, then it acts like an HMO and covers everything in the hospital. Most HMO's are not doing a good job.

The Los Angeles Times Newspaper reported in the July 18, 1993, issue, that the average cost an employer pays is $3,300 per year for a full-time employee and his family for Medical Insurance. On top of that, the employee pays an additional $1,680 per year. This averages out to $96 per week, total. Guess who gets to pay this $96/wk. when they are self-employed? You do. In 1996, the IRS lets you deduct 12.5% of this per year, or a whopping $623. Big deal. Meanwhile, you have to select your health insurance and get ready to apply for it *after* you start your first consulting job. Some Consultants use their spouse's insurance, if their spouses are working. Others continue their previous medical plan after they leave their captive jobs. Both methods are usually cheaper than getting new insurance. So, shop around and get ready.

In addition to Medical Insurance, you may want some Dental Insurance, also. These plans are usually 80/20 plans that pay 80% of normal checkups and fillings. More complex operations such as caps, root canals, and so on, are not covered at all. Start calling some of them.

Life Insurance is another type to consider. If you die, your family may be left out in the cold to fend for themselves. Life insurance can be used to give them a head start, and/or it can be used to make them rich. It depends on how much coverage you purchase. It should be enough to pay off all of your mortgages and debts, and still leave a good deal for your family to live off of. An insurance salesman will recommend that you purchase at least five times your yearly income worth of insurance. That's one whopping amount if you're a Consultant. Life Insurance can be purchased in at least two ways. The first way is to pay a monthly fee forever. The fee is relatively low. The second method involves paying a much higher fee for a fixed period of time, usually about 15 years. After that, you actually own the money and the insurance payments stop. Be careful to fully check out the life insurance field. Life insurance will cost somewhere around $80 per month, for a 20-year term, at $500,000 pay out. Hopefully, after you've saved a lot of money, you won't need any life insurance (yeah right).

Some clients can require Disability Insurance before you walk onto their premises as a Consultant. It is intended for accidents and dismemberment while on the job. For a 90-day kick-in, at 5000/month, for a period of 2 years, you are looking at a rate of something like $250 per month. Personally, I have decided that it is far cheaper to put this money into a mutual fund for myself, and hopefully I won't need it. I am assuming though, that in my case, I would have to be pretty badly hurt not to be able to run a computer. Also, I am assuming I could learn a new way to make a living in any two-year period. But, that is a gamble that you will have to work out for yourself. Since we are all paying Social Security (W2) or Self-Employment (1099) Tax, we are entitled to Social Security payments that kick in 6 months after we are hurt.

Later, if you convert the company to a corporation, you may be required to carry more insurance, especially to work for Job Agencies on a Corp-to-Corp basis. The first one is General Liability (G&L), usually for $1,000,000. G&L is used in case you mess something up. It costs about $300 to $500 a year. The second type of liability, that may be required, is called Errors and Omissions Insurance (EO). This is needed in case you leave something out. Some clients require these so they can have a way of suing your corporation. EO Insurance costs much more, about $1300 to $1700 a year. A third type of insurance that may be required is Workman's Compensation. This normally is required if you have employees. However, some clients and Job Agencies that pay Corp-to-Corp require that your corporation appears to have employees!

Remember, since you have a risk-taking type of personality like most Consultants, there could be a strong tendency for you to waive all these types of insurances. Don't do it. You must have them for your own peace of mind, and your family's peace of mind. Besides, you want the same benefits as those with captive jobs, PLUS, the benefits of being on your own. You are not trying to make trade-offs between the two.

Step 6.5: Select Insurance Plans Now.

Establish Good Credit

When you start freelancing, the financial institutions view you as a high risk, compared to the captive employees. You "skip from job to job" or "You don't know where your next paycheck is coming from," they will say. You are very unorthodox and are "taking risks" in their view. Yes, even though you are making a great deal more money, you are not conforming to their view of a financially stable person. Don't worry though. If your consulting takes off, the banks will be itching to help you invest your money. Before then, you've got to have good credit.

In addition to good credit, you really need a company credit card. To get one, you can open a C.D. (cash deposit) account at a bank, like Citibank. Based on the money you put in there, they will give you a Visa Card with that same cash limit on it. This is called a Secured Credit Card. If you pay the entire balance every month for 1.5 years, you will get your cash deposit back. Then you will have an Unsecured Credit Card. After paying, on time, for one more year, you will have earned a good credit rating. Soon after that, other banks will send you unsecured credit cards.

Another way to get credit is to buy a company car through a credit union. Credit unions were meant to help the employees of the respective company that runs them. Some of them, however, allow outsiders to belong. One of these was the Sears Federal Credit Union, now known as the South Western Credit Union. Practically anyone can join by depositing money there. They operate much like a bank. A Credit Union can give good deals on car loans. Once you establish credit with one of these institutions, you should keep some money in your account there, to stay a member with them forever.

I found out the hard way, once, that your good credit rating gets erased every 7 years by TRW and every 2 years by most credit unions. It can be difficult to re-establish your credit if it gets erased and you didn't buy anything big for 7 years. Become and stay a member of a credit union, forever.

Credit Unions have great parking-lot car sales. A company such as Hertz Rent-A-Car will bring in 50 cars in good condition into the Credit Union's parking lot on a Friday night. There you can select a car that you like and go inside and get the loan instantly. This is a good way to buy a used car that comes with a warranty. It is also a great way to get credit.

Step 6.6: Start A Credit Strategy Now.

Start Keeping Records

Don't forget to keep all the receipts for your purchases. Our tax system is founded in receipts! The IRS doesn't believe anything that you say without the receipts to back it up.

Our goal throughout this book is to plan on being audited, and win. Keep your receipts and the monthly bank account summaries in a filing cabinet. It is not very difficult to justify to the IRS car mileage, home office, and business entertainment deductions so long as you have the receipts to back it up. The IRS recommends that we keep these records for more than 15 years. You will need a large filing cabinet for this at some point.

The best way to keep records of spending is to have a personal credit card and a company credit card. Buy everything for the company, with the company credit card. This is much more convenient than writing checks. Plus, it gives you 2 receipts, one from the cash register and one from the credit card company. If you don't qualify for credit cards, use your separate checking accounts. Take good notes on what each check was for.

Step 6.7: Start Keeping Records of Purchases Now.

Prepare Your Family

One of the major difficulties in beginning a consulting career is trying to get your spouse, family, and your parents to understand what you are doing. Spouses can become insecure when it comes to the notion of their counterpart taking on temporary job assignments. There is only one universal talisman that works in this situation. That is the discussion of PROFIT. Begin by showing them how much more you will be making compared to how much you were making (about double plus overtime)! Explain all about how the insurances will be in place. Explain how you will be able to afford to take more vacations. Also, briefly mention some of the possible negatives, such as how more car travel will be required. Explain that there will be some downtime in-between some jobs. Find out what they expect from your new "risk". Then prepare to rebuttal with them as you get more ammunition from this book. Talking it over will also help you answer new questions in your own mind, and build confidence in the new endeavor. Please don't let this be your downfall as a Consultant. Keep re-discussing the money issues. You must not give up hope. Remember that many bright, deserving people fail to improve their lifestyle by consulting.

Step 6.8: Talk To Your Family Soon.

Start Up Your Database Of Job Agencies

To be successfully employed as a Temp, you must have a good database of job agency addresses. **I cannot stress this enough!** There is no such thing as having too many agencies working for you! Every time you run across an agency name, write it down. A good database of job agencies takes a few months to collect. Try to get their FAX and email numbers. Call them to see if they have a website. If they do, log in and check it out. See where all of their offices are. Are they within driving distance? Also, keep track of every agency that calls you. Sometimes they call out of the blue. Ask them if they hire Temps in your field. Also ask if they hire on a 1099. Try to build up your database.

I started my first database of agencies by purchasing a book called **"Directory of Contract Service Firms,"** by Contract Engineering Publications (CE Publications) in Kirkland, Washington. I ordered the book for $10, and in 3 days, had a list of technical, professional job agencies, organized by state. This was a good start. These days, however, there is a wealth of information on the Internet. CE Publications is on the net now and so is part of their directory, for free. It's at *www.ceweekly.com*. My current database has 105 agencies in it, that specialize in Engineering jobs in the Los Angeles/Orange County Area in Southern California.

Another group of useful sites on the Internet are the various Yellow Page listings. Yahoo at *www.yahoo.com* has a good Yellow Page site.

Here you can type in your address, and then find businesses close to you, including job agencies. It gives you the mileage away from you, as well as a map. With it you can search for any category, that would normally appear in the phone book, and get the latest phone numbers and addresses for companies or agencies. These searches can be done by area code, zip code, city names, business name, business category, and so on. Try it out! Since every company that orders a company telephone gets a free listing in the Business-To-Business Yellow Pages, they are likely to appear in your search results.

Yellow Page searches under the subjects Employment Technical or Employment Temporary will locate many agencies to suit you. Using Yahoo Yellow Pages you can search for Temporary Employment Agencies or any other category, much quicker. You can start out with the ones in your area code, zip code, or your city. The search results can be saved into text files that can be imported into database files.

To further enhance your database, you need even more agencies! You can never have too many! Trade magazines, the Sunday newspapers, and other publications, similar to **"Contract Engineering Weekly"** by C.E. Publications, do have more listings for your area. Some agencies have so many openings that they run ads in the Sunday Paper Classified Section, under Jobs Offered. These are the ads that don't have a paragraph, but, instead, look like a list of 10 to 15 job titles with the price range next to them. Don't forget that the personnel department where you presently work can also tell you which job agencies they use. I must stress the importance of collecting a good database of job agencies. Only one of these agencies has your next job! You can't overlook a single one.

There are hundreds of agencies on the Internet, too. The Monster Board is a great source for captive and temp job openings, at *www.monster.com.* It is one of the oldest job boards on the Internet. Sometimes the jobs link to companies, other times they link to agencies. DICE is also great source of job openings for Temps at *www.dice.com*. It links many job agencies together in a job search engine. With these types of electronic job bulletin boards, your resume is sent via email to the company or agency with the job opening in about 5 minutes. Just click the job you like. You can also post your resume on these sites and clients can search for you, all for free! There are many others, too. A newer one is at *www.headhunter.net*. There are new ones popping up all of the time.

Try this job search sequence, for instance. Go to the Yahoo search engine (at *www.yahoo.com*). In small print near the top, click on "Classifieds." Then when the new page comes up click on "Employment." Then push the button called Search. If you entered a reasonable job type, a list of many jobs should have come up. These jobs are cross-referenced to other agencies, companies, and other job boards like DICE, Headhunter, and Monster! They are all hooking together!

By the way, many of the agencies are nation-wide. If you accidentally, or on purpose, tell them you are willing to travel, they will broadcast your resume over the entire country overnight by computer. Once these people all over the country have your resume, they will call you, all hours of the day or night, for years to come. It is very hard to erase this, so be careful when you explain your travel criteria to an agency.

It would be highly advisable to enter the list of agencies into a database program, such as Microsoft Access™. This will allow you to print out mailing labels, address envelopes directly, make mailings by geographical area, or automatically send out faxes through an email program. By the way, some printers can directly print on envelopes. Alternatively, a separate, dedicated label printer peripheral can be purchased and added to your computer system. If you FAX your resume, some agencies will require you to also mail them the original. Normally, agencies scan your resume into the computer and perform word recognition on it. This doesn't work well for faxed resumes.

Eventually, all agencies will have email. This will allow the agency to receive a perfect resume that is already in character format.

If you don't have a computer, you can manually keep track of your database. You can also look up agencies in the regular yellow pages, just like I used to. Don't let this stop you. The quickest way to get a computer is to increase your pay by Temping, Contracting, or Consulting! Don't give up before you've even started.

When creating a database by computer or by hand, it is important to maintain a certain structure for it. The database should have columns for name, address, phone number, fax number, and the people contacted there, their email address, the companies website address, and whether they hire on a 1099 or not. Leave room to record, later, a description of each job offered to you, and how much they were going to pay. Start researching!

Step 6.9: Start The Database Of Agencies Now.

Temporary And Contracting Jobs On The Internet

There are many other job sources on the Internet. Go to **Yahoo: Business and Economics: Employment: Jobs** at URL *http://www.yahoo.com/yahoo/Business/Employment/Jobs.* This will give you access to hundreds of job banks, directories of jobs, and upcoming job fairs. Many of the jobs listed are for captive employees. Some are for job agencies. Some are for Consultant's.

Later on, you will be applying for all of the job openings that you like with a resume that says "Contractor" on the end of your title. You can send this resume to *any captive* job opening and wait for someone to take the bait. It usually gets to the right person or gets handed to someone else at a different company. When sent to captive job open-ings, they frequently call back. The conversation usually goes like this:

Client: "Don't you realize this opening is for full-time employment?"
Consultant: "Sure.
Client: "But your resume says you are a Contractor."
Consultant: "That's right,"
Client: "So would you consider full-time employment?"
Consultant: "No, I'm looking for Contracting work."
Client: "Oh. Well how much do you charge."
Consultant: "$75 an hour."
Client: "Oh. <Big pause> Well, when can you come down for an interview?"

There are also Contracting and Consulting Networks on the Internet. At the same Yahoo URL above, there is a search tool. Type in the word "consultant" and many more Business categories will come up for Consultants. Start looking at these sites. As you advance into consult-ing more, these will become very important. In fact, you will need to have your own website.

More Resources On The Internet

There are many other resources on the Internet, some particularly handy for Consultants. Look at this site *www.resumesonline.net*. This site offers to broadcast your resume out to 1000's of companies for you. You can even automatically have them enter your resume into about 8 job boards, like Monster. It is not free, however. Make sure you really like your resume before you do this.

Another very useful and fun site for consulting is Janet Ruhl's site at *www.realrates.com*. Here, Janet has set up a way for Computer

Consultants to enter their billing rates into a database! Look how much these Consultants are getting. This information is virtually impossible to get, since the U.S. Government stopped collecting this data in about 1988 for Temps and Consultants. Don't forget to look at the Message Board she has set up. Up to date thoughts from Consultants can be found here.

Completely Scouring The Internet

Surfing the Internet, in general, can prove quite fruitful. Completely SCOURING it can be even more educational! Every top domain level for names on the Net, ending with .com, .net, .org, or .edu used to be registered with InterNIC. Now, the InterNIC functions as an index for several Domain Name Registrars. Wild card searches at these sites are usually not allowed.

One site allows wildcard searches on domain names called Namedroppers at *www.namedroppers.com*. Go to this site and type the word "contract" by itself. Push Search and you will see all the domain names with the word "contract" in the domain name itself. This list can be cut and pasted into another file for future reference.

Search Namedroppers for other key words in your field including, of course, variations on the word "consult". Keep printing out the resulting lists. After you have several lists, take a yellow highlighter and highlight the websites that might be good resources for consulting information. Now you've got something to surf.

Step 6.10: Surf the Internet With A Purpose Now.

Setting Up Your Office For Contracting And Consulting

We have now covered the items that need to be prepared, before doing Temporary work. Contracting or Consulting work, however, requires much more preparation than Temp work. For one thing, a full-blown, operational company is required. Computerized Accounting and Online Bill Paying is required to do Contracting or Consulting, as mentioned earlier. In addition, Consulting also requires a registered website. Needless to say, this all requires the ownership of a computer.

Business Computer Hardware

The following is recommended as a business computer:

1. An IBM PC Clone Computer. (Sorry, but most businesses don't use Apple Macintosh-type computers.)
2. A PENTIUM CPU, running at 300 MHz or higher.
3. 128 Megabytes of DRAM.
4. An 8 gigabyte Hard Disk or larger.
5. A 3.5 inch Floppy Disk Drive.
6. A Color Deskjet or Laser Printer.
7. A Color Monitor, 1024x768 resolution, preferably a 17 inch diagonal, flat screen, non-interlaced type, or larger.
8. A CD-ROM player.
9. A built-in Sound Blaster equivalent sound.
10. 56K Dial-up Modem or high speed DSL Modem.
11. A backup device such as a Read/Write CDROM drive.

Typical systems from Dell, Compac, or Gateway have all of these normal hardware features.

Business Computer Software

The minimum use for the business computer is to write invoices, pay all of your bills electronically, do your own taxes (initially), and do your normal work which requires word processing, spreadsheets, databases, and possibly CAD or publishing software. The operating system that comes with the computer is also important. Of the three choices: Windows 95, Windows NT, and Windows 98, the later is the best one.

Basic Office And Internet Software

Microsoft has bundled WORD™, EXCEL™, ACCESS™, and a few other programs into this expensive program called Microsoft OFFICE™. Microsoft Office YYYY Professional is certainly the choice for systems these days. Note that the YYYY is the year it was released. Office 2000 is the latest release. It contains the following software, all of which will be needed for doing regular work:

> WORD: Word Processing program.
> EXCEL: Spreadsheet program.
> ACCESS: Database program.
> OUTLOOK: Email and Organizer program.
> EXPLORER: Internet Browser program.

Mastering the business software will be a **major** advantage to you and your clients.

EXCEL™ is a spreadsheet program that allows you to prepare budgets, proposals, business pro-formas, or keep track of the total running costs of a project. It also helps you to prepare excellent graphs for your reports.

ACCESS is a database program for collecting names of contacts and printing either mailing labels or envelopes. It works very well. This total collection allows you, not only to do your business, but also to generate output in the format that you clients require.

Internet and Email are mandatory. This requires that you have an Internet account, a web browser like Microsoft Explorer and very fast Modem. Being able to send your work or your resume via email is also very important. To use the Internet, Microsoft's Internet Explorer and Outlook Email programs can be used. If you are a novice to computers, don't let other people talk you out of these Microsoft products. They work well and are simple to use. Plus, they fully integrate with Office. With this capability, you will be able to look up other people's research on the internet, cut them out (pictures and all), place them into a WORD document, and Email that document to your boss 5 minutes later. Then, he will think you did all of this research! Nifty, eh?

Courses on the most popular software packages are offered every semester at local junior colleges. In many states, the registration fee for these is very low. They have to offer these software courses because they are the foundations of businesses today.

> **Step 6.11: Learn How To Use The Internet And All Of The Above Softwares Now.**

Accounting Software

In order to maximize your tax write-offs, it is important implement Online-Banking. This service will be necessary at some point in building up a consulting practice. Online Banking is the most advantageous way to keep records, using an accounting program like QUICKEN™ or QUICKBOOKS™. The accounting software allows Checks to be written on the computer screen. After filling out the checks on the screen, the computer calls up the bank and tells it to print and mail the checks for you. The advantage is that when you write a check electronically, it is automatically assigned to a category. Examples of categories are Office:Stationary, Office:Online Services, Office:Computer Software, Auto:Fuel, Auto:Repairs, Bank:Service Charge, and so forth. This makes it easy to track where the company's money is going and helps you prepare tax strategies.

QUICKEN is the most popular accounting software today. It allows online banking with most major banks. The Small Business Version allows the writing of invoices. If you are planning to work as a 1099, you will need to invoice your client for services performed. Once the expenses (checks) and the income (invoices) are entered, reports about your company's financial status can be automatically generated. QUICKEN can generate a Profit and Loss Statement for your business in less than 5 seconds. Learning an accounting software package is required for running a legitimate business. Furthermore, you are not going to have a spare two hours a week to do this by hand. Learning QUICKEN is pretty easy, but courses are also available on it. At the end of the year, QUICKEN data can automatically be exported to your Tax Software. This saves several weeks of time per year.

Step 6.12: Start Learning Quicken Small Business Version Now.

Online Banking is required for Contracting or Consulting, but also recommended for Temping. Both the personal and the company bank accounts need to be online, especially if the company's office is in the home. Most banks support online bill payment using QUICKEN.

Step 6.13: Decide If You Can Handle Online Bill Paying Now.

Tax Software

In the first two years of the business, it is better to try to do your taxes yourself, first. Then take them to a taxman and see if they do it the same way. As a sole-proprietor, you should experience doing your own taxes. You will find out that most tax preparers don't like to include things that may red-flag the IRS, such as Office In The Home. They are also loosing money for you by "Not Asking" you the right questions about your business. For example, they may ask you if you bought a computer this year. If so, they depreciate one-fifth of that cost each year for five years. Whereas, they could have deducted the full price this year, if it cost less than $10,000. You are allowed to take this much deduction every year. Above that, you then must depreciate. They forget to tell you this. You deserve every deduction, even if it flags the IRS. Of course, the deduction will have to be legitimate and you will have to have record keeping to pull it off. The bottom line is that you will have to do your own taxes to receive maximum benefits, while you are a small-time operator. Recently, the laws were changed so that the IRS has the burden of proof now. So, in order to audit you, they have to prove first that you fibbed on your taxes.

TURBOTAX™ is a good tax program for tax preparation. First, it imports all the data from QUICKEN that you've been typing in all year. Then, it fills out the tax forms by interviewing you, asking you questions about your business. One thing you must do right now is to get a copy of TURBOTAX from last year, and enter the data for last year. Once that is done, enter your projections for your new company and its expenses. Pretend that you have a home office that is 25% of your house and your car is a company car. Put in double your income. You will be pleasantly surprised. Playing "What-If" is what computers are good for. Enjoy it.

Step 6.14: Go Through a TurboTax Interview Now.

Making A Backup

Backing up the hard disk on your computer, regularly, is mandatory. After learning all of this software, loading it, setting it up, and using it, you are not going to be able to afford loosing it if your computer or disk breaks. You should back up your computer once a week. Writable CDROM is the best way back up your computer. The CD's last very long if they are not exposed to the sunlight. Work for each client can be stored on separate CD's. CD's are very convenient. Besides, this drive can be used for reading CD's also.

As hard disks get bigger these days, it is impossible to fit the disk image on one CD. Multi-CD backups also take a long time. So, it is advisable to keep most of your work in the same directory. Windows 95 used to have such a directory called "My Documents." If you keep all of your work in a single directory, then you can make a quick backup of your recent work. Then, on a weekly or monthly basis a full backup can be made.

As you use the computer to keep bank accounts, taxes, contacts, emails, etc., making backups will become extremely important!

The Golden Rules Of Computing

No matter what type of system you put together, remember these Golden Rules Of Computing:

1. In computers, there is a price for waiting to buy what you need. Know the price for waiting (i.e. try not to wait).
2. In computers, more money fixes everything.
3. In computers, it always takes longer to use it the first time. Time savings occurs the following times that you use it.
4. In computers, it is 100 times easier to learn new software by watching someone else, instead of reading the manual.

Main Computer Skills

Once you learn the basic skills to operate both a sole-proprietorship and a computer, the amount of work you can get is enormous. The amount of work you can produce is likewise astounding. The output you produce is also of professional quality. Here are some categories: writing resumes, writing ads, writing invoices, writing manuals, writing books, writing articles, submitting proposals, drawing schematics, drawing blueprints, designing logos, Circuit layout, writing C programs, circuit simulation, doing accounting, doing taxes, collecting databases, preparing business plans, writing flyers, sending faxes, uploading advertisements to bulletin boards, downloading job offers, solving equations, drawing graphs, tutoring in computers, putting together computers for others, buying and selling products over the net, sending email, surfing the net,...to name a few. First you've got to get one! Be patient, work hard, and it will come true.

If you don't have a computer and can't afford one, you probably need more money. Well, don't feel bad. Many of us became motivated to become Consultants because we couldn't afford what we considered the basic tools of our trade.

If you do not have a computer, or know how to use the fundamental business programs, I do not recommend that you Contract or Consult at this time. You should consider Temping for a while, first. Build up some equity, learn some computing skills, then go out on your own.

However, that doesn't mean it can't be done. If you have the extra drive, you can do anything.

Premeditated Preparedness

Well, that is a pretty extensive list of things to prepare. At this point you should have a company with a mission and a name. The company should have a database of names and addresses of people and agencies to contact. It should have a way of sending out advertisements, flyers, or your resume. A method of receiving voice and email messages should also be up. If you are Contracting or Consulting, the company is ready to go into operation with an accounting method using online banking.

Preparing this much stuff can take several months, or even years, if you don't have enough money. Try to get as much of these done before you accept your first job. You are going to be busy making money soon. You will be continuously asked to work overtime. You need to keep every hour free, in case you need to work. You need these systems in place so you can concentrate on your work. It can all be accomplished manually if you can't afford it, but it will take much more of your spare time. Don't get discouraged if you can't afford all of these things now. Soon the price of a new computer will be a less than a few weeks of profit!

Chapter 7:
Your Portfolio On Paper

Preceding every Consultant is his reputation and his portfolio on paper. Your portfolio should include a resume, a list of personal references, a business card, a flyer (or Blurb Sheet), and a list of past clients. The preparation of these paper credentials is important for success. This chapter will analyze and present the best ways to prepare your portfolio on paper.

Writing A Resume For Consulting

It takes a special kind of resume to land Temp, Contracting, or Consulting jobs. After reading eight books on how to write resumes, I could not find a format that met my basic criteria. So, I developed a special format for the resume, which is based on a modified "Functional Resume." It is called the "Skill Bullet Resume." Before going into that format, lets examine some of the rationale used to develop it.

Resumes Are Searched By Computers

Nowadays, a computer, not a person, may examine your resume. Long before a stranger gets to read your resume, a computer may have examined it several times. The computer is asked to search all of the resumes, in a database, for certain key words that appear in the job description. These keywords are called buzzwords. Buzzwords are the phrases used in your particular industry. For example, in my field of electronics engineering, DRAM, DSP, and RISC would be very common buzzwords. Your resume must have as many buzzwords in it that can possibly fit, so that a searching computer will trigger on them. The Human Resources (HR) person might call the top five people selected by the computer. The client, your future boss, may decide to trust the computer match, and not read your resume at all, until he meets you! He is satisfied that the proper buzzwords appear on your resume. So, a resume for Temping, Contracting, or Consulting must be loaded with industry standard buzzwords.

Clients Only Have 20 Seconds

A good resume format better tell a client what your experience is, in about 20 seconds. When I first began consulting, I started to notice a pattern developing, in many of my interviews. Many times when I went on an interview, the client read my resume, for the first time, after I was already present. So, I made it a game of watching their eyes. They seemed to read every word for about 20 seconds, then accelerate rapidly down to the bottom of the page. I've had many interviewers, then, look up and ask me, "So what do you do for a living?" (Can you believe that?) At first, I thought they were just kidding, trying to break the ice. But after it kept reoccurring, over and over, it started to really eat at my emotions. Sure enough, after several more interviews, clients had all kinds of excuses for not reading my resume. When they did, they did it in front of me, and spent no more than about 20 seconds.

Very few clients will have the patience to read an entire resume. When they do, it is usually because they liked what they read in the first 20 seconds. As you gain experience, you begin to realize that most clients, with a job opening, are in crisis mode and rarely have a spare 20 seconds!

A Resume Must Impress In 20 Seconds

After analyzing several resume formats, I concluded that not one of them portrays much information in the first 20 seconds of reading! I was going to have to invent one to cover this aspect. Furthermore, resumes are factual and have very little entertainment value. Resumes can't hold an average person's attention for longer than about 20 seconds. Although you may think your resume is exciting, it can be very boring to someone who has been reading resumes all day.

Resumes Must Be Single Page

The length of the resume must never exceed 1 page. The reason for this is multifaceted. Clients are usually in crisis mode. They certainly don't have time to read a multi-page resume. In fact, most clients won't read a single page resume, until you get there for your interview. Clients prefer single page resumes because they can easily scan them while they are asking you questions. This allows them to think of questions quickly, without loosing their concentration. If you have a multipage resume, the interviewer will have to keep flipping the pages back and forth, trying to think of questions to ask you. It will become evident that the interviewer was not prepared to ask you questions. This action may become so distracting, that they may get embarrassed, at themselves. The end result is that they inadvertently forget to ask you the proper questions, and actually cut your interview short. By reducing your resume to one page, you are allowing the interviewer to be more casual! Besides, how does it look when an Advanced Consultant, with 30 years experience, comes in with a one-page resume and a beginner comes in with a two-page resume? Does this imply someone is trying to stretch the truth?

Every resume will fit onto a single page. I have written over forty of them for myself and over one hundred for other people. Keep your resume to a single page. It is the defacto, industry standard (i.e. thee standard format). It is easy to FAX or email. It is easy to scan into a computer and perform buzzword recognition. It is easy to cut-and-paste into an online search engine. It is far less boring than a multipage resume! Most of all, it will help you during your interview. You won't be reminding the client that they forgot to read your resume before you arrived. These are only a few of the reasons for keeping your resume to a single page.

The format chosen for the resume has to have an intrinsic nature to it that allows it to be kept on one page, forever. Remember, all of your resumes, from now on, must fit on one page! It can be very difficult for a beginner, to fill up a one-page resume. However, a Consultant could conceivably have a more difficult time. Trying to fit 20 or more companies on a single page is impossible. So, the particular format of the resume that we decide upon should be easily updated to fit on a single page.

Cover Letters Are Out

Almost every book written on resumes requires that you have a Cover Letter. What is it that the Cover Letter basically says? Read between the lines. It says something like, "Hi, I am me. I like the field I'm in. I'm good at it. Most of all, I'm looking for a good company to work for. I hope to contribute normal work and get rewarded handsomely for it. Please call if your company can do me this tiny favor. Sincerely..." If you leave it up to the interviewers' imagination, a cover letter can sound very disastrous! If you send a client a resume only, he knows you want work. You don't need an additional letter to say that. Your are looking for a job and you are ready to start. The cover letter can only damage your chances of finding a job.

What can we do to fix the function of a cover letter? The cover letter is so open for ridicule and miss-interpretation that there is only one thing we can do. Leave it out! It throws away the first, most valuable 20 seconds that the client has, by describing the applicant's needs, instead of his skills! Cover letters are good for teething puppies.

There is only one situation to ever use a cover letter. It could be used to announce your future availability. It might say you have been given a notice that you have 1 month left on your assignment, but here is your resume now.

Say Bye To The Objective

Look at any book on resumes today and you will also find that the Objective section is supposed to go at the beginning of the resume. But, again, this is where the most valuable 20 seconds is located. A typical Objective is a paragraph saying something like: "I'm looking for a good job, at a great company, with all kinds of opportunity for advancement, and rewards for hard work, in a pleasant environment, and I want my title to be something impressive." What the objective really needs to say is, "I'm looking for any kind of work, in my field." In fact, the resume should say that without the Objective section. Later it will be shown that your "Title" says what kind of work you want. The Objective, like the Cover Letter, is subject to mis-interpretation of the interviewers' imagination! Although you may be an excellent worker, you have not yet mentioned that fact. The reader of your resume, so far, thinks you only care about yourself! You are asking them for a favor before they even know your qualifications. Never, never, ever put an "Objective" on a resume! It is just like the Cover Letter. The new resume format must tell potential clients what kind of work you want, without having an objective section. This leads us to another problem with resumes that we must watch out for.

Avoiding The Client's Negative Imagination

Clients and agencies are trying to find flaws in your personality, and punch holes in your resume. Because they are scrutinizing everything, a resume cannot leave anything up to the client's negative imagination concerning philosophy, religion, and politics. If you drift away from the "business facts" and start getting into philosophy, religion, politics, etc., then you most likely won't get a job with that resume. You are stimulating the client's imagination, in a negative way. This works against you, 9 times out of 10.

Consider the Objective example we talked about earlier. It begins, "I'm looking for a good job..." This is philosophical in nature. What does "a good job" mean? Does it imply you are willing to work hard? No. Does it say you are looking for a company that really needs your help? No. Does it say you are selfish? Yes, this seems to be the most likely! When the objective talks about benefits, does this mean you are looking for more sick days and vacation days? If left up to the client's negative imagination, yes it does! There are many other examples of this in Objectives.

Lets say you are a good salesman and your resume talks about the trips you have made instead of the dollar amount of sales you have made. Does the client think you just want to travel to more places? Probably so.

Let's say your resume states that you belong to the National Rifle Association, and like Salsa Dancing. Is the client going to need to know this to hire you as a tech-writer, publisher, technician, accountant, or engineer? Maybe he's going to think you might be carrying a concealed weapon on your interview. Maybe he will imagine that you will stay out late at nightclubs. Does this mean you will be wasting time at work arguing about religion, gun rights, and organizing social gatherings? Does this mean you are highly opinionated? It could. If you put things like this on your resume, you will only hurt yourself. Why take that chance? You may not ever get an interview with a resume like that.

Hence, items such as hobbies, likes, dislikes, age, religion, color, marital status, number of children, creed, objectives, articles published, scholarships won, awards won, speeches given, countries visited, security clearances, patents granted, etc., all make the client suspicious. They make the client's imagination go haywire! They have no business on a resume because they are not about business. They work the client's negative mind into frenzy. If their negative imagination kicks in, they will conclude that you are too much of a social person and not enough of a worker. So, you're out of there. A good resume only has enough room on it for the business facts of your life, no mater how boring.

Tapping Into The Client's Positive Imagination

A resume can make use of the client's positive imagination concerning your work skills, however. The first time I stumbled across using the client's imagination in a positive way was on my education status. When I first began consulting, my resume stated that I went to 3 junior colleges. Now even though, by that time, I had accumulated 20 years of experience, as well as good references, some interviewers actually told me that I needed to complete my degree to be employed with them. They did assume that I had an A.A. degree though, but not a Bachelors degree. I didn't have either one of those. So, I asked myself, "Why do they assume I have an A.A. degree?" Simple, because I went to junior colleges, and only had junior colleges on my resume. Later on, I took two courses given by the University of Southern California (USC). As soon as I put USC on my resume, clients stopped asking me about my degree! The clients and the job agencies all ASSUME that now I have Bachelors degree. "He must have one, since he has so much experience and good references," their sub-conscious mind concludes! This proves that if the subject seems to be skill-related, business facts, and not of a philosophical, religious, or political, in nature, then, the client's positive imagination will work in your favor.

Skill Bullets Deliver The Punch

The best way of using the client's positive imagination is by grouping your skills into Skill Bullets. Skill Bullets are paragraphs that are **not attached to any particular company**.

With a Skill Bullet Resume, the client cannot tell **WHERE** you acquired each skill. For example, suppose I wanted to put "book publishing" on my resume. I have written a book, correct? [Don't get smart]. No one has hired me to do it, though. So, on a normal resume, there would not be a place for it. But on a resume containing Skill Bullets, paragraphs that name skill after skill, "book publishing" could appear non-chalantley. The client cannot tell which company, or "where", I did this work.

With a Skill Bullet Resume, the client cannot tell **WHEN** you acquired each skill, either. Skill Bullets are not listed in chronological order. They are grouped by skill-types. Let's suppose there is a job opening for someone to design a stereo amplifier. Let's also suppose that from 1980 to 1990 you designed stereo amplifiers. With a standard resume, the client would know how long ago you did this. So, he would assume that if you were good at amplifier design, you would still be doing it now. Therefore, you wouldn't even get an interview. On the other hand, when a client reads a Skill Bullets Resume, he doesn't know how long ago you did this. With a Skill Bullet Resume, his positive imagination fills in the blank. The client assumes that you have recently been doing this type of work! You are just the person he was looking for. So, you would at least get an interview.

Skill Bullets are a good way to trigger the client's positive imagination, in your favor, by disassociating your skills from the time that you performed them.

Note: **Skill Bullets are not designed to help you lie about your skills. You must have the skills you have written down in your resume! It is also assumed that you can execute these skills in a timely manner with confidence and precision.**

A Special Skill Bullet Section

A good resume format has to have a compact way of presenting all of the PC-related software packages, and any other special tools you have experience with. A normal resume would have these skills scattered throughout. A Skill Bullet resume focuses these skills into a dedicated Skill Bullet paragraph. This particular Skill Bullet is dedicated to software and tools. One advantage, as mentioned earlier, is that no one knows how long it has been since you last used these tools. A second advantage is the ease of locating a particular tool skill. This becomes very significant when dealing with software type tools. For example, if you were applying as a tech-writer, your client would want to know if you have Microsoft WORD™ experience, without reading your whole resume. A good resume would allow the client to scan for this WORD (no pun intended). Remember, if you force the client to actually "read" the whole resume, then he might loose interest and chuck it!

Resumes Must Be Pleasing To The Eye

Since humans tend to scan the resume instead of reading it, the resume must have ingredients in it that will catch their eyes. The eyes are caught by Indents, Bullets, Font Changes, Bold Characters, Capitals, Italics, Underlines, and Buzzwords. These types of enhancements are easy to incorporate with today's computers. Your resume must look at least as good as the next guys. A Skill Bullet resume automatically uses a lot of bullets and indents.

Don't consider typing a resume on a typewriter. It must be word-processed. If you do not have a computer, hire someone to straighten it out for you, after you type it. You can also go down to a copy center, such as Kinkos™, and rent their computer for about $10 per hour. They will be glad to assist you with your resume and the computer.

Don't use unusual fonts on the resume. If the resume is emailed electronically, then the receiving computer must have that font installed on it. Use only the fonts that come with Microsoft Office™.

The Skill Bullet Resume

Well, now I hope you can see why the resume formats of the past are dysfunctional, especially as consulting resumes. Let's summarize what we need in our new, Skill Bullet Resume:

1. It must have as many buzzwords on it that can fit, so it will trigger a computer search.
2. It cannot be more than one page long, because it has to allow an interviewer to be more casual when asking questions.
3. The format must allow for it to be kept to 1 page in length, forever.
4. It must tell what your experience is in the first 20 seconds!
5. It must never have a Cover Letter, unless you cannot accept employment right away.
6. It must never have an Objective statement on it. The objective is replaced by your title.
7. It cannot leave anything up to the client's negative imagination concerning philosophy, religion, and politics. Items such as hobbies, likes, dislikes, age, religion, color, marital status, number of children, creed, objectives, articles published, scholarships won, awards won, speeches given, countries visited, security

clearances, patents granted, your own company, etc., all make the client's negative imagination go haywire.

8. A resume needs to make use of the client's positive imagination concerning your work skills. Doing this makes the client read positive things into the resume that aren't there. The Skill Bullet format itself takes care of this. With this format, the client cannot tell where or when you acquired each skill. He will have to interview you to get more details.

9. A resume needs a special Skill Bullet Paragraph to gather software and tool skills.

10. Since humans tend to scan the resume instead of reading it, the resume must have some eye-catching ingredients.

After years of research, I have developed a resume format that incorporates all of the basic principles above. It is an example of the Skill Bullet Resume. This particular example is the 29th consulting resume that I've done for myself. It is shown on the next page.

Jimmy Moore
Electronic Hardware/Firmware Design Engineer—Contractor
dba Explore Electronics Inc., 641 Buena Vista Dr., Fullerton, CA 92633
(714) 123-4567 Office   Email: info@ee-consultants.com

DESIGN EXPERTISE
- Extensive Analog, Digital, Microprocessor, FPGA Hardware Design.
- Firmware and Software Design in High-Level and Assembly Language.
- Member IEEE, Orange County Consultants Network, Altera Partner.
- Specialize in Video, Imaging, Communications, and Process Controls.

CAREER HIGHLIGHTS
30 Years of Experience in Design, Test, and Mfg. of Commercial Electronic Products.

Digital Circuit Designs
- Computers, Embedded Controllers: CISC, RISC, DSP types, on PCI, PC104, ISA, VME, buses, based on 68360, i960, 80486, 80186, 80196, 68360, 68020, 68331, 320C25, 80251, Z180, etc.
- Memory: DRAM, SRAM, CACHE, VRAM, NVRAM, FLASH, PCMCIA, and Disk Interfaces.
- Data Communications: T1/T3, FDDI, ETHERNET, ISDN, EPP/ECP, I2C, RS232/485, etc.
- ASIC, FPGA, PAL: CPU Glue, DRAM, DMA, Interrupt, UART, Parallel, Drawing, Rasterizing, Scanning, Stepper, Math, ECC, etc. Devices: Altera 20K, Xylinx, Lattice, Actel.

Analog Circuit Designs
- Data Acquisition: A/D and D/A Conversion, AGC, OpAmp, Comparator, Sensor, Isolation.
- Optical Circuits: CCD Camera, Scanner, Detectors, Laser, Displays, Fiber Optics.
- Communications: VHF RF, Video, Audio, TV, T-Line, PLL, Modem, FAX, FCC, EMI, ESD.
- Power Circuits: MOSFET Amplifier, Stepper, Regulator, High-Voltage, Magnetics, SMT.

Software Designs
- Assembly and C Programs: Real-Time Embedded Control, Image Compression Expansion Forward Error Correction, Digital Image Processing, Data Communications, PCMCIA Card and Socket, BIOS.

Hardware and Software Tools
- Software Languages: C, BASIC, and Assembly: i960, 80X86, 68XXX, 80X51, PIC, ZXXX.
- Schematic, PCB: ORCAD, PCAD, VIEWLOGIC, VALID, PROTEL, TANGO, PCGERBER.
- Simulation, Timing: PSPICE, MATHCAD, MAXPLUS II, and CHRONOLOGY.
- ASIC, FPGA, PAL: MAXPLUS II (4 Years), AHDL, VHDL, SYNOPSIS, ABEL, PALASM.
- Machines Used: IBM PC, Logic Analyzers, Emulators, Oscilloscope, Current Probe, etc.
- PC Applications: WINDOWS 98/NT, WORD, EXCEL, ACCESS, SLICKEDIT, Internet, etc.

EXPERIENCE (partial list)
8/92- 5/93 SYNC RESEARCH, Irvine, Ca, EE Consultant, **Data Communications.**
1/91- 10/91 OCA APPLIED OPTICS, Garden Grove, Ca, EE Contractor, **Space Cameras, Lasers**.
7/90- 1/91 UNISYS/TIMEPLEX, Los Angeles, Ca, EE Contractor, **FDDI Data Communications.**

EDUCATION
1986- 1991 CALIFORNIA STATE UNIVERSITY FULLERTON (CSUF), Fullerton, Ca.
1985- 1986 UNIVERSITY OF SOUTHERN CALIFORNIA (USC), Los Angeles, Ca.
1970- 1985 CYPRESS, ORANGE COAST, and FULLERTON COLLEGES, Orange County, Ca.

Thank You For Your Time and Consideration.

Well, how do you like the format? Did you learn anything about me in 20 seconds? Was it easy to scan? Was it easy to keep reading? Did it keep your attention all the way to the end? Probably not. But that's Ok. All I really wanted to get across was the first 20 seconds. Lets analyze this format so we can make note of how all the basic functions were incorporated.

Your New Self-Appointed Title

The second line of the new format replaces the Objective with your new, self-appointed title. It states directly what field of work you are looking for. It can rarely be misinterpreted. Try to give yourself a title similar to those at a captive job. Carefully choose your title. It must state what you want to do for a living, not what you have been doing.

The trend these days is to call Temps, Contractors, and Consultants by the term "Contractor," as mentioned in an earlier chapter. It is very important to put this word on the end of your title so that people will know you want to be Freelance. If the job opening is for a captive and they like your resume, they may call anyway.

Also, drop any references to the level of the title. Words like "Senior" should never be included. For example, Senior Accountant would become "Accountant—Contractor".

By the way, never give yourself the title of president or sole-proprietor. This does not tell of your occupation. Sometimes, when people see that you are a Temp, and that you know how to run a company, then they imagine that you are there to steal their ideas.

Now that you know your objective, you must begin to prepare to write the rest of the resume. The rest of the resume must sound like you have been doing what your title says, for quite some time. For example, if your previous title was Test Engineer, and you want to become Design Engineer, then your entire resume must be written to sound like you have been designing, not testing. You could, also, throw in your Testing experience and make it sound like a second task that you were asked to perform, on occasion. If you want to do both Testing and Designing, change your self-appointed title to read just "Engineering—Contractor."

Note, that I'm not saying that you should tell a lie. I am merely assuming that you know how to design, in this example, and feel you have been and should be doing this.

Putting the "ing" on certain words in your title can make you feel more comfortable with it. Experiment with adding "ing" on the words used for your title.

The First 20 Seconds

The EXPERTISE section, is the most important part of the resume. It is the part that has teeth. It will always be read. Most of the time it will be the only thing read! It must clearly state what you do the best. In this section, you must state what you know in 3 or 4 sentences. If the potential client sees the skill he is looking for in this section, you probably will get an interview. These sentences should be worded like a Yellow Page ad or a Business Flyer. They need not be complete sentences. Organize them from the best thing you like to do to the least. In the last sentence, try to put something that makes you unique from all the other people in this field. What makes you better than anyone else? I like to start this last sentence with the phrase "Specialize in..." Consider the rest of the resume to be background data used to support these 3 or 4 sentences!

Career Highlights Section

The CAREER HIGHLIGHTS section is the meat of the resume. This section begins with the number of years of experience. Be sure to include any work experience including college courses that provided on-the-job training, as well as volunteer work. Also, include any time that was spent at your office doing intense research or work on a particular project that preoccupied your life for several months. If you have 2 unique skills that you've spent your career on, then you may need to use 2 sentences for the "number of years" of experience.

Skill Bullet Sections

In this section, you will find neatly organized groups of Skill Bullets. Note that they are not really paragraphs. Nor do they contain complete sentences. However, most items are bulleted. Thus the name "Skill Bullet."

Each group of Skill Bullets has a title. At least one of the groups is about software and tools. A human can find the Skill Bullet they might be interested in because the group title is in bold type and underlined.

Inside of each Skill Bullet group, there are bulleted lines. These are not sentences at all. Each line has a category title, followed by a colon. Each line contains a barrage of buzzwords that will light up any computer! These buzzwords and phrases are normally used throughout the industry. Be sure to use capital and small letters carefully when typing out the buzzwords. If you are not sure, use more small letters. Misplaced punctuation and spelling can cause the computer to skip over the correct buzzword. Read a few want ads, in your field, to figure out how to phrase some of these. Notice how no one can tell WHEN I acquired these skills! For example, I haven't written any software in three years, now.

Experience Section

This EXPERIENCE section has a couple of subtleties in it. First, the dates are contiguous, except for jobs that overlapped. There are no gaps in time. Interviewers like to look for flaws so they can make you feel bad, and try to get you to lower your price later. By taking out the gaps, you are helping the interviewer to concentrate on your good qualities. If you leave gaps in the dates, your interviewer will want to know what you did during that time. They assume you were in jail or something similar, of course. I merely stretch the amount of time from each job by 1 month or so, to make the gap disappear. Employers do not care about an adjustment of a month. I fill in the gaps and they don't ask questions. Very, very, rarely do they check the dates. Even if they did, they would probably call your old boss and ask him when you were there. He won't be able to remember exactly, anyway.

If you have a big gap, you must put in a line that states what you have done. If I needed to, I could put down my own company name, and what I worked on at the time. You may have to get creative on this. If you have a big gap of unemployment, in recent times, you could be in real trouble. This keeps many people from finding work. You must have something to put in there. Fill it in with volunteer work, took a few classes, retrained, or whatever. Make sure you fill it in. The interviewer may not actually notice.

Job agencies are not too concerned about your experience history, because they want to employ you more than you want to. If they find the right buzzword in your Skill Bullet, and your references are good, you will get submitted to clients.

Continuing with the EXPERIENCE section, the second thing to notice is that the company names are capitalized but not the job-titles. If you capitalize or highlight your title, subconsciously you are telling the interviewer that you think more about yourself than the companies you worked for (which, luckily for the mankind species is true). So, my technique is to do the opposite. Stress the company name, with capitals, and not your title. Neither of them is going to mean anything once you start your new job, anyway.

The third item to notice in the EXPERIENCE section, is the simple phrase at the end, describing your work at those companies. These phrases are your only company-dependent skills. Notice these are very general. They tell what the company made. They hint at what you worked on. They do not tell how many other people worked on them with you. They also do not tell what part of them you were responsible for. That part is kind of vague. By keeping your company-dependent skills vague, the client will have to call you in and interview you, if they want more information.

A final requirement for the EXPERIENCE section is that is has to be updateable, easily. Notice that the title of this section says "partial list!" This allows us to put only the past few companies on the resume. As you complete more and more jobs, you will be able to quickly and easily update your resume using this format. Simply drop off the last company on the list and add a new first one. This gives us a way of keeping the resume limited to one page.

Education Section

Proceeding onto the last area, the EDUCATION section, we see a list of schools. In the Education section, they just want to know if you went to college at all, and how long you could stand it. In general, it should state that you have a degree, but only if you have one. If your degree is "Bachelor Of Science in Underwater Basket Weaving," and you do not want to be a weaver anymore, then just put down "Bachelor of Science Degree." If you do not have a degree, try to put down as many trade schools and colleges that will fit. Don't ever put down high schools. If high school is all that you have, leave this entire section off the resume. One reason for putting this section at the end of the resume is that they may not read down this far.

After having many years of experience and good references, the degree will loose some of it's worth. The degree should always mean something important to you, however. Remember that it is harder to go to school than it is to actually work in industry. It should be a continuous, self-confidence boost having a degree, even if others do not think it is important.

A Final Thanks

The final ingredient required on a good resume is a nice, non-orthodox, "Thank You". I have always received good vibes while sitting there waiting for someone to read my resume, as they run across that last line. It implies, "Hey, I know you are busy, I know you are a person like me, and I really want you to know that I appreciate the time you have spent reading this. Thank You." Putting a Thank You on your resume can only do positive things. It could set your resume apart from everyone else's. If the Thank You is on the actual resume, instead of on the Cover Letter, it will get Faxed to the client by the job agency. Then the client will receive the Thank You also. The actual phrase I like is the one on my resume. It takes up an entire line, but I think it is worth it.

That completes the resume. You have a lot of work cut out for you, now. Get started on it know before you forget how this format works.

Step 7.1: Write A Skill Bullet Resume Now.

The Personal Reference Sheet

Hand in hand with the resume goes the Personal Reference Sheet. It is essential that the reference sheet be prepared before the resume is sent out. When an agency calls and says, "The client likes your resume and now they want us to check your references," you have to be ready. Being able to FAX the references to them within the next five minutes, can greatly improve your chances of getting the job. The timing here is crucial. Other agencies may be bidding on this job. We don't want to loose this opportunity because of a few minutes of lag.

Companies usually require three personal references. These references must be in the same field that you are in. They must also know of your work record and capabilities. Preferably, you met them while working together on a project. Carefully choose the best three of these acquaintances. They will be your primary references.

Sometimes clients want to here from your past three supervisors. These references can be much harder to come by. Normally these would be three department managers. Now, most of the time, department managers are too detached from the actual work, to do you much good. They are the ones that lay people off or fire them. Typically, avoiding department managers as references would be wise. It is much better to use the next guy under them as a reference. This middle manager, although he was not in full control of your destiny, he does know more about your performance. Normally these individuals are known as "lead men." Carefully choose the best three of these middle managers as potential references. If you can't think of any managers that will give you a good reference, then leave this section off.

In addition to the standard categories of references, I have found that references from other job agencies can be very helpful. On paper, these job agency people actually were your supervisors, because you were their employee. Many times they know a lot about your work because the client reported to them on a regular basis. They tend to be very positive with their recommendations because they want to do business with you in the future, by employing you again. Throughout all time, Headhunters and Mercenaries have helped each other!

Now that we have a group of references in mind, we can prepare these people. Calling each reference, before using them, is important for many reasons. First, any negative feelings that they may have about your work may show up. Second, if they say they will give you a good reference, but do not appear to be enthusiastic about it, then maybe you shouldn't use them anyway. If they like the idea, and they are enthusiastic to help you, then you need to give them one more test. Ask them if you can use their home telephone number. This is the final test they have to pass to insure they have no qualms about giving you a reference. You will need both the work and home phone numbers from your personal references. Home phone numbers from your supervisor references are not required, but they will help you immensely if you can get them. Having a home phone number from your previous supervisors tends to make people think you are a well-liked worker. When clients or agencies see this, they tend to not check your references at all! You should promise your references that you will be careful giving out their home phone number. For other business acquaintances, such as a job agency reference, a home phone would never be important to have. They will only need to know that you are intent on using them as a reference.

Before proceeding further, I must point out the difficulty many people have had with references. It can stop your whole career for months, if you have a problem.

Sometime in the past when I was doing captive work, I used someone for a reference that I had worked with. Everytime someone called him, he would say that I always kept up with state-of the-art techniques, which was good. But he would go further and say that I did this by having several jobs going all the time! Well, this doesn't go over too good with clients. Clients want to think that you will be totally dedicated to their company.

Another time, a friend of mine had an extremely difficult time with our boss. So he asked another fellow if he would pretend to be his supervisor. Being a "close" friend of his, he said, "Sure, no problem. Tell me what you want me to say." Later when an agency called this reference, he said, "No, I'm not his supervisor. No, I don't think he was a Design Engineer, I think he was a Test Engineer. No, I do not know what kind of work he did. He worked in a completely different building." Surprise! This is another example of the millions of ways your references can mess you up.

If you are not getting job offers that you know you are qualified for, and it keeps happening over and over, my friend, you are getting a bad reference! Have someone, like your dad or brother, call all of your references for you. If they don't give overwhelming referrals, don't use them any more.

Coming to grips with a bad reference can be devastating to your ego. Finding out that one of your so-called friends is not recommending you is very hard to accept. Many people fail in consulting because they refuse to believe that they are getting a bad reference! Don't be one of them!

Preparing your Personnel Reference Sheet is straightforward.

References For Jimmy Moore

Personal References:	Days	Evenings
Mark Martella, Project Engineer	(714)472-1867	(714)894-4006
Alan Moore, Software Engineering Contractor	(310)631-8603	(310)838-9358
Dave Springer, Hardware-Software Consultant	(714)838-7126	(714)997-6109
Manager References:		
Richard Leslie, JBS Controls	(310)736-2962	(310)637-2692
Fred Hesse, OCA Applied Optics	(714)449-2874	(714)449-4728
Terry Benson, Magtek	(213)631-7363	(213)136-3637
Harlan Rogers, Interstate Electronics	(818)639-0783	(818)936-3870
John Bailey, Unisys	(602)739-8987	(602)937-7898
Victor Kostrukoff, Excellon Photonics	(310)736-2992	(310)637-2992
Ron Crawford, Sync Research	(310)736-4498	(310)637-8944
Job Agency References:		
Bob Roen, Engineers Exchange	(310)103-0012	
Jerry Gallenson, Tech-Aide Corp.	(213)236-3633	
Michael Ruchman, Mini-Systems & Associates	(714)897-6105	

Notice that the Personal Reference Sheet looks much better when it is in table format. Also, notice how the commas line up and the font changes really accent its professional look. Most beginners would not have this many references, so table format would not be necessary. However, if you do have quite a few references, put them into table format. It is much easier to read.

Many people find it hard to get good references from managers. I had the same problem when I was a captive employee. It never crossed my mind to nurture my references while I was working. Now I consciously collect everyone's' phone number, not only for references, but so I can keep in touch. Its fun to keep in touch with your friends and supervisors of the past, especially when you are much happier as a Consultant. If you do not have good references from managers, leave off the manager section. Remember, if you are planning on Temping, the job agency wants you to get a job more than you do! They want you to give them only 3 of your best personal references.

The reason I have listed more than 3 references is psychological. When a potential client sees that you are not afraid of giving him all of these references to call, day or night, especially past supervisors, they assume you are a very good worker! Also, the more references you give them, the less likely they will check any of them (not that we have to worry about it). Good Luck with your references and your Personal Reference Sheet.

Step 7.2: Write Up Your Personal Reference Sheet Now.

Prepare Your Business Card

Now that you are a company, you can start to take advantage of some of it's benefits. You see, job agencies like to hire people that are Consultants to do Temp work! It makes them feel more confident in your ability when they see that you are already a company. To appear like a company, you will need several more items from your portfolio, beyond the Resume and Personal Reference Sheet. A Business Card is the first thing you are going to need.

Before designing a business card, we must understand it's purposes.

First, it identifies your name with your company name, and possibly company logo. Second, it has elements of your company's mission statement in it. This is a summary of what you want, and can do. It must specifically point out if you are a developer or a researcher. Third, it must make your company sound as if there are several employees in it. Hopefully, there will be some day. Fourth, it gives you the title that you've always wanted. And finally, it has an address, a phone number, and an email address on it. If you do not want others to know where you live, then you will need a Post Office Box. Here is an example of a business card:

Business Cards are ment to be somewhat vague. Yet, if someone in your field gets it, they probably can tell what it means. Referring to the example, can you tell how large this company is? Can you tell what the company is involved in? Can you tell what I do for a living? Those of you in Electronic Design probably can. Keeping you business card a little vague will get you more phone calls.

Business Cards are primarily a closing act for a referral. When someone comes to you and asks, "Do you know a good electronic hardware engineer?" You can say, "Well, not personally, but I have this card from a friend of a friend. I've never worked with him, but I here he is good. I do know that he charges a lot." So, the card, or at least the phone number, is passed along. Situations always come up where you need a business card. Some examples are, when you make contact with a past friend, when someone you work with is moving on, when you just finished an interview, when you want a salesman to send you a quote, etc. It is a convenient way of passing out your phone number and email address. You are competing with other people that have business cards. Therefore, you need one too.

Making the Business Card stand out by using art and a logo implies that you are creative. Most people prefer to see art. Look at other people's cards before you begin your graphics design. There are many examples of other people's business cards at the places where the make them. Many of your larger copy centers, such as Kinkos™, makes Business Cards. Their prices are fairly reasonable, too. For about $100, you can get 500 cards. If you use art, color, or a complex logo, the price can double. I have found, however, that 500 cards can last a few years. I think it is worth the extra expense to spice it up with graphics art and a logo, if you can afford it. Get your cards done today, before you loose another potential client!

These days you can design a good business card on the PC. Go get some 24lb. Card Stock from Office Depot™ and drop it into your

Inkjet or Laser printer. WORD knows how to support those sheets of business cards.

Step 7.3: Design Your Business Card And Have Them Printed Now.

Preparing a Blurb Sheet

One of the more useful forms of advertising for the Contractor or Consultant is the Blurb Sheet. A Blurb Sheet is a fancy list of services that your company (your schizophrenic self) regularly provides.

The Blurb Sheet is a single sheet flyer. Many of the basic resume writing rules apply to the Blurb Sheet. In addition, a few other ingredients must be added.

- It must have a company logo on it. Logo's cost about $250 to have designed.
- It must be printed on thick, 24 pound, glossy paper.
- It must be in color.
- It has some wording similar to a high-powered advertisement.
- It contains a list of your basic and expert services.
- It gives the impression that many people are employed at your company.

An example of a black and white Blurb Sheet is shown on the next page.

EXPLORE
ELECTRONICS
Design, Test, & Manufacturing Consultants
... taking your ideas into mass production

Specializing in Reliable, Commercial Product Designs

Product Design Services
- Micro Computers RISC/DSP
- Digital, High-Speed
- Analog, High/Low Power
- Embedded Controllers
- ASIC/FPGA/PAL Design

- Windows/DOS Applications
- C++ , Visual Basic, Assembler
- R&D Project Management

Design Support Services
- Schematic Capture
- PCB Layout & Fab.
- SPICE & Timing Analysis
- DeskTop Publishing
- Engineering Model Fab.

- Design Review
- Reverse Engineering
- EMI/ESD Protection

Manufacturing Support Services
- Test Equipment Design
- Manufacturing Management

- On-site Manufacturing Liaison
- Assembly Jig Design & Fab

Jimmy Moore
EE Consultant / President
P.O. Box 1752, Fullerton, CA 91748
Email: info@ee-consultants.com
Serving the Southwest since 1984
(714) 526-3991

The Blurb Sheet provides a quick and easy way of presenting all of your capabilities to the client. It should accompany your resume whenever you apply for a Contracting or Consulting position. As mentioned earlier, some Temp agencies are interested in the Blurb, also.

Many times writing the Blurb Sheet is easier than writing the resume. It can help to organize your thoughts about you skills, what you want to offer, and what you want to avoid. You may, after writing your Blurb, want to go back and tweak your resume.

After designing the basic black and white version, take the Blurb and some pictures that you like to a graphic artist. Let them design the real thing. Remember, it must be in color and look professional.

Step 7.4: Design Your Black & White And Color Blurb Sheet Now.

The Client Reference Sheet

A Client Reference Sheet is a list of all of your past clients. It also states what you worked on at each company. The style used for a Client Reference Sheet is quite vague. It need not mention your title nor the dates you worked at these companies. It merely states which companies you have been at. It is more of an instrument to brag about some of the things that you have done for other companies.

The Client Reference Sheet gives the potential client a feeling of the depth of your consulting experience. If you have worked for well-known, large companies the client could be impressed. Some clients really don't care where you have worked before. Most of them, however, are easily impressionable. Sometimes the Client Reference Sheet will help your future boss justify your exorbitant wages to upper management. In others words, you are giving them something to brag about to their bosses. Frequently, clients will see some of the past companies they have worked for in your sheet, or they will know someone that presently works at one of the companies listed. This tends to make them feel more comfortable about hiring you. An example of a Client reference sheet is shown below. Notice that the company names are in alphabetical order.

List of Past Clients for Jimmy Moore

ALPHA PERIPHERALS, PCMCIA Card Peripherals.

CALCOMP, Mass Storage and Imaging Systems.

COMPUAIRE, Heating Ventilation Air Conditioning Control Systems.

COCHRAN CONSULTING, Semiconductor Wafer Fabrication Controls.

DATA TECHNOLOGY, Data Acquisition and Instrumentation.

EXCELLON PHOTONICS, 10,000 DPI Direct Laser Imaging Machines.

FLUOR, Data Communications and International Telephone Systems.

INTERSTATE, Graphics Displays for M1A1 Tank and Trident Submarine.

JBS CONTROLS, Heating Ventilation Air Conditioning Control Systems.

LAZER MICRO, Apple II Video Games and 16-Bit Personal Computers.

LAWRENCE LIVERMORE LABS, Space-born Sensor Systems.

MAGNAVOX, Military Spread-Spectrum Modems and FAX machine.

MAGTEK, Color Credit Card Printers, Ticket Printers, Mag-stripe Readers.

MILTOPE, Airline Ticket Reading Machine.

NEWPORT ELECTRONICS, Instrumentation and Controls.

NORTH AMERICAN PHILLIPS, Laser-Disk Data Archival Systems.

OCA APPLIED OPTICS, CCD Cameras for Star Wars.

PAIRGAIN TECHNOLOGIES, T1/T3/E1 Telecommunications.

PARROT COMMUNICATIONS, Automatic Cable Test Systems.

PERKIN ELMER, Military Laser Range Finder & Camera Instrumentation.

PERTEK ENGINEERING, Design & Development Consulting Firm.

PLAYERS WEST AMUSEMENTS, Arcade Games.

POWELL INDUSTRIES, Process Control Systems.

PROCESS SYSTEMS, Programmable PLC Controllers and Valve Systems.

SIEMENS, Data Communications and Telephone PBX Systems.

STANDARD INDUSTRIES, High Power Conversion and Lighting.

SYNC RESEARCH, PCMCIA and Data Communications.

Now is a good time to write your Client Reference Sheet. Put down every company that you've ever worked for, even if you were a student at the time, into the format shown.

Step 7.5: Write Up Your Client Reference Sheet Now.

Step 7.6: Combine Your Resume, Client Reference Sheet, and References Into One File For Emailing Now.

Summary Of Chapter 7

Your entire portfolio on paper should be looking pretty good by now. You can present yourself as a person looking for work or as a company looking for work. You can now email things out that will find you work, while you keep your present job. Potential clients can study your qualifications and check your references before they offer you a job.

Are you ready to accept a new job? Not yet! Before you start advertising your services to a cheapskate world, you need to have a good idea about how much to charge and how to haggle for it. These are the subjects of the next few chapters.

Chapter 8:
What's It Worth To Ya?

People forget, sometimes, that the main reason for going to work is to get money (believe it or not)! They get highly involved in their company's projects, excited about their field, and forget about how much they are getting paid. Earning money, so we can be happy after work, weekends, and holidays (and so can our families), is what going to work is all about. You've got to remember, first and foremost, you are working for money.

It's fantastic that, sometimes, the people we work with can provide great entertainment and comradeship. One can become good friends with many of their coworkers, and even a few managers. Also, a job can become too easy. It can feel very comfortable and laid-back. These types of distractions can help you forget about the money aspect of your job. Making friends and experiencing successes at a job site are fringe benefits. So, keep that in mind, while you are at your job.

The first step in avoiding stale business relationships is to really know how much your work and your expenses are worth. This builds a strong defense mechanism inside of your brain. In order to confront potential con-artists and cut-throat clients about money, you must be able to have confidence in the amount of money you are asking for.

Knowing how much it is costing you to be in business, is the only way to gain confidence in the amount you are charging. It is not an outrageous amount you will be charging, but in fact, is the fair market value, a defacto industry standard.

In order to instill this confidence in yourself, you must study, for several hours, all of the calculations that go into establishing your hourly rate. You must also know how much money others are getting in your field. We will cover both of these areas in this chapter.

We will also step into a fantasy world, for a moment, to figure out what would be a pleasant amount to make—our Dream Rate. You will be able to make this much in a few years. It can be a good goal for yourself.

This chapter could, literally, be worth thousands of dollars per year to you. Study it carefully.

How Much Do We Need To Break Even?

In talking about how much we need, we are referring only to breaking even with our equivalent captive employee wages and benefits. To figure out how much we need, we must, first, calculate how much we are getting on our present job. This calculation must take into account all of our benefits. Then, we will calculate how much more money we will have to charge, as a minimum, for becoming a Temp. After that, we will expand the calculation to cover any extra costs that will be encountered when becoming a Contractor or Consultant. By studying how these calculations are done, you should be able to personalize them to fit your specific situation. After establishing these minimum rates, we will research the "going rates" for people in our particular profession. Finally, we will calculate the extra profit we are going to make!

To help you get started with your own calculations, four spreadsheets have been put up on my website *www.ee-consultants.com* in the section called "Downloads." The files are in Microsoft Excel format. You must have Microsoft's Excel on your computer in order to make use of these files. If you do not have the proper hardware or software, or if you do not know how to use Excel, by all means, get someone to help you. They could literally save you months worth of work. The names of the files are:

Captive.xls	Calculates worth of captive employee's benefits.
Temp.xls	Calculates extra expenses incurred while Temping.
Consult.xls	Calculates additional expenses found in Consulting.
Dream.xls	Calculates Consultants entire budget including living expenses, savings requirements, and after-tax profit for a sole-proprietor with office in the home.

To keep this discussion simple, let us start out with an example of a captive employee making $25 an hour. We will also assume, for insurance purposes, that this person also has a family of three or more. Furthermore, this person has been at the company for some time because he or she is getting 3 weeks of vacation per year, as well as stock options. Let us examine the next three spreadsheets to see the differences between Captive, Temp, and Consulting from a wage and benefits standpoint for this situation.

The first spreadsheet, below, captive.xls, shows the worth of the benefits paid to the captive (full-time) employee, in our example. In order to pay for the employee's benefits, the company actually pays $31.82 per hour, as shown at the bottom of the sheet. Taking $31.82 per hour and subtracting $25 per hour, we get a difference of $6.82 per hour, as shown at the bottom of this spreadsheet. This is the worth of this employee's benefits. The company is actually paying this amount to the employee. Notice that your employer must pay half of your Social Security and Medicare taxes. Note that these taxes are only approximated in these spreadsheets. The official formulas are somewhat complicated.

Worth of Benefits For a Full-Time, Captive Employee - Worksheet					*Hours*	*Amount*	*Totals*
Full Time Employee Wage Calculation:							
	Captive Hourly Rate					$25.00	
	Hours Actually Worked Per Year				1816		
Pay For Hours Actually Worked:							$45,400
Hours Paid For By The Company:							
3	Weeks	Vacation/Year			120	$3,000	
12	Days	Holidays/Year			96	$2,400	
6	Days	Sick Leave/Year			48	$1,200	
Total Hours Per Year and Cost Of Hours Paid For:					2080		$6,600
Benefits Paid For By The Company:							
$96	/ Week	Health Insurance (Entire Family)				$4,988	
$25	/Month	Dental Insurance (Entire Family)				$300	
$1,000	/Year	Education Reimbursement				$1,000	
3	%/Year	Retirement Contribution By Company				$1,560	
3	%/Year	Stock Option Plan				$1,560	
3	%/Year	Christmas Bonus				$1,560	
6.2	%/Year	One Half Of Social Securit (approx)				$3,224	
Total Benefits Paid For:							$14,192
Equivalent Yearly Pay Rate (what the company actually pays):							$66,192
Equivalent Hourly Pay Rate (what the company actually pays):							$31.82
Hourly Worth Of Benefits:							$6.82

The next spreadsheet, temp.xls, shows how much the Temp, on a W2, will have to charge in order to recover the benefits he lost when becoming a Temp. Note that the numbers shown in parenthesis are negative numbers.

To make the equivalent amount of a Captive employee, the Temp must charge $5.65 more per hour to pay for his own benefits, as shown. Keep in mind that since the job agency is his W2 employer, the agency is still required to pay half of the Temp's Social Security taxes.

Temporary Employee Minimum Hourly Rate - Worksheet				Hours	Amount	Totals
Equivalent Wage Calculation:						
	Full Time Hourly Rate				$25.00	
	Hours Actually Worked Per Year			1816		
Pay For Hours Actually Worked:						$45,400
Hours Lost Due To Temping:						
3	Weeks	Vacation/Year		120	$3,000	
12	Days	Holidays/Year		96	$2,400	
6	Days	Sick Leave/Year		48	$1,200	
Total Hours and Cost Of Hours Lost:				2080		$6,600
Benefits Lost Due To Temping:						
$96	/ Week	Health Insurance (Entire Family)			$4,988	
$25	/Month	Dental Insurance (Entire Family)			$300	
$1,000	/Year	Education Reimbursement			$1,000	
3	%/Year	Retirement Contribution By Company			$1,560	
3	%/Year	Stock Option Plan			$1,560	
3	%/Year	Christmas Bonus			$1,560	
Total Benefits Lost:						$10,968
Benefits Not Lost Due To Temping						
6.2	%/Year	One Half Of Social Security Tax (approx.)			$3,224	
Total Benefits Not Lost Due To Temping						($3,224)
New Expenses Incurred Due To Temping:						
$1,000	/Year	Seminar Costs			$1,000	
$1,000	/Year	Increased Travel Expenses			$1,000	
$2,000	/Year	Office Expenses (in home)			$2,000	
Total New Expenses Incurred:						$4,000
Minimum TEMP Yearly Pay Rate Needed:						$63,744
Minimum TEMP Hourly Pay Rate Needed:						$30.65
Equivalent Hourly Cost Of TEMP's Benefits:						$5.65

The third spreadsheet, below, consult.xls, shows that a Contractor or Consultant, on a 1099, would have to charge an additional $12.31 an hour more than the Captive Employee to remain at the $25 per hour income level, after recovering his benefits. This may sound excessive right now, but in most professional and technical occupations, Consultants wages easily make up for this extra amount.

Contractor/Consultant Minimum Hourly Rate - Worksheet						*Hours*	*Amount*	*Totals*
Equivalent Wage Calculation:								
	Full-Time Hourly Rate						$25.00	
	Hours Actually Worked Per Year					1816		
Pay For Hours Actually Worked:								$45,400
Hours Lost Due To Contracting/Consulting:								
3	Weeks	Vacation/Year				120	$3,000	
12	Days	Holidays/Year				96	$2,400	
6	Days	Sick Leave/Year				48	$1,200	
Total Hours and Cost Of Hours Lost:						2080		$6,600
Benefits Lost Due To Contracting/Consulting:								
$96	/ Week	Health Insurance (Entire Family)					$4,988	
$25	/Month	Dental Insurance (Entire Family)					$300	
$1,000	/Year	Education Reimbursement					$1,000	
3	%/Year	Retirement Contribution By Company					$1,560	
3	%/Year	Stock Option Plan					$1,560	
3	%/Year	Christmas Bonus					$1,560	
6.2	%/Year	Half Of Social Security Tax (approx.)					$3,224	
Total Benefits Lost:								$14,192
New Expenses Incurred Due To Contracting/Consulting:								
$1,000	/Year	Seminar Costs					$1,000	
$1,000	/Year	Increased Travel Expenses					$1,000	
$2,000	/Year	Office Expenses (in home)					$2,000	
1	Month/Y	Unemployment Benefits Lost (approx.)					$2,167	
2	Hours/W	Book Keeping Time				104	$2,600	
2	Hours/W	Marketting And Selling Services				104	$2,600	
Total New Expenses Incurred:								$11,367
New Taxes Incurred Due To Contracting/Consulting:								
0	%/Year	State Tax Increase (California, approx.)					$0	
$50	/Year	City Business Tax (approx)					$50	
Total New Taxes Incurred:								$50
Minimum CONTRACTING/CONSULTING Yearly Pay Rate Needed:								$77,609
Minimum CONTRACTING/CONSULTING Hourly Pay Rate Needed:								$37.31
Equivalent CONTRACTING/CONSULTING Hourly Cost Of Benefits:								$12.31

In the examples above, we have attempted to calculate how much more a Captive Employee will have to charge in order to do Temping or Consulting. We've tried to include the obvious benefits that most companies offer to their employees, these days. We have calculated that to break even with a Captive, making $25/hour, the Temp must add $5.65, or 23% and the Contractor/Consultant must add $12.31, or about 49%, in our example. These percentages are the costs of recovering your benefits and encountering new expenses.

Many captive employees, as in our example, do not receive as many benefits as shown in the first spreadsheet. For instance, some employees are single, so their medical insurance is much less. Some companies require 5 years of service before they give 3 weeks of vacation to their employees. Many companies don't give Christmas bonuses or stock options, and so forth.

Check out the example, on the next page, about a Captive employee, who is single (thus lowering his insurance), and working at a company that has little or no benefits (alias, a "sweat shop").

Worth of Poor Benefit Package, Captive Employee - Worksheet						
					Hours	*Amount*	*Totals*
Full Time Employee Wage Calculation:							
	Captive Hourly Rate					$25.00	
	Hours Actually Worked Per Year				1992		
Pay For Hours Actually Worked:							$49,800
Hours Paid For By The Company:							
1	Weeks	Vacation/Year			40	$1,000	
6	Days	Holidays/Year			48	$1,200	
0	Days	Sick Leave/Year			0	$0	
Total Hours Per Year and Cost Of Hours Paid For:					2080		$2,200
Benefits Paid For By The Company:							
$33	/ Week	Health Insurance (Employee Only)				$1,715	
$0	/Month	Dental Insurance				$0	
$0	/Year	Education Reimbursement				$0	
0	%/Year	Retirement Contribution By Company				$0	
0	%/Year	Stock Option Plan				$0	
0	%/Year	Christmas Bonus				$0	
6.2	%/Year	One Half Of Social Securit (approx)				$3,224	
Total Benefits Paid For:							$4,939
Equivalent Yearly Pay Rate (what the company actually pays):							$56,939
Equivalent Hourly Pay Rate (what the company actually pays):							$27.37
Hourly Worth Of Benefits:							$2.37

In comparing spreadsheet number 1 with spreadsheet number 4, you can see quite a difference in the worth of benefits. The difference is $6.82 minus $2.37, or $4.45 an hour.

Keep in mind that is possible for both of these employees to be working at the same company, in the same occupation. That is one reason why companies do not want their employees to discuss their pay with each other. Usually, discussing wages is considered as sufficient grounds for being fired.

Because of these wide pay differences, for employees in the same field of work, it would be impossible for someone else to calculate how much you are making. You must do this on your own. When personalizing your own calculations, you may find out, like I did some time ago, that your benefits are only worth $2.50 an hour and not $6.82 as shown in the first spreadsheet.

Notice that the first three spreadsheets build progressively on the data in each previous spreadsheet, respectively. It is, therefore, important to accurately profile your situation as a Captive Employee, or equivalent, before doing calculations for Temping, Contracting, and Consulting.

Keep in mind, that none of the spreadsheets above show how your paycheck gets spent. The spreadsheets only attempt to explain the worth of benefits or recovery of benefits. They do not show, for example, that most Captive Employees pay 35% of their income to the IRS in federal taxes, whereas, many Consultants are usually in a 25% tax bracket. Increased taxes are another factor to consider when you move up the pay scale. Remember too, that increased tax write-offs also come into play, however. It will take further more complicated analysis to get the complete picture.

Your task, for the next day or two, is to personalize these three calculations to exactly fit your situation. You will probably be amazed at how little your benefits are worth, like I was. More than any other subject, "loss of benefits" is what most people are concerned with when considering a career in consulting. Knowing exactly how much everything costs will build your confidence, when it comes to negotiating your pay.

> **Step 8.1: Download And Personalize The Spreadsheets To Match Your Situation.**

How Much Can You Get?

From this point on, you should have a solid idea of how much it is going to cost you to pay for your own benefits. Now you need to know how much other people are getting. Unfortunately, for all of us, there is no magic table or equation in existence, that will tell us how much we can charge. Needless to say, this will require more research, on your part.

Start Asking Others

In order to find out how much you can charge, you need to start asking people, in your field, that have come in contact with Temps, Contractors, or Consultants.

Start by asking captive employees in your field how much they "think" Temps make. Ask them in groups. Then ask the Temps that work there how much people in their field are getting paid. Most mercenaries will be glad to help a newcomer join the invisible army. If they don't want to tell you, ask them how much they charged when they first started out. Ask them how they got started, while you're at it. Ask the personnel office how much they company pays for Temps.

While doing your research, you will find a wide range of pay. Some people that are not good workers will be making $100 an hour, and some that are excellent workers will be making $30 an hour, doing the same thing. There is a wide range of pay, but there is only one average pay that most people in your geographical area are getting. Your challenge, in doing this research, will be to determine the average amount you can charge, not the most you can charge. Remember, if you charge the average, you will get much more work.

Search The Net

Remember Janet Ruhl's site at *www.realrates.com*? That's perfect for software engineers needing rate information. Try to find a site like this for you. Also, you can find some government wage data for captive employees that may help.

Be Careful About Asking About Money

You must promise, however, never to tell anyone how much others are making. This could lead to some very bad feelings all around. Here is an example of what happened to me once.

Once upon a time, I was working at a company for several years at $50 an hour. The company started up a large project and hired many other Consultants. One of my tasks was to manage these other Consultants, since the company trusted me. A couple of months later, someone told me how much the others were getting paid: $65 an hour. I was terribly distressed by this. My performance and work quality immediately dropped. In a short time, I had to get out of there. In retrospect, I wish I had never known how much the others were getting paid. But, when I left that company, I started charging much more. I cried all the way to the bank.

Step 8.2: Ask A Few People About Temp, Contractor, And Consulting Wages Today.

Ask The Agencies

Another source for wage information is from the job agencies themselves. I called agencies and asked them how much I could get as an Electronic Engineer. Most of them said that the minimum in this field was $30 an hour! Even a fresh-out (also known as a recent college grad) could get this much. They also said that most experienced Engineers get about $45 an hour. Keep in mind that agencies rarely tell you the truth about money. Most of their replies are a little on the low side. If you average out what they are telling you collectively, you could get some valuable numbers.

For example, let's say there is an opening at a company, and that company is willing to pay the agency $75 an hour. Now, normally, the agency would find someone willing to work for $50 an hour, keep $25 for themselves, and everyone would be happy. Then let's say that you happen to call them and start asking all these questions about pay. Obviously, they realize you are new to this field. They ask you about your experience and soon realize that you are a perfect match for that job. They could then tell you that they have a great job for you, but the most they could pay you is $35 an hour. That could be a lie! They just want to make $15 an hour more than they normally would! Greedy aren't they?

Notice that when a client or an agency lies about money, they call it negotiating. But when the worker bends the truth about money, it is called a lie. Is this fair to the working class to give the employers the right to lie, and not the employees? No! It is all part of the game called negotiating that we will investigate later.

Confusion About "Contracting"

Some of the recruiters, I had first called, commented that since I did not have any experience as a "Contractor," they wouldn't consider hiring me. How can you be a Contractor if you are a W2 employee of an agency, I wondered? And, if you are supposed to have experience working for an agency, how are you supposed to get that experience then? It's the same old "chicken or the egg" problem. In retrospect, this problem of not saying that I had done "Contracting" before delayed my consulting career by several years. But, it shouldn't have! I figured out some years later that job agencies, trade magazines, and fellow mercenaries frequently swap the term "Contracting" with "Temping"! Now, 20 years later, no one refers to working for agencies as "Temping." I had no clue, back then, how much money I was going to loose because of this confusion.

It took me more than five years, after this, to try Temp work. In that five-year period, I lost, at least, $20/hour for 49 hours a week (based on national averages), for five years, or $254,800. Yes, I lost thousands of dollars. That's $51,000 a year! I could have bought a house with that, and paid cash! Don't let this happen to you! When an agency asks you if you've done "contract" work before, what they are really asking is if you have done Temp, Contracting, or Consulting work before.

You must be able to answer YES, if they ask you about prior Contracting experience. If you can't honestly say "yes," get one of your friends to hire you, for one hour. Then, buy them dinner with the money they paid you! Finally, you can say you've done Contracting work.

Temp work, or whatever you want to call it, is no different than captive work. Don't let an agency fool you. They are already negotiating when they ask you this. Did I ever mention that Temp work is no different than captive work? It takes no additional experience to do Temp work, than captive work. You do have to carry your own benefits. And, it is much more fun and rewarding. But, you do not need more work experience than you now have. Please remember one thing, Temp work is not different than captive work. You must be able to say "yes" to their question.

The Degree Problem

When I was calling agencies for the first time, many of them answered my questions about pay. After that, they wanted to know right away, what my skills and education were. They wanted to give me a job right then. When they found out that I didn't have a college degree, most of them gave me advice to go back to school. They said this without realizing the many years of experience I had with microprocessors and electronics. I had the knowledge and the experience to fill a niche that many companies needed back in 1977. I was on the leading edge of technology (sometimes referred to as the "bleeding edge"). What I had learned, wasn't being taught in schools yet. In fact, the schools are still way behind in the computer/electronics fields. These agencies seemed to ignore the 147 college units I had received as a physics major! Believe me, that's nothing to sneeze at.

So, I laughed when these, so-called, "Job Finding Experts" told me I couldn't get a job without a degree. I may not have a degree, but I did have the knowledge.

Here is an example of what happened to me once. After several years of consulting, a headhunter told me that he wouldn't be able to find me a job because I didn't have a degree. Instead of working, I should go back to school and get my degree! A few days later, that same headhunter took some vacation. A much wiser recruiter, in that same office, realized the experience I had on my resume. She sent me on an interview the following day. I won the interview and got the job, the next day. When I went to the agency to sign all the papers, I saw this same lady recruiter saying goodbye to everyone. It turns out, that was her last day to work, since she was 9 months pregnant! So, the headhunter in that office, that told me that he couldn't possibly get me a job because I didn't have a degree, is the one that actually signed me up! A few months later he commented, "Jimmy they sure like your work here. We could have gotten you much higher pay for this job, huh?" Now it sinks in, I thought!

Average Out What Agencies Tell You

So, don't get too depressed when asking these agencies about pay. They are already working on angles to pay you less when you talk to them. This is what people do when they negotiate money. You're not prepared to get too involved with them yet. Don't send any of them your resume yet. Tell them you were merely curious about Temp jobs. Ask them to mail you some information on it.

Start calling agencies. Average out what the agencies are telling you. Compare the results of all of these groups. Are they dealing with the same range of pay?

Step 8.3: Call A Few Agencies And Talk To Them Now.

Rules Of Thumb For Pay

After doing the leg work you will probably find that the average most people charge can be found by my general rules of thumb:

- **To start Temping, charge about 2 times your Captive Rate.**
- **To start Contracting, charge about 1.3 times your Temping Rate.**
- **To start Consulting, charge about 1.3 times your Contracting Rate.**

This formula will work for most people, unless you are at a very high captive rate already (i.e. $80K or more). However, if you charge

10% to 20% less than the formula, you will get more work than most, and you will probably be happy with that amount.

Step 8.4: Determine How Much You Are Going To Charge Now.

Calculating Your Extra Profit

After all this work, we have reached a point where we can calculate your extra profit! If you have done your homework, you should now have in mind how much you are going to try to ask for. You should also, now, know how much you need to recover lost benefits, and how much others are charging in this field. By subtracting how much you need from how much you are going to charge, the result will be your extra profit.

Keep in mind that this profit is for each and every hour you work! No more free overtime! I hope you are pleasantly surprised like I was! What are you going to do with all the extra money?

Don't worry, the world has a developed a few surprises for people with extra money. Let's play "what-if" in the next section, to give you an idea of the magnitude of these surprises.

Caution: Please be sure this subtraction is not a negative number. If it is, your chosen field for Temping is one that will not work out.

Step 8.5: Calculate Your Yearly Profit Now.

Budget Planning For Non-Captive Work

Would it be too much to ask to have a good retirement plan, good medical coverage, money for the kid's colleges, a little savings account, a house, and a decent car? Probably so, if your just starting out as a Non-Captive!

I define a good retirement plan to be something like 10% of my earnings, since I'm 40ish and only have about 20 years to go. A college fund of say $5000 a year would be a minimum, for each child. Saving $100 a week in a savings account would be nice too. Well, believe it or not, $50 an hour won't buy you these basic dreams as a Temp or a Consultant. But it is a heck of a lot better than $25 an hour!

On the next page, you will see another spreadsheet called a Temp's Budget Planner. It is included on my website as another Excel file called tempplan.xls. It is good for playing "what if" scenarios, if you know what amounts to put in for your taxes and bills. It attempts to take into account ALL of the expenses encountered for a whole year's worth of Temping.

The example shown on the next page is for someone making $50 an hour. You can see down near the bottom that a decent retirement and a little lunch money is attainable. However, a general savings account and adequate college funds are still not a reality.

Temp's Budget Planner - Worksheet

						Hours	Amount	Totals
Wage Calculation:								
	Hourly Rate						$50.00	
	Hours Actually Worked Per Year					1888		
0	Hours/Week Of Overtime (Average)					0		
Gross Pay For Hours Actually Worked:								$94,400
Pay Lost To Time Off:								
2	Weeks	Vacation/Year				80	($4,000)	
12	Days	Holidays/Year				96	($4,800)	
2	Days	Sick Leave/Year				16	($800)	
Total Hours & Cost Of Time Off (although not actu						2080	($9,600)	
Expenses for Living And Self Employment:								
$2,500	/Month	Housing & Utilities					($30,000)	
$96	/ Week	Health Insurance (Entire Family)					($4,988)	
$25	/Month	Dental Insurance (Entire Family)					($300)	
$1,000	/Year	Seminar Costs/New Books					($1,000)	
$2,200	/Year	Travel & Vehicle Expenses					($2,200)	
$2,000	/Year	Office And Computer Expenses (in home)					($2,000)	
Total Expenses:								($40,488)
Taxes To Be Paid:								
29	%/Year	Federal Taxes (approx)					($27,376)	
6	%/Year	State Taxes (approx)					($5,664)	
$0	/Year	County Taxes					$0	
$35	/Year	City Taxes					($35)	
8	%	Sales Taxes on Puchased Items					($416)	
Total Taxes To Be Paid:								($33,491)
Net Profit for TEMPING:								$12,491
Savings Plans:								
8.4	%/Year	401K Retirement Plan					$7,930	
$40	/ Week	Childrens College Savings					$2,078	
$0	/ Week	Personal Savings Account					$0	
$40	/Week	Lunch Money					$2,000	
$0	/Week	Entertainment					$0	
Total Savings Plans:								$7,930
Total Cash Spent:								$2,000
Petty Cash Left Over:								$483

Now, let's see what happens when we try to Consult at this low rate. Look at the next spreadsheet called the Consultant's Budget Planner. It is called conplan.xls on my website.

Again, we can see that Temping, first, is a lower risk way to start out in the consulting business. As you can see, the Self-Employment taxes, and the hours lost due to bookkeeping and marketing yourself, change the picture drastically.

Consultant's Budget Planner - Poor Rate Example						*Hours*	*Amount*	*Totals*
Wage Calculation:								
	Hourly Rate						$50.00	
	Hours Actually Worked Per Year					1784		
0	Hours/Week Of Overtime (Average)					0		
Gross Pay For Hours Actually Worked:								$89,200
Pay Lost To Time Off:								
2	Weeks	Vacation/Year				80	($4,000)	
12	Days	Holidays/Year				96	($4,800)	
2	Days	Sick Leave/Year				16	($800)	
2	Hours/W	Book Keeping Time				104	($5,200)	
Total Hours & Cost Of Time Off (although not actu						2080	($14,800)	
Expenses for Living And Self Employment:								
$2,500	/Month	Housing & Utilities					($30,000)	
$96	/ Week	Health Insurance (Entire Family)					($4,988)	
$25	/Month	Dental Insurance (Entire Family)					($300)	
$1,000	/Year	Seminar Costs/New Books					($1,000)	
$2,200	/Year	Travel & Vehicle Expenses					($2,200)	
$2,000	/Year	Office And Computer Expenses (in home)					($2,000)	
Total Expenses:								($40,488)
Taxes To Be Paid:								
1) Business Expense Deductions: includes 20% use of Home							$15,946	
for Office, 1/2 Self Employment Tax, 1/8 Medical.								
2) Net Income After Business Deductions							$65,761	
10	%/Year	Self Employment Taxes (approx)					($8,171)	
29	%/Year	Federal Taxes (approx)					($19,071)	
6	%/Year	State Taxes (approx)					($3,946)	
$0	/Year	County Taxes					$0	
$35	/Year	City Taxes					($35)	
8	%	Sales Taxes on Puchased Items					($416)	
Total Taxes To Be Paid:								($31,638)
Net Profit for CONSULTING:								$9,581
Savings Plans:								
8.4	%/Year	Keough Retirement Plan					$7,493	
$0	/ Week	Childrens College Savings					$0	
$0	/ Week	Personal Savings Account					$0	
$40	/Week	Lunch Money					$2,000	
$0	/Week	Entertainment					$0	
Total Savings Plans:								$7,493
Total Cash Spent:								$2,000
Petty Cash Left Over:								$88

At the rate of $50 per hour, consulting is out of the question! Looking at the bottom section of the sheet, you can see that all you can afford to buy is lunch. You have no savings and no entertainment money.

Consultants May Be Starving

Consulting costs a lot more than Temping! I have met several Consultants that do not understand this concept, and they are perpetually starving. Literally, they can barely afford lunch.

The reason they haven't figured this out, yet, is twofold. First, they haven't done the calculations we have done in this chapter. Secondly, since they are good, they are asked to work alot of overtime. Working overtime masks out income shortfalls. If you work enough overtime, you can make a profit at any rate, but your home-life suffers.

!Downtime Warning!

Temping, Contracting, and Consulting all have periods of layoff, or Downtime. Downtime savings accounts were not included so that these worksheet comparisons wouldn't get too complicated. Assume that your retirement money will go into your downtime account until it is filled up with a certain amount of money. Then, your regular retirement account will begin growing. The spreadsheets we have investigated thus far assume you already have this money. Your regular savings account can also be used to fill up a downtime account. But, it is better to have a line item for downtime savings, to show that it is separate from retirement and other savings accounts. Downtime is listed as a type of savings plan in the Dream Rate spreadsheets shown later. It has to be a liquid cash asset, cash that you can get to. Downtime Savings has a cap to it. Once it reaches a certain value, say 3 months worth of living expenses, there is no need to add more money to it. You must have some amount of money put aside for downtime occurrences.

The amount of downtime actually needed depends if people are nice to you or not. They may come up to you and say, "Well, in about two weeks we will be wrapping this project up. You can start looking for more work if you like." If that's the case, the downtime will be very minimal. On the other hand, if they come up to you on Friday at 4:55pm and say don't come to work on Monday, you may be looking at a 2 month unscheduled vacation. Most people are decent folks and will give you some kind of warning, particularly if you are working through an agency. Only the ones that are mad at you will surprise you with unexpected layoffs. But, if they are mad at us, we should have quit earlier anyway, to protect our reputation, right? Both instances count as downtime, however.

Step 8.6: Calculate Your Downtime Cash Requirement For Three Months.

The Dream Rate

By playing "what if" it is easy with the next spreadsheet to calculate how much we would have to charge to reach our "Dream Rate". Playing "what if" is the most powerful use of a personal computer, in the business world.

In the third spreadsheet below, we have set our "Dream Rate" goals in the categories down on the bottom of the spreadsheet, first. After filling in all of the values for all of our bills, the cost of our new dream home, and our savings goals, then we can increase the hourly rate, at the top of the spreadsheet, until the petty cash number, at the bottom is between 0 and $1000. The result in this example is approximately $86 an hour. Remember, this result is without overtime.

In this example, we did not itemize our tax deductions or take tax credits for owning a home. We also stayed inside the previous tax bracket. However, be sure to take into account which tax bracket you will be in when you personalize yours.

The Dream Rate Spreadsheet is included on my website. It takes into account, office in the home and company car deductions. It does not take into account being incorporated, since that is much more complicated.

Consultant's Dream Rate Calculation - No Overtime					Hours	Amount	Totals
Wage Calculation:							
	Hourly Rate					$86.00	
	Hours Actually Worked Per Year				1784		
0	Hours/Week Of Overtime (Average)				0		
Gross Pay For Hours Actually Worked:							$153,424
Pay Lost Due To Time Off:							
2	Weeks	Vacation/Year			80	($6,880)	
12	Days	Holidays/Year			96	($8,256)	
2	Days	Sick Leave/Year			16	($1,376)	
2	Hours/Wk	Book Keeping Time			104	($8,944)	
Total Hours & Cost Of Time Off (although not actually lost):					2080	($25,456)	
Expenses for Living And Self Employment:							
$3,500	/Month	Housing & Utilities				($42,000)	
$96	/ Week	Health Insurance (Entire Family)				($4,988)	
$25	/Month	Dental Insurance (Entire Family)				($300)	
$1,000	/Year	Seminar Costs/New Books				($1,000)	
$2,200	/Year	Travel & Vehicle Expenses				($2,200)	
$2,000	/Year	Office And Computer Expenses (in home)				($2,000)	
$1,000	/Year	Life Insurance (approx.)				($1,000)	
Total Expenses:							($53,488)
Taxes To Be Paid:							
1) Business Expense Deductions: includes 20% use of Home						$22,165	
for Office, 1/2 Self Employment Tax, 1/8 Medical.							
2) Net Income After Business Deductions						$115,917	
10	%/Year	Self Employment Taxes (approx)				($13,808)	
29	%/Year	Federal Taxes (approx)				($33,616)	
6	%/Year	State Taxes (approx)				($6,955)	
$0	/Year	County Taxes				$0	
$35	/Year	City Taxes				($35)	
8	%	Sales Taxes on Puchased Items				($416)	
Total Taxes To Be Paid:							($54,830)
Net Profit for CONSULTING:							$29,764
Savings Plans:							
$15,000	Total	Downtime Savings				$15,000	
10	%/Year	Keough Retirement Plan				$15,342	
$100	/ Week	Childrens College Savings				$5,196	
$100	/ Week	Personal Savings Account				$5,196	
$40	/Week	Lunch Money				$2,000	
$39	/Week	Entertainment				$2,028	
Total Savings Plans:							$35,538
Total Cash Spent:							$4,028
Petty Cash Left Over:							$1

Let's look at one more example of the simplified Dream Rate Calculation, but this time include the national average for overtime, of 9 hours per week. Keeping all expenses the same, we can see that we can charge $16 dollars an hour less now!!! We only need to charge $70/hour to achieve our Dream Rate, at 49 hours per week. Keep that in mind! The file is dream.xls.

Consultant's Dream Rate Calculation - Average Overtime						Hours	Amount	Totals
Wage Calculation:								
	Hourly Rate						$70.00	
	Hours Actually Worked Per Year					1784		
9	Hours/Week Of Overtime (Average)					468		
Gross Pay For Hours Actually Worked:								$157,640
Pay Lost Due To Time Off:								
2	Weeks	Vacation/Year				80	($5,600)	
12	Days	Holidays/Year				96	($6,720)	
2	Days	Sick Leave/Year				16	($1,120)	
2	Hours/W	Book Keeping Time				104	($7,280)	
Total Hours & Cost Of Time Off *(although not actually*						2548	($20,720)	
Expenses for Living And Self Employment:								
$3,500	/Month	Housing & Utilities					($42,000)	
$96	/ Week	Health Insurance (Entire Family)					($4,988)	
$25	/Month	Dental Insurance (Entire Family)					($300)	
$1,000	/Year	Seminar Costs/New Books					($1,000)	
$2,200	/Year	Travel & Vehicle Expenses					($2,200)	
$2,000	/Year	Office And Computer Expenses (in home)					($2,000)	
$1,000	/Year	Life Insurance (approx.)					($1,000)	
Total Expenses:								($53,488)
Taxes To Be Paid:								
1) Business Expense Deductions: includes 20% use of Home							$22,355	
for Office, 1/2 Self Employment Tax, 1/8 Medical.								
2) Net Income After Business Deductions							$119,521	
10	%/Year	Self Employment Taxes (approx)					($14,188)	
29	%/Year	Federal Taxes (approx)					($34,661)	
6	%/Year	State Taxes (approx)					($7,171)	
$0	/Year	County Taxes					$0	
$35	/Year	City Taxes					($35)	
8	%	Sales Taxes on Puchased Items					($416)	
Total Taxes To Be Paid:								($56,471)
Net Profit for CONSULTING:								$31,917
Savings Plans:								
$15,000	Total	Downtime Savings					$15,000	
10	%/Year	Keough Retirement Plan					$15,764	
$100	/ Week	Childrens College Savings					$5,196	
$100	/ Week	Personal Savings Account					$5,196	
$40	/Week	Lunch Money					$2,000	
$39	/Week	Entertainment					$2,028	
Total Savings Plans:								$35,960
Total Cash Spent:								$4,028
Petty Cash Left Over:								$1,733

Thinking in terms of these high rates can be upsetting to someone that is not at this point in their career. Don't get discouraged if you cannot charge this much, yet. You have to pay your dues in society first. Charge less and work a little overtime for a while. Then, gradually raise your rates.

I have written this book to help you get to your Dream Rate. Don't give up on your dreams. Right now, by studying these charts, you should have just realized that these dreams will be reality, in the not-to-distant future.

The Dream Rate calculation should be one of the most enjoyable calculations about money that you'll ever make. It helps you visualize your financial future, and realize why consulting is so important for it. If only someone would have showed us this earlier!

Step 8.7: Calculate Your Dream Rate Now.

Personalize The Math

You must personalize your own bills and goals in these Spreadsheets to fit your exact situation and dreams. Have your taxperson and accountant give you additional advice while your are working on them. Use the files supplied from my website as a starting point. Then, think about it overnight. Work on this for a few days. Are you going to be comfortable asking for your new rate? Do you really know what others are getting in your field? Are you able to be flexible with your new rate? If so, by how much? These are some of the questions that agencies and clients will soon be asking you.

Many items in these examples are over-simplified, approximations for demonstration purposes only. The numbers they give may not be exact values, but they can be compared to other calculations for relative differences.

Please do yourself a favor and work hard on these calculations. They are worth hundreds of thousands of dollars to you. Check them every 6 months. Make sure you are charging enough to pay your taxes and reach your goals, at all times.

Summary Of Chapter 8

Well, we have performed several investigations and financial calculations in this chapter. We calculated how much our benefits are worth. Hopefully, you've realized that your benefits aren't worth all that much, especially compared to the profit you could be making. We've researched how much people are getting paid for Temping, Contracting, and Consulting. We planned some budgets for Temping, Contracting, and Consulting for a whole year. You have probably felt a surge in your confidence in asking for more money, especially after realizing where much of your money is going. We are about ready to go out and get this money!

Getting the pay rates that you want requires forceful negotiation. In the next chapter, we will establish the rules of war for wage negotiation. Are you ready to pump up your paycheck?

Chapter 9:
Basic "Negotiating" Principles

In this chapter, the techniques used for pay-rate negotiation will be explained. Please note that the word negotiating has been put in quotes for a special reason. Later you will realize what this incredible reason is.

General Negotiation Principles

Let's establish some basic principles used in all wage negotiations.

If a person went to an open-air market, swap-meet, or garage-sale, they could experience negotiation first hand. There, a potential buyer can learn what happens when trying to buy something at the lowest possible price.

Here is an example of what the negotiation involves. Let's say a buyer sees an item he would like to purchase. He feels that $2.00 would be a fair price for this item. The negotiation might go like this:

Buyer: "So, how much do you want for this?"
Seller: "How much do you think it is worth?"
Buyer: "$2.00."

Seller: "No way. I paid ten times that when it was brand new, and it is still in good condition. So, how about $4.00?"

Buyer: "I only have $2.50." (While pretending to dig through his pockets).

Seller: (starts walking away slowly) "Too bad, the lowest I could go would be $3.50."

Buyer: (quickly adds) "$3.00 is my last offer."

Seller: (bursts into an ear-splitting smile) "Sold for a mere $3.00!"

Thus, the price agreed upon ended up somewhere in-between the price that each person originally wanted.

Most negotiations are a compromise like that. There is no set price on items for sale. *Likewise, in the job world, there is no set price for your services! You have to negotiate your price.*

Notice, also, that each person in the negotiation was "telling lies." For example, the buyer said he only had $2.50. The seller said he would not go any lower than $3.50. But, these aren't considered to be lies, when it comes to negotiating! These are mearly "test answers" to see what the other person will respond with. It is not considered to be "lying" but more like playing a strategy game. That is also why the title of this chapter has the word "negotiating" in quotes. "Negotiating" is very close to lying.

Realizing this, you are now beginning to see why, most likely, you are probably underpaid at this moment time. You did not "negotiate". You merely told the truth. You took it too seriously. The recruiter or personnel representative negotiated you into a less favorable salary and you couldn't negotiate back, because you were afraid you would be lying.

Let's see how we can do better on our next negotiation.

The Four Rules Of Negotiating Pay

First of all, did you know that it is virtually illegal for your previous employer to tell a recruiter (or anyone else) how much you are making right now? The only time they are allowed to do this is when you have sent them a signed release form, or filled out a job application and signed it. We can take major advantage of this when negotiating our pay!

Before we can use this principle to our advantage, we have to make sure that we never, ever, give anyone, verbally, or in writing, permission to call others to find out our current, or past, rate of pay. For example, if you fill out a job application, it will have little boxes on it for your salary at each job. It will also require that you sign it, giving them permission to get any information they want. Therefore, never fill out an application (until after the wage negotiation). Give recruiters a resume only.

If you go to an interview, and they insist that you fill out an application first, tell them you don't have time to. Tell them that you have another interview in one hour (negotiate your way out of that). If you can't get out of it, put down on your application to "see attached resume for details" in the experience section and sign it. Never put your salary on your resume, either.

Negotiation Rule #1:
Keep your current or previous rate of pay a secret, at all costs!

Whatever we charged in the past has nothing to do with what we are asking for now. The only reason agents and clients want to know our past wage is so they can leverage it against us.

Let me demonstrate the power of not letting anyone know how much you made before. When I was a captive employee, I discovered this system for getting higher pay whenever I changed jobs. If I was making $50K (i.e. $50,000 per year) and I wanted $55K, I would tell the new company that I was making $55K and that I was due for a 10% raise. They would think that I was making $55K, and was asking for $60.5K. After several days, the personnel department would usually get back to me, and say, "Sorry Mr. Moore, but we can only *afford* to offer you what you were making before, $55K." So, I would get my $55K! This technique worked time after time. In fact, sometimes the new employer would even give me the extra 10%, on top of that! Is this fair of me to do this?

Is it fair of them to lie and say they "can only *afford* the $55K?" What do they mean by "afford?" Aren't they a multi-million dollar corporation? Do you think they can control their millions down to the nearest $5K?

Is everything fair in "negotiation"? Do you think it is fair for them to "negotiate" while you are required to tell the truth? If you do, you are probably grossly underpaid at this time. Sorry, I know this is concept is hard to grasp for the honest people out there. How do you think I felt after going to Catholic school most of my life? Anyway, lets see if we can justify this a little better.

Usually, when accepting a captive job, the new employee has to completely fill out an application after being hired. On this application, he *must* put down the truth about how much he was paid in the past. By signing the application you are swearing that the information is true. This brings the salary history all out in the open.

After I "negotiated" my new pay rate, I would always have to put down the truth on the application. Funny though, on job after job, no one has ever commented to me that I lied or deceived them, in any way, during the "negotiation". I guess some recruiters don't read the application. I watched recruiters that did read that section of the application. They looked up at me and smiled. I called their bluff, out-negotiated them, and they knew it. They didn't care, however. The "negotiation" process was over. I was already signed up to work, and they were happy. This was the ultimate proof to me that, indeed, we were negotiating, and it wasn't considered as "telling a lie." I guess they figured I was on their side now and could use my negotiation skills for their company. Conclusion: It is a semantics game. Don't take it so seriously. It is called negotiation, not lying!

What gives the agency or client the right to base my new salary on what I was making before, anyway? Hey, just maybe, I have recently advanced in my field, or received a new college degree. Perhaps, that's why, I was looking for a new job in the first place. So what, if I just found out everyone else was making more than I was. Why can't I seek work elsewhere to get more money? Do these people think we work for the shear pleasure of it?

Some people have a difficult time negotiating this way. In their honesty, they decide it is better to argue with the interviewer. One friend tells them outright, "What I am asking for now has nothing to do with what I was making before. I want this new amount and it is not negotiable." Sometimes it works, but more often, you will not get hired for the job because you have already started an argument. It makes you seem arrogant. It, also, makes you seem like you are changing jobs just to get a large pay raise. So, they may decide that you are lying about the real reason that you left your last job. Or, they may conclude, that all you really want is a lot more money, and so you are also lying! So, therefore, you are a liar, anyway! This technique, of being forcefully truthful, does have a better chance of working when you negotiate with a job agency, as opposed to negotiating directly with a client. However, you should really, really, avoid using this technique, altogether, really.

Now let's get back to negotiating. In the swap-meet, negotiation example, the buyer made the first mistake of telling the seller how much he thought the item was worth. This gave the seller a basis from which to start the negotiation. The seller's only goal was to get more than that original offer. That is what people who sell things do. That's how they maximize their profit. They won't stop haggling until they have gotten the better end of the deal. A buyer, on the other hand, does the opposite. The buyer's only goal was to pay less than the seller's original price. This is the principle that personnel recruiters use. They are taking the buyer's role. From this, we can see why the next rule for negotiating is so important.

Negotiation Rule #2:

Always ask for more than you really want. Anticipate being haggled with. Factor it in.

If you want $50 an hour, plan on asking for $55. An agency will usually ask, "How much do you want?" Say you tell them $55 an hour, without hesitation. Then they immediately ask, "What is the lowest you will go?" You need to again say, "$55 an hour". See, they are already haggling in the first few seconds of talking to you on the phone. After you win a job interview, the agency or client will still offer less than the amount that was previously established as your absolute minimum.

Most humans that negotiate frequently cannot control this nasty habit. They have a second-nature compulsion to bump you down one more notch, even after the first verbal agreement. *But that's O.K. for us! We have factored all this in, ahead of time!*

They usually come back and say, "Sorry Mr. Moore, but $50 an hour is the most I could get for you from this client. He won't go any higher, and we do a lot of business with him, so we don't want to make him angry. If you take this job, we will get you a better rate next time, O.K.?" This is a very typical agency response. My response to this is fine:

☺

Now, what if, for some reason, you need to get a higher rate, than what you had previously asked for? Perhaps you just learned something new about the job requirement that makes you more valuable. Or maybe your availability has changed because you've negotiated higher pay from a different company. Maybe one of your friends called you and wants you to come and work with him, which would be more fun. Maybe you learned something from your interview that the agency didn't know about or forgot to tell you about, that you really would not prefer to be doing. Here are some other examples of what can occur:

1. Another recruiter has offered you a better deal, but you really want this first job because it interests you more.
2. The recruiter is giving you your rate, but the job is much farther away than you thought.
3. You told the recruiter some ridiculously, low rate a few days ago, before you found out, how easy it was to get much more.

This brings us to the third basic rule of negotiation.

Negotiation Rule #3:
Always have several excuses memorized to boost your pay rate back up to a higher level.

These types of excuses or rationalizations are called "Squeeze Factors." They are used to "Squeeze" more money out of the people that want to hire you. Let's review how some common ones can be used.

My favorite Squeeze Factor is the "travel distance" syndrome. Recruiters don't actually know how "far" you think is far. Nor do they know exactly where you live and how crowded the freeways are around you. "Far" is subjective. It's easy to say, "Wow, that client is pretty far away from my house. To go that far I would have to charge more." This is usually good for about a $5/hour boost-up.

An interesting side-effect of this syndrome, by the way, is that by traveling a great distance, you can usually get the client to give you additional freedoms. The trick is to get the extra travel pay from the agency, first. Then, after you are on the job for a short time, mention to the client that it would be much more "productive" if you could work at home. There you could put in at least 2 more hours per day in overtime, instead of sitting in traffic. So, that's at least 10 more hours per week of work." They usually agree. So, you get the best of both worlds, more pay for traveling far but you don't have to go anywhere. So, travel distance makes a good Squeeze Factor.

The best Squeeze Factors are found during the interview. Below are examples of Squeeze Factors found at most job sites. They can all be used as believable Squeeze-Factors, because most of them are true.

"I'm really over-qualified for the job, it will be very boring for me working there."

"The schedule they have for the project is already blown, it will be very stressful working there."

"The boss there seems like a very uptight person, I will be very uncomfortable working there."

There are many other Squeeze Factors you can invent. Unfortunately, most of them are real! Keep in mind this is a required part of negotiating. *Your Squeeze Factors must be on the tip of your tongue, ready to use at any time during the negotiation process.*

Stall for time, if you must, just to think of more Squeeze Factors. Tell the headhunter or client you need to think about the offer and do some calculations. Tell him you will call him back in an hour. Then, let him stew for half of a day. This lets the recruiter know, without a doubt, that you are not happy with the offer. They may feel guilty about haggling with you so hard. Sometimes, they will call you back with a better offer.

If the first three rules didn't help you get what you want, the next rule might.

Negotiation Rule #4:
Always be prepared to walk away from an offer you don't like.

If the agency or client insists on tying other things to your pay, then you should refuse them and walk away. For example, they could throw in things like we will pay you less for the first three months then pay you what you want after that.

These "strings attached" negotiations are easy to spot. You'll be asking yourself, "Why are these people trying to avoid paying me my regular pay?" When you get that feeling, get up and walk away. Usually, walking away indicates to them, that they went too far. After thinking about it for a day, they may call you back and give you what you want.

Step 9.1: Memorize The Negotiation Rules Now.

Keeping A Proper Frame Of Mind During Negotiation

It always seems odd to me that the people that really need your skills treat you like dirt during the negotiation phase. This can be confusing to a novice at negotiation. Before you even start working for them, recruiters, agencies, and clients act like they don't like you. If you are not used to this game, it can really make you feel depressed. Don't worry, its just part of the game.

The reason for this behavior is that you have done a great job of preparing for the negotiation. You've kept secret your previous pay rate. You've filled all the holes in your resume. You've have avoided stirring up the recruiters negative imagination. So, a recruiter has nothing left to use against you. So, the only recourse a recruiter has, is to try to make you feel like dirt, so that you will lower your price.

Negotiation doesn't work unless both parties have something to haggle about. If you have not given them a negotiating angle, all they can do is get a little angry. They will only have one available course of action to take, to try to get you to lower your price. That is, to try to make you feel bad. But, that's okay. Remember, we are going to let them haggle our price down once, to make them feel better. We've already accounted for it.

The negative feelings that occur during the negotiation, however, can be quite distracting. To stifle these negative feelings, we have to keep the proper frame of mind. So, remember this golden rule:

"He who has the gold makes the rules"

Who do you think has the gold, the Agency or the Temp? Who has the gold, the Client or the Consultant? Well, the agency would be out of business if they couldn't find skilled Temps to send to the client's office. The client would be out of business if he couldn't find skilled workers. It's that certain knowledge, that know-how, that is generating profit. This knowledge is the gold. Therefore, we have the gold, because we have the knowledge!

With this knowledge we can get a job anywhere. We do not have to work for this particular client or this agency if we don't want to. There are many competing companies out there that need our knowledge. Companies need us more than we need them! We have the gold so we get to make the rules. We will work for this client on our terms, not theirs. Remember you have the knowledge they are seeking.

Some companies act like they are going to do you this big favor of hiring you. They make you feel like you are going to cost them lots of money. Yes, you will cost them quite a bit, but they're going to make a huge profit off of your work! Otherwise, they wouldn't be in the business. They need us. They should be nice to us. Yet, agencies and clients will treat you like their bitter enemy until you finish negotiating pay with them. Sure enough, as soon as you accept their pay offer, they will act like they are you're best friend! Once you pass the negotiation, they will treat you like royalty. Don't forget you have to knowledge they are seeking.

Step 9.2: Meditate On The Golden Rule Now.

Summary Of Chapter 9:

Negotiating for money should be easier for you, now that you know it is really about haggling, and not lying and cheating. You may not feel totally comfortable with the haggling concept until you try it a few times. Don't worry about it too much, haggling is something that you do only a few times a year, at most.

Negotiating as a Temp is very simple. There are only a few extra things to watch out for, beyond these basic negotiation concepts. Getting training as a Temp first is the best way to get used to negotiating. Let's look at some conceptualizations of these in the next chapter.

Chapter 10:
Negotiating For Temp Jobs

Applying the four basic rules of negotiation, good pay can be achieved for Temp work. This chapter shows how to apply the four negotiation rules to Temporary jobs.

Never Fill Out An Application

If you are Temping, you should never have to fill out an application at the client's office. Tell the client that your agency has already done an extensive background search on you and they will be glad to send them a report. Usually the agencies claim that they have researched your background, but usually they don't bother, either, until the client asks for this report.

If you are Temping, never fill out an application at an agency, until after you have negotiated your wages. If the agency requires that you fill one out before sending you to an interview, then that agency probably doesn't know what they are doing. Some ancient job agencies require this. They are usually small-time agencies and do not process Temps in high volume. In addition to wasting your time, these ancient-ones do not know what the going pay rates are. Avoid them completely. You should only need to fill out an application, at an agency, after you are offered a job, and have signed something stating how much you will be paid. The only time I ever had to fill out an application for an agency, at all, was when the client wanted me to have a Security Clearance. That was done after I had signed the pay offer and was already working at the job site. Remember, never let anyone know how much you are making or made before.

Never Discuss Rates With The Client

A second problem arises if the Temp discusses pay with the client. *A Temp should never discuss wages with the client company. The agency is solely responsible for this.* It is not your right to negotiate on behalf of yourself as a Temp! The agency must negotiate for you.

Don't let the client trick you into telling him how much you charge. If you do, he can do a little subtraction, and calculate what the agency is trying to make from the deal. This puts the agency in a predicament where they have lost all of their negotiation angles.

If the client tries this on you, tell him, "Sorry, but I am under contract with my agency, and I can't discuss my wages with you. If my agency found out about this, I could get into a lot of trouble." Although this is true, the amount of trouble one can get into, is really nothing. It just means the agency will have to pass their loss on to you. Again, though, you can turn down the offer, if it is too low. Note that if a client tries to do this, it indicates that this particular client is somewhat shrewd and could be hard to work for.

This is another nice feature of Temping. You only have to negotiate with the agency. Then, after the agency knows what you want, they try to get it for you. That is their responsibility. If they can't get the amount that you want, then you have the choice of not accepting the offer.

Never Get Submitted By Multiple Agencies

A common occurrence when Temping is that two agencies will try to submit your resume to the same potential client. Agencies are supposed to call you on the phone and ask if you want to be submitted to a particular company. It is imperative that you keep notes of all the places you have been submitted to, so you won't get mixed up.

When a second agency offers to submit you to the same company, tell them that you have already been submitted. If, for some reason, things go awry, and 2 agencies have submitted you to the same place ask the second agency what they intend on doing about it. Frequently, it will be forgiven. Once in a while, there will be an argument about it. If this takes place you may have to resign to keep everybody happy.

A corollary to this is to make sure you never send consulting materials such as Flyers, Business Cards, Blurb Sheets etc. to the same companies that the agencies want to send you to. In summary, never get submitted to the same company twice. If you do, other people might get angry.

Always Have Your Squeeze Factors Ready

When an agency sends you to an interview, you are required to call the agency back and tell them how it went. First, go to the interview and find out why they are hiring a Temp. After the interview, take plenty of time to list the Squeeze Factors found. The agency is going to start haggling with you as soon as you call. Go eat a salad somewhere while you think of some good Squeeze Factors for this situation.

Remember, the best squeeze factors are found during the interview. These squeeze factors have to be on the tip of your tongue. Headhunters are good at arguing about money. Memorize what you are going to tell the headhunter before you call him back.

You can use the "It's too far" syndrome, the "It's already a disaster" complaint, the "It's too boring" whine, the "They want me to manage a bunch of people, Yech," gripe, the "Somebody just got fired," fear tactic, the "The boss is a ruthless bastard," situation, and/or the somewhat complicated "I have to think about it" pressure function.

Keep in mind that if you postpone too long, it could work against you. Four hours is a very long time to stall for a Temp work. You may not get the job because someone else, more hungry than you, has moved in, for far less, while you weren't looking.

Step 10.1: Write A List Of Possible Squeeze Factors Now.

Summary Of Chapter 10

Negotiating as a Temp is very simple. There are only a few extra things to watch out for, beyond basic negotiation concepts. These negotiations are usually done over the phone in a few minutes. Getting training as a Temp, first, is the best way to get used to negotiation.

Being able to "negosh" won't do much good if you can't pass an interview. A sure-fire interviewing technique is presented in the next chapter.

Chapter 11:
Picture Perfect Interviews

Having a great resume and good references does not guarantee that jobs will be offered to you. Many highly skilled people have failed in Temping, Contracting, and Consulting because they can't pass interviews. This chapter will explore the various aspects of successful interviewing.

The Main Interviewing Principle

People, not experienced with a lot of interviewing, believe they can get hired by the "aura they radiate." They assume that they will be hired for the way they look, their disposition, their energy level, their sensitivity, their outspokenness, their sense of humor, and, in general, the "vibes" that they can project. Rarely is this true. In fact, a person cannot depend on these "good vibes" or "showmanship" to get a job!

Instead, it is your **SKILLS** that will get you a job. Therefore, in the beginning of the interview, you must keep the interviewer focused on your skills, as much as possible. If you prove your skills first, and then impress the client later, with your showmanship, your showmanship will work for you. If, however, you try to impress them with your showmanship, first, they will think you are a fake! This will make them doubt everything you have to say about your skills. This is the main principle of interviewing.

Main Interviewing Principle: Prove your skills first.

Interview Sequence

Strategically, it is very important that you try to control the sequence of events that take place on the interview. In order to make the Interviewing Principle work, you need to get and keep the client focused on your skills. Don't let him off of the subject until he is convinced that you can do the job. After that, you will need to get more of the low-down on the actual tasks that you will be performing. You need to see what the company looks like. What equipment will you be using? Where will you be working? Who will you be working with? You have to figure out if you even want this job. You need to review all the aspects of the company. Then, if everything is satisfactory, you can haggle about your pay, and any other stipulations that you will require to do the job.

This is the proper sequence that the interview should follow:

1. Present your skills.
2. Get the task specified.
3. Tour the company.
4. Haggle about money.

Some clients will not follow this sequence because they are disorganized. If they are disorganized, then their department is probably in chaos too. This is normal. Many non-captives are hired because the company is disorganized and can't seem to get anything done. Whatever the case, all clients must be kept on track, during the interview.

So, in the first half of the interview, keep the client focused on your skills. Don't let the client get sidetracked. If he asks, "How do you like the boat pictures on my wall?" he is trying to get you to talk. Just say, "they look good." If he wants to blab let him. Just sit there quietly and smile. This will eventually signal him that you are serious about getting this job. Usually, later in the interview, when the client has made up his mind to hire you, he will relax and start talking of other subjects. He'll talk about the news, the weather, or the industry. It's O.K. to indulge in conversation at that time, but not in the beginning of an interview.

After he is convinced of your skills, you must postpone discussions about money. You still need to see if the company, environment, the equipment, and the people are all normal. Insist that the client take you on a tour. This will give you insight into the company. It will also allow you some time to try to figure out if you really want this job.

Finally, if you are satisfied that the job is worth doing, and the company is normal, then, it is time to haggle about money, flexibility in hours, work location, etc.

Purpose Of The Interview

Interviewing for non-captive jobs is not the same as interviewing for a captive job. When Temping, Contracting, or Consulting, usually, your reputation arrives at the client's site way before you do. Whoever recommended you has practically talked the client into hiring you, before you walked in the door! So, what is the interview for?

The main purpose of the interview is to determine if:

1. Your skills really match this particular job.
2. You are a normal person, and not a psycho.
3. You are eager to work on their project.

If you can convey these three concepts properly, you will pass the interview.

Keep Quiet On The Interview

Before getting into how to go about presenting your skills, an important underlying rule must be adhered to during the interview. This is it: speak as little as possible during the interview. Many Consultants are not hired because they talk too much. Their talking distracts the interviewer. The interviewer has important things to ask. It is important that the interviewer be given the chance to ask whatever he or she wants. Remember, at all times a Consultant must have Two Ears and One Mouth. Listen carefully, and talk only when necessary.

This presents a challenge to the way we must interview. How can you present you're skills without talking very much? We shall see in the following sections.

Presenting Your Skills

Do you really have the skills that your resume says you have? Are your skills a good match for the job you are being considered for? After Temping, Contracting, and Consulting for many years, you will be skilled in practically every aspect of your field. However, it won't do you much good unless you can convey this fact to your new client. So, if you can do this job, you better make sure that the client is convinced that you can. Presenting your skills is the most important part of the interview. You have to be talented and appear confident in those talents. You have to appear very experienced. You have to present your skills in an exciting, imaginative way. The following technique works much better than any other technique.

Present your skills during the interview by:

1. **Showing photographs of past projects.**
2. **Showing samples and documentation of past projects.**
3. **Showing samples of past notebooks.**
4. **Showing samples of your computer skills.**

Presenting Photographs

The best way to convey your skills is to bring in Photographs of your previous accomplishments. Since a picture is worth a thousand words, presenting a picture book with 10 or 20 photographs of past projects can be very impressive. One picture book can be worth a thousand jobs! Besides, while the client is looking at a picture, you can describe the pictures. He will be able to associate what you are describing, with the real image of the product. The brain works better when it can associate with images. This will allow him to remember you better, and your accomplishments. Don't forget to take pictures of the things you are working on now, before you leave the company you are at.

In the picture book, also put in the product data sheet or marketing brochure. Companies usually put together nice product data sheets with more pictures of people using the product. These fit well into the picture book and help the interviewer associate the companies you were at with more images. Furthermore, it makes your story more believable.

Presenting Paper Samples

Bringing in drawings, software, charts, documents, circuit boards, spreadsheets, schematics, math analysis, timelines, budgets, and other actual SAMPLES of your work, will also be of great benefit! It is more real than just reading a resume. People like to touch real things.

Keep your paper samples loose in a manila folder. Open the folder up and give the folder to the client. Let them hold them. Holding samples of your work will relieve most of the doubt they have about your skills. Bring enough paper samples for 4 people to read at the same time. Several people usually interview consultants at once. Many of them, the quite ones, will like reading and studying your samples.

Present The Physical Product

Bring physical samples of your work. In my field, I give them a circuit board I designed. They hold it and look at the surface mount technology, ask what kind of processor is on it, ask about the memory chips, and ask how long the project took. It makes the interview go quickly giving them actual samples. Bringing physical samples for them to hold reinforces the concepts found in your paper samples. It makes your paper samples more believable.

Present Your Notebook

Bring in one of your past notebooks. Flip through the pages, while you explain different things that you were doing at the time. It is beneficial to explain how you go about doing your job. You need to prove that you are organized. Clients like people who write things down, and paste things into their notebook. Those types of people are organized. They don't loose things. The client assumes that since the notebook is organized, then the consultant's brain must also be organized.

Present Your Computer Skills

The next step is to present the fact that you are computer efficient. Bring in samples of your computer skills. Put together samples of your work and burn them onto a CDROM or a floppy. Talk about the types of computers you have used at other client's sites. Before the IBM PC came out, I had already used 24 different operating systems! Bring in a picture of your computer, your desk, and book shelves. Talk about the computer and the kinds of software you are running on it. Bring up all of the tax and accounting software you use. Refer to your Internet skills and how useful the Internet has become. Mention how long you have been using computers. Memorize a little speech about your computer skills. If you are really eager, you can put together a POWERPOINT presentation slide show!

Putting The Samples Together

Presenting your skills with pictures and samples is quick and easy. With all of your samples ready, you can complete an interview with four or five people in about an hour! Since most people don't use this technique, the client thinks you are imaginative. You saved his company a lot of time, already.

Start making your picture book and gather your samples now. Get product data sheets from your old companies. Include all the companies where you were a captive employee also. Try to go back into those companies with your old friends and take pictures. Your friends will be interested in helping you with your new career.

Print out your paper samples of work, from various jobs. You need to start on this right away. It takes several days to put together a set of samples. You may have to load older versions of software to get these hardcopies.

After showing all of your pictures and samples, the interviewer will then focus in on specific questions about the particular task he has for you. Some of the questions are normal and one or two are totally ridiculous. In the next section, we will prepare to answer them.

Step 11.1: Put Together Your Picture Book And Work Samples Now.

Preparing For Different Types Of Questions

To really convince someone that you are an expert in your field, you have to answer their questions in a QUICK manner. Not answering questions fast enough is another common failure in interviewing.

When interviewing, the client will ask you many different questions. These questions will cover a wide range of subjects. There will be many questions about the skills stated on your resume. There will also be questions about what you like to do.

Most interview questions fall into 3 categories:

1.   General questions about your resume.
2.   Standard questions used in your field of expertise.
3.   Ridiculous questions of the skills or circumstances required for the job.

Let's see what the differences are between these categories and go over how to deal with each type.

General Questions About Your Resume

These questions are the result of words that the interviewer saw on your resume. To convince the interviewer that you are telling the truth on your resume, these questions must be answered *quickly*. Note that answering quickly means that you cannot hesitate before you answer. It does NOT mean talking real fast. The basic form of these types of questions is "What company did you use {a particular skill} at?" Or, "How long ago have you been doing {a particular skill}?"

With some practice, answering these types of questions, properly, is a matter of memorization. Since these questions stem from words that the client saw on your resume, they are easy to anticipate.

Take your resume, and pretend that you have never seen it before. For every Buzzword on your resume, ask yourself two questions:

"What company were you at when you worked on {Buzz-word}"

"What did that company need that {Buzz-word} for."

Write down all of your answers. After completing your list, memorize it, by writing it down again, on a second piece of paper. It may be difficult at first, but once you memorize the responses for one version of your resume, adding to it later will be simple.

The client, usually ill-prepared, will ask these types of questions while reading your resume. Certain Buzzwords on your resume will remind him of things that need to be done, at his company. Some, he hasn't thought of, in a while. This will make the client shift gears, and start to talk of a different subject. Don't get alarmed when this happens. You did not mess up. The client is just realizing that he needs you more than he first thought. You are a better match than his original job requisition. This shift in thought will usually trigger another series of questions.

For example, if my resume says that I had designed a High Voltage Regulator, the interviewer may ask questions like these, in succession, "How high was the voltage on that regulator you designed?" "What was that regulator used for?" "What company were you with, when you designed it?" Then they may summarize, "Oh, so you designed a 380 Volt regulator to be used in a graphics display system at General Systems." "How long ago was that?" Then they may add, "Good, that is similar to what we need, only our product requires a 600 Volt Regulator for a Laser product." "Have you ever worked with Lasers before?" With my experience I can reply, "Sure, I've designed a 10,000 volt, flashlamp power supply, for an Nd-Yag Laser, at Laser Technologies, but it didn't have to be regulated." "Good," he responds excitedly. Thus, he merged two requirements. Then he progresses to other parts of your resume for more questions.

Standard Questions Used In Every Field

There are, also, many standard questions used in every field of expertise. These questions are used to indicate, in general, the amount of experience that you have. If you answer them quickly, you will appear to have a high level of experience. Figuring out what these questions will be, may take several interviews. After you are interviewed, make sure that you keep a list of questions that were asked to you, that you weren't prepared for. Come up with a definite answer for all of these questions, to use on future interviews.

For example, in my field, I am frequently asked, "What is the fastest clock rate you have ever designed a digital circuit to run at?" Even though the job may not require a fast clock rate, they still may want to know my answer because it gives them an idea of my past experiences.

Having 2 or 3 of your colleagues interview you, is another, real good, way to prepare for the standard questions about your resume and your field of expertise. Most of the people that you work with have never seen your resume. They can discover questions pretty easily. Of course, you may have to invite them to dinner, to get them to do it.

The Preposterous Questions

More times than not, the client will OVER-SPECIFY the type of person he is looking for. This will lead to a pretty precarious situation, where, you will be required to answer a ridiculous question, with style and finesse. Furthermore, if you stall in answering, you may loose the interview.

Typically the interview will be going very well. You've been able to answer questions about all of the Buzzwords on your resume. You've properly answered all of the standard questions that they ask of people in your field. It seems at this point that the interviewer is getting close to running out of questions. But, something seems to still be bothering him. Then, as if directly from the psycho-ward, comes the most ridiculous question you have ever heard of (and you thought you were done)! But that's O.K. You don't flinch. You were prepared for strange questions. That's common to the non-captive field because most jobs are OVER-SPECIFIED. You are prepared to answer the preposterous, with seriousness.

There are several levels of ridiculousness. Some questions are mildly weird, others can get extreme. Some questions have to do with your skills, others have to do with your schedule or your pay.

Here is a mild example. I have designed more than 100 different computers for various companies. My resume mentions several 8, 16, and 32 bit microprocessors, that I have designed circuits for. If a new computer chip came out, say a 64-bit, P8 chip, the client may ask me, "Have you ever designed a circuit for the P8 chip?" Well how could I have? It just came out a week ago. Thus, you see, this is, indeed, a ridiculous question. But, I am "prepared for the preposterous", so I answer this way: "No, not yet, but one of my previous clients was considering using it on a new project, so I went to a seminar on it, at Intel, a few months ago. I have also designed several products based on the P5, the P6, and the P7 chips." Then, I will usually throw in a very general statement about my skills like, "Besides, after designing computers for 25 years, a new processor only takes me about a day to learn."

(Slick how I answered that, eh?).

It can be demonstrated, over and over, that the way you answer these ridiculous questions will turn out to be the most valuable part of the interview!

How To Handle Answers To Ridiculous Questions

1. Mention how your long history of experience has lead up to the involvement with this new product, and that it is just a matter of time, before you will be required to know it, by this client or any other client.

2. Mention that you have read up on the new product, but have not had the opportunity to make use of it.

3. Mention something equally complicated that you have completed in the past.

4. Make a statement, in general, about how you are a fast learner in this particular subject.

5. Mention how, in general, there will always be a need to learn new skills or new software tools like this.

6. Mention how, in general, Consultants are used-to keeping up-to-date with all of these changes.

These ridiculous questions can and will make you quite angry, sometimes. It will be very tempting to just tell a lie in response to a ridiculous question. It certainly would be a quick response to lie and say, "Yes, I've designed a computer based on the P8 two months ago. I don't know if the design works, yet, because I've been waiting to get one of the parts. It just became available a week ago."

But, this is a discussion of your actual experience. It is not proper to tell the client a lie about your experience, under any circumstances, even if it is in response to his ridiculous questions.

To answer ridiculous questions properly, you do have to word the truth very carefully. It is important that you are able to explain why you are qualified to do this new task. Most of the projects you will be encountering will require something very new. You are on the cutting edge of your field. That is one of the qualifications of being a Consultant. The client understands that you are more qualified to pick up something new, faster than his own employees!

You must be able to explain why you can do a job better. You must be able to explain why you can pick up a concept faster than anyone else can. Your explanation is based strictly on your experience. Your experience is already established, and is listed on the resume that the client is holding in his hands, right now. If he didn't like your listed

---

experience, believe me, he wouldn't have called you down to this interview. Base your answers on your experience. Try not to get upset. On the other hand, don't laugh in his face for being stupid, either. Pretend that you care about his problem and answer very seriously.

Breaking A Stale-Mate With Blatant Honesty

If the client insists on finding out if you have the experience to satisfy his ridiculous question, over and over, be on guard! You are about to loose the interview. *You have reached a stalemate.* You will notice a stale-mate is happening when you get a feeling that you are being asked a ridiculous question, over and over, from what is beginning to look like a very ridiculous client. If you get to this point, you have to take drastic measures.

To argue with a loony client, when the interview goes off-track or when you reach a stalemate situation, you need to display some sort of blatant honesty. *Blatant honesty is honesty that is made to jump out at the client.*

To display this blatant honesty:

1. You need to get a little riled up.
2. You need to talk loudly and appear slightly upset.
3. Then, you must summarize, in no uncertain terms, why you are easily qualified to do this job.
4. And finally, then you blame yourself by saying something like, "But, honestly, I don't think I have convinced you of my skills, yet."

Being blatantly honest means that you will have to say phrases like: "Look. If you are looking for someone to do task A and Task B then I'm the person that can do it. But, honestly, I don't think that I've done a very good job of convincing you of that, yet."

For example, one client kept asking me if I knew what "Double Correlation" ment. I told him, over and over, that I never heard of the term. Now, the job that was described to me was to debug a product that was already designed. It appeared to be too late to put in this Correlation feature. Instead, they needed someone with both analog and digital design experience, which I have plenty of. So, after talking with the client and one of his partners for over an hour, the client asked me that ridiculous question, for about the tenth time, "But are you sure you have never heard of Double Correlation?" "Why did he keep asking me about a concept, when the product was already designed?" I thought to myself. So, I jumped out of my chair, rushed over to the drawings that were shown to me earlier and said, "Look. If you are looking for someone with analog and digital design experience to debug this design (as I waived my hands over the drawings), then I am the best guy for the job. The problem is that I apparently have failed in convincing you of that." I was hired in the next 30 seconds.

Another example is when I told a potential client, on the telephone, that I had no experience designing a PCMCIA card. I did tell them, however, that I had designed a PCMCIA socket for such a card. The client said that was good enough, and to come on down to his company. When I arrived, I was taken to a conference room with four people in it. They asked right off, have you ever designed a PCMCIA card before. I answered, "Like I told your boss, no, but I have designed a PCMCIA socket." They proceeded to tell me how they needed someone to design a card, not a socket, and to write the software for it. After about the tenth time of asking me if I had ever designed a card, I pretty much yelled straight out, "If you want someone that has designed a card before and has written the software for it, then I am NOT your man. But I am a good design engineer, experienced in both hardware and software, and I'm sure I can read a specification and design this card for you. But, honestly, I don't think I've convinced you of that, yet." They hired me in less than two minutes.

> **Step 11.2: Get Help From Your Friends And Make A List Of Interview Questions Now.**

Summary Of Presenting Skills

We have now covered how to present our skill on the interview. Here is a review of the procedure:

We will use pictures and samples of our past work. We will let potential clients touch them. We will flip through our photographs and describe each project. As we do this, we will pause quietly, waiting for their questions. We will answer their questions quickly about our skills because we have practiced answering the standard ones. If they ask a ridiculous one or two questions, we will answer them very seriously, based on our past skills and history of rapid learning. Finally, if they keep asking a ridiculous question, over and over, then we will jump up and in a loud voice say, "I am the best person for this task A and task B that you described, but apparently I haven't convinced you of that, yet."

Now let's now look into two other important aspects of interviewing.

Appearing Normal On An Interview

Appearing "normal" to someone else is really a relative concept. If you were being interviewed to set up equipment for a rock concert, i.e. a "Roady," then appearing normal would probably include having long hair, and wearing a leather jacket and Levies. You should also be able to speak a jive lingo, be able to argue about which bands sound good, and have big muscles, like you've done this work before. Appearing normal for a job, depends on the interviewer's "frame of reference" of what he thinks is normal. The interviewer expects to see and hear certain types of responses from the person he is interviewing. The job-applicant must appear normal to the interviewer, not necessarily normal to his or hers own self-image.

Since this book is specifically about Temping, Contracting, and Consulting in Professional and Technical Fields, the scope of what appears normal, or not, can be narrowed down, further. Dressing and talking like a "Roady" wouldn't work for any kind of job classification we are talking about.

Most Professional and Technical Work require the "Office-Type" of appearance. Most of these types of jobs are what are referred to as White-Collar, or desk jobs. To appear normal, the Temp or Consultant must dress normally and speak normally for an office environment.

Dressing Normally

In the olden days, companies used to require Formal dress for interviews and office environments. Today, this is not so. In fact, if you dress formally, for an interview, you will distract the whole company. The proper dress code these days is Semi-formal.

For men, this means that a tuxedo is definitely out. A suit and tie is also probably not a good idea, either. In fact, most companies are starting to realize that ties cause low blood circulation to the head! So, although a highly controversial issue, I do not recommend wearing a tie, unless you are very comfortable doing so. A full suit and tie is definitely not a good idea, unless you are in some sort of sales or human resources field.

The best way to make a good impression with appearance is to go out and buy new clothes for this interviewing time period. New clothes can be detected by the subconscious mind of the interviewer. For men, this would be a pleasant-looking, long-sleeve shirt, or a polo shirt, and slacks. For women, a mid-length skirt, dress, or matching outfit would be fine.

There are two very important rules about clothes, that a normal person must be always take care of, before an interview:

- Always make sure your clothes are ironed!
- Always make sure your shoes are shined.

These are requirements for appearing normal, on an interview, and even, in an everyday office situation.

The rest of your appearance is equally important, as well. Here a few more things you should try before an interview.

- Get your hair slightly cut, just so that is looks even.
- Take a shower.
- Wash and dry your hair.
- Don't use very much perfume or cologne.
- Get at least 8 hours of sleep the night before.
- Use eye drops to make sure your eyes aren't red.
- Take a nap before you go to the interview.

Don't Slouch

During your interview, you must move around and sit normally. Make sure that you walk with your back straight and sit-up straight in your chair. Slouching is considered the same as being lazy, and lazy people are not hired.

The World Smiles With You

Smiling as much as you can, on the way to the interview, will ease some of your own self-induced nervousness. It can be a great benefit to your confidence level. Smile as you think of the new money you will be making and the new things you will be learning.

Smiling during the interview a few times is also very good. It tends to indicate that, internally, you are a normal, happy person and the environment you live in at home is also normal. Smiling is part of being normal.

Speak Normally

The biggest failure of all, in interviewing, is to talk too much. Clients don't like people that talk too much! They get the impression that:

- You talk all day instead of working.
- You are a "showman" and are trying to fake your way into the job.
- You are so busy talking that you won't be able to listen to instructions, on the job.
- You are going to distract the whole company because you talk too much.
- You remind them of the last person that was fired for talking too much.

Other than the first greeting and the description of your pictures and samples, the applicant shouldn't talk at all, for the majority of the interview. Be extra quiet on the interview. In general, speak only to answer the questions of your skills or to direct the conversation away from talking about money.

When you do get to speak, you must make it count. Some people are too soft-spoken to be Consultants. Talking too softly is second on the list of interviewing failures. Make sure the client and half of the people in the next room can hear you. Talk as loud as you can without straining.

Some people have a hard time consulting because they were born in foreign countries and have heavy accents. If you can't speak clear English, then you will have some extra difficulty on interviews in America. Keep in mind that if the client can't understand you right away, then he probably won't hire you, no matter how good your skills are. If you have a heavy accent or poor English, speak slowly and loudly.

Look Them In The Eyes

It is very important to look the client in the eyes, when answering questions. Many times clients won't hire someone that could not or did not look them in the eyes. Eye contact indicates, to them, that you are telling the truth. If you forget to look the client in the eyes, you may be telling the truth, but some outlandish clients out there may not think so. Eye contact is very important for answering ridiculous questions and using blatant honesty techniques. Make sure to make eye contact with all of the interviewers in the room, if there are more than one.

Appear Eager To Work There

In addition to questions about the company, make sure that you complement a few things about the company, as well! Tell the client that the project looks challenging and exciting. Point out that the people there seem friendly and happy. Complement everything good about the company that you can think of, eagerly.

For example, if they say they have a 4-day workweek, tell them, "I've always wanted to work at a place that has a four day work week. That would be great to get 3 day weekends once in a while!"

Interviewing The Company

At some point in the interview, the client will say, "So, do you have any questions about the company?" Of course you do. Before you arrived, you made a list of questions to be sure to ask, right? Well, hopefully, you have.

Don't forget to ask why they have a job opening, all of a sudden. They may say, "Oh, because the last guy started on the project, got it half way done, and then quit." This is important to find out about before accepting this job! You may need to stipulate your feelings about this, before taking this job. Find out if the client is flexible, willing to start the project over if the previous person really messed up. Their answer could indicate that there are more internal problems with the company than you care to deal with, at this time.

Summary Of Chapter 11

Interviewing is about appearing normal and answering questions. Most people fail by using too much showmanship or talking too much.

During the interview, we must try to get the client to follow a certain order. It is essential that we present our skills first. This is easily accomplished by the use of pictures and actual samples of our work.

There is a wide range of questions asked on an interview. These questions must be answered rapidly and honestly. We can prepare for questions triggered by our resume, with a little practice. We can also anticipate certain questions frequently asked to people in our particular field.

Many times we will be asked some sort of ridiculous question. These have to be answered with honesty and seriousness. Sometimes we have to resort to blatant honesty, honesty with force. This occurs when the client asks you the same crazy question, over and over.

Passing interviews takes practice, however. Get your friends to help you. Don't be alarmed if you can't pass the first few. Keep notes on how well you did, and the questions that you weren't prepared for. Soon you will be a professional interviewee. All successful Temps, Contractors, and Consultants are.

Chapter 12:
Adrift On A New Job

Starting a new job is no picnic in the park. New companies scrutinize every move you make for the first few weeks. This is a time when the non-captive could feel very vulnerable. Combining their crisis situation, with their scrutiny, beginning a new job involves a lot of pressure, for the inexperienced. An experienced Temp, Contractor, or Consultant, however, knows what to do. Non-captives enjoy changing jobs. This chapter will cover how to survive this confusion during the first few weeks.

The Law Of Perpetual Consulting:
Since the majority of clients change their mind alot, they cause a lot of chaos and calamity. Because there is a lot of chaos and calamity, the client really needs to change his mind alot.

Chaos and calamity are the things that keep Temps, Contractors, and Consultants employed all over the world. It is never more obvious than on the first few weeks of a new job. The reason for this is because most non-captive job openings are time-pressurized situations, as mentioned in an earlier chapter. Non-captives are hired at companies that are undergoing a crisis situation, going into a new field, just lost a key person, and/or are trying to get to market in a big hurry. Why else would somebody hire a Temp, Contractor, or Consultant? If everything was planned out, and ran smoothly, then non-captive personnel would rarely be needed.

In fact, the more confusing the first few weeks are, the greater the chaos in the company as a whole. The greater the chaos in the whole company, the more they will need your common-sense, savvy and calmness. You can tell if your going to be in for a little roller-coaster ride or a giant, free-hanging, full-twisting, looping, 5g, 80 mph, backwards-moving, roller-coaster ride.

After consulting for a little while, you will realize that the Law Of Perpetual Consulting is really working for you. If you don't find confusion and chaos at the new job, then they probably won't need your services for very long.

Remembering and focusing on the Law Of Perpetual Consulting should bring you a calm feeling. You can remain relaxed because you expect chaos and calamity to be there. You are not afraid of it. It guarantees that these people really need your help. It should make you feel secure. You won't have to look for a new job for a while.

The First Few Days Are Really Confusing

The first two or three days on a new job can be very traumatic, especially if you are not used to changing jobs. Many times, by the time you start working there, your assignment will be something completely different than what you were interviewed for. Yes, the client already changed his mind! Don't let this get you down, either. In the first few days, you must accept anything they throw at you, and do it cheerfully. It will take a week or two, for the dust to settle, before you can really realize what you are supposed to do. Don't worry, it usually will take management even longer to figure out what you are supposed to do. It will also take you a while to figure out who is going to help you, and who is going to hinder you.

Always remember to look forward to the unknown! Don't be afraid of it! It is exciting! Remain cheerful! Say "hello" to everyone. If anyone introduces himself or herself, then you probably will need to know them. Stop and converse with them for a few minutes. Ask them what their title is and what they do around there. Tell them about your background in a sentence or two.

You must portray that you are a normal person. A normal person is someone that is a little lost and/or confused the first few days on the job. A normal person is not totally lost, however.

You must not appear to be a loser. Losers have car problems the first few days. They are late to work. They get lost on the way to work. They wear the same clothes, often. Their clothes are wrinkled. They don't take showers everyday. I'm sure you know the type.

The First Few Weeks Are Critical

Even as a Temp or Consultant, you still have a "probation" period to go through. Upper and Middle management will be watching you closely. They want to make sure that you do not turn out to be a time-waster. It is, therefore, important that you trust no one (yet). At this point in time, you do not know if management is messed up, if the workers are messed up, or neither, or both.

Don't Be Too Friendly

The best approach, for at least the first three weeks, is to not be real friendly with anyone. Avoid chatting in the halls about the latest football scores or the stock market. Take breaks alone. Don't do anything that might be interesting to someone else because you will have to stop your work and explain it to them.

Don't Take Sides

It is crucial, in the first few weeks, not to appear to be "taking sides" with anyone. Bring your own lunch, daily. Eat your lunch in your car, alone. If you are invited to lunch just say, "Sorry, I brought my lunch." Don't go to lunch with anyone, unless the whole department goes, management and workers. When you need to find the bathroom, the stationary, or the network printer, ask a different person for each item. In that way, you are not depending on a single person.

Don't Attract Attention

Don't attract attention to yourself, unless you are solving work-related problems. Be self-sufficient. The main thing to do is to understand your assignment, get the documents or information you need for that, and then block out the rest of the distractions, for three or four weeks. If you can avoid contact with everyone, then do it. Concentrate on work. Become a robot.

Do Keep A Log

Keep a log of everything you do, preferably in a notebook or computer. Write down everything that you are told to do. Write down everything that you started. Ask your boss which one task has the highest priority. Work on that task first.

Don't Write Status Reports

Do not write a weekly status report, unless you are asked to do so. Status reports, in the beginning, will show many weaknesses about your understanding of the assignment.

Don't Relax

Don't relax until you receive some compliments from your boss. Eventually, your boss should come around and show some kind of appreciation. It is at this point that your probation period is over. When this happens, you don't have to worry about your job security anymore. If it doesn't happen within a month to 6 weeks, you may have to put the company on probation and consider looking for another job. Maybe your boss is too busy and just forgot to tell you. Go ahead and ask bluntly, "How do you think I'm doing?" If he still doesn't compliment you, then at least now you know the truth. Go ahead and start looking for work elsewhere, but don't quit yet. Make it a point to start asking him "how you are doing" more often.

Step 12.1: Memorize This List Of "Do's and Don'ts" Now.

One New Beginning

Once I interviewed for a new job at a small company. Five people interviewed me all at once. Naturally, I was hired after I showed them my photos. On my first day on the job, my boss gave me an assignment. Later that day, one by one, each one of the other guys also gave me an assignment.

- First, the president came in and gave me an assignment. Surely, I must do what he wants, I thought for a while. I figured out that the last guy was fired because he didn't complete this task for the president.
- Then, the marketing guy came in and said "we" have a problem getting this older product market. It works, but it needs some

minor changes. It was supposed to be selling 8 months ago! Surely this was a serious profit loss, being late to a market with millions of dollars of potential profit.

- Then, a software guy came in with his project. It was a newer project capable of making even more millions of dollars worth of profit. It wasn't quite working yet. I felt that this software guy's project was the most important and the most behind schedule.

This all became too confusing to me, so I decided to work on each project a piece at a time. I also decided to keep a log of all of these assignments. At this point, Outlook 97™ by Microsoft was picking up in popularity, so I decided to start logging all of my tasks into the Task Manager part of that program.

About three weeks later, my boss came in and asked, "What the heck have you been doing all this time?" I immediately printed out my log for him, which shows "tasks completed" and remaining "tasks in progress." He took this to the president and came back 5 minutes later. He said, "Good List. Pack up your things. You're going to work at home. This new project is way behind schedule. Don't answer your phone. Don't answer anyone else's email except mine." So, I worked on the software guy's project for the next two months. That was the project I was hired to do. That's the project I knew was the most valuable. It was soon making a profit.

So, try to remain calm. Try to weigh everything and stay afloat for the first few weeks. Eventually things will come into focus. When your first paycheck gets cut for umpteen gillion dollars per hour, believe me, management will all of a sudden get focused on how to use you more effectively!

Summary Of Chapter 12

Keep to yourself the first few weeks. Don't fraternize with anyone. Do only what your boss tells you. Don't take sides. Keep a log of everything you do. Don't write status reports, just yet. Tell your boss when other people are giving you assignments. Above all, stay calm. Chaos usually leads to long term employment.

Chapter 13:
Beginning By Temping

Well, are you ready to begin your new career path as a Consultant? You should be since you have kept up with the assignments in this book. Of course, you will have to put in a few years as a Temp, first. Let's review why you should be ready now to Temp, at this point in time:

- You're not afraid of the unknown. You are looking forward to it. You are eager to improve your lifestyle. You are eager to help more people. You are eager to learn new things. You are eager to accept new challenges.

- Your office is set up. It is ready to communicate in many forms. You have a real company name. You've set up bank accounts and an accounting system for this company.

- You have a powerful, Skill-Billet Resume and good references.

- You know how to find Temp jobs. You have a database of job agencies and websites. Your database is expandable and ready to log more contact names as they begin to call you.

- You are ready to sign up with several job boards, such as the Monster Board, DICE, Headhunter.Net, etc. You are prepared to find more contacts on the Internet.

- You know how much your bills are going to be, while Temping. You've analyzed how much it will cost to recover your medical, vacation, and retirement benefits. You've called and found some medical insurance plans that you like and are ready to sign up with them.

- You know how much others are getting paid. You've, carefully, talked to other Temps, Contractors, and Consultants about how much they charge. You've called agencies and asked how much they think you could get.

- You know how much you need to charge. You've analyzed spreadsheets and played "what-if" with overtime and pay scales.

- You know you are going to make a profit. You've subtracted all of your new costs from your new wages and have profit left over.

- You've learned a simple way to pass interviews. You've prepared a picture book of many past projects. You've printed out hard-copy samples of your previous work and put them into a manila folder. You've got a physical sample of previous work.

- You've bought some new semi-formal office clothes. You washed and ironed them. Your shoes are polished and waiting by the door.

- You know how to play the negotiating game and use the four rules of negotiation.

- You have confidence in asking for higher pay because you know how much it costs to be a Temp.

- You know, in particular, how to handle negotiating for Temp jobs.

- You have realized that Temping takes no more skill than a captive job. What is normal to you, is the golden skill the client needs.

- And finally, you know how to survive the first few crazy weeks on a new job.

Well, then, it is time to take action, my friend!

> **Step 13.1: Email, Fax, And Mail Out That New Resume Now. Post It Up On Those Internet Job Boards. Get Some Interview Appointments. Pass Those Interviews. Prepare Your Squeeze Factors. Negotiate With That Agency.**

Exciting isn't it?

Now, while you're waiting, be sure to read the rest of the book. It is about setting up the business and establishing connections throughout the industry.

Chapter 14:
Contracting: Running Your Own Company

As defined by this book, Contracting means working for job agencies on a 1099 basis, although the term is used for many other situations. After Temping for a while, Contracting will start to look more attractive. Although it will cost you much more to Contract than to Temp, the tax advantages should outweigh that cost. At some point, the added expense of Contracting will look more feasible and be worth the extra hassle.

Moving Into Contracting

The only difference in Contracting verses Temping is that the work is done on a 1099 basis with the agency, instead of a W2 basis. But that is a big difference! For one thing, the Contractor has to pay more in taxes. Now the Contractor has to pay the full 15% of the Social Security and Medicare Tax. The IRS gives this tax increase the name of "Self-Employment Tax." By paying this, the Contractor looses 7.5% more of his income.

The Contractor will get more tax deductions, however. These deductions better add up to more than the 7.5% increase in taxes, or else it will not be worth it. It usually turns out that it is worth the trouble, since the Contractor is allowed to take many more tax deductions.

204 Advancing Into Temp, Contract, And Consulting Jobs

Contractor's Additional Tax Deductions

A Contractor or Consultant has the right to take more tax deductions because the IRS classifies them as "Independent Contractors". This means that by acting as a company, instead of an employee, more deductions are allowed. Check all of the latest laws by reading the brochures at the IRS website, *www.irs.com*. Here are some of the major deductions.

Office In The Home Deductions

If you can justify having your office located in your home to the IRS, a big tax benefit will result. The deductions are based on either square footage area or number of bedrooms. For example, if you use a 500 sq. ft. room, in a 2000 sq. ft. home, you qualify for using one-fourth of your house for your office. If you are using 1 bedroom of a 3-bedroom home, then you qualify for using one-third of your house, regardless of square footage. Note that this is true even if you rent your home. Also, the same proportional amount of the utilities, such as electricity, natural gas, water, trash, and necessary repairs to the home are deductible as part of the office expenses.

The IRS has recently changed the requirements for justifying an Office In The Home. On January 1, 1999 the IRS relaxed the rules for office in the home. Now the office can be claimed as "principle place of business," even if it is used just for the management and administration functions of the company. An office no longer has to be the primary location for where the work is being done! This is a major change in policy in the Independent Contractor's favor.

The latest information about Home Office Deductions can be found on the IRS website called Publication 587. Study it at *http://www.irs.ustreas.gov/prod/forms_pubs/pubs/p587toc.htm*.

Office Equipment And Supplies Deductions

Regular office equipment can be deducted such as computers, printers, monitors, desk, tables, book shelves, telephones, fax machines, furniture, and file cabinets, etc. Stationary supplies and computer supplies are also deductible such as printer paper, floppy disks, and my favorite, blank CD's. Computer software, a major office expense, is also deductible.

Educational Deductions

One of the best deductions realized is that for educational purposes. Books, Seminars, Technical Courses, and College Courses that apply to the business are also deductible.

Company Car Deductions

Basically, if your company is located in your home, then everywhere you drive for the business is a deductible expense. Normally, if you are a W2 Temp, working for an agency, only the second place you drive to is deductible, according to the IRS. If you are driving a company car, even more tax benefits can be realized. The company car deduction is one of the most overlooked. There are some minor requirements, but most families meet them. For example, there must be a second vehicle that is used primarily as the family vehicle. Note that the company vehicle can be used 49% or less for family functions as well. Check the latest laws on this at the IRS website, or talk to a taxman about it. Some tax preparers are too chicken to take this deduction for you.

The company vehicle must be paid for with company checks. This is how you prove it is a company vehicle. Nothing else is required for proof. If you've already been paying on your vehicle, you may have to sell it to your company and pay tax on that sale. Consult a taxman before converting your car to a company car.

Here are the tax benefits. First of all, you get to depreciate the cost of the vehicle for five years. This means that if the vehicle costs $30,000 you get to deduct $6000 a year! Second, you get to deduct the interest on the payments. If your payments are $500 a month, about $400 of that will be interest! Over 12 months that adds up to $4800 a year. Then, you can also deduct either the mileage or the maintenance. The maintenance figure also has the fuel and oil costs. This is usually about $3500 a year, or so, depending on how far you drive. This all adds up to a $14,300 deduction per year, for five years. Wow! Now, that's a whopping deduction for a normal priced car. What if the company car was an expensive $50,000+ Mercedes. Now, you can begin to see how self-employed people can afford to own those types of cars. If your taxman doesn't want you to take this deduction, fire him!

Now, remember that deductions don't save you the total amount in taxes. If you are in a 30% tax bracket, you will save 30% of the $14,300 in actual tax owed. That's about $4,920 actual money saved. In actuality, it is better to buy an expensive company vehicle on a 3 year payment plan to get the most deductions. Paying off the loan in 3 years will allow you to resell the car back to the dealer before it gets worn out. That way, every 3 years you can get a new company car without using out-of-pocket cash for a downpayment.

Contractor's Additional Taxes

The downside to Contracting is having to pay the additional 7.5% in Self-Employment Tax, as mentioned earlier. That's a large number too!

Is Contracting Worth It?

Get the latest version of Turbo Tax—Deluxe™ or Small Business Edition™, and take the built in interview. Pretend to do your own taxes.

Estimate how much you will spend on your office, education, equipment, and company vehicle, for one year. Don't forget to include paying the Self-Employment Tax. After doing your taxes both ways, W2 verses 1099, print out all the forms and compare the two sets. The bottom line should be obvious. Usually it is worth it.

Advantages To Contracting

Elevating to Contractor status after Temping a few years allows the Temp to save more on taxes, while getting used to running a business. The Contractor, while still working through the agencies, will not have the extra problems of looking for clients, like a Consultant does. The real challenges in this Contracting phase will be learning about tax deductions, keeping records, and tax planning. Developing a business sense, paying taxes on time, and making a profit are very important business skills to learn before going on your own as a Consultant. Working as a 1099 employee of an agency is a safe way to develop these skills.

Step 14.1: Discuss 1099 Conversion With A Tax Person Now.

Incorporating

After you have been successful at 1099 work for some time, and you want maximum tax advantages, then changing to a corporation may be good for you. As mentioned before, the corporation pays you a small salary and pays for all of the company equipment and expendables. Then it transfers any remaining money into your retirement account where it sits tax-free. The corporation then makes a net profit of zero and pays no taxes.

Incorporating can have some ill side-effects, however. Since the profit of the corporation is usually dumped into the retirement plan, the profit isn't liquid. It is hard to use it after that. Also, since the corporation pays you a tiny salary, then it will be very hard for you to get a loan. On paper it will look like there was a huge drop in your income, from a six figure 1099 income, back to five-figure W2 income. If you were thinking of buying something big in the near future, like a house, you'd better put off incorporating. Incorporating takes a lot of up-front lifestyle and tax planning. Be thorough and careful. Don't try to do this by yourself. Involve your family, accountant, and tax preparer.

I incorporated just after I bought a new house. I thought I was wise. Then, when I went to build a pool in the backyard, no one would give me a loan!

Step 14.2: After A Few Days, Discuss Incorporating With The Same Tax Person.

Requirements For Contracting

The only additional requirements for becoming a Contractor, beyond those for Temping, is that the company's accounting and banking must be done online, electronically. By doing this with a program like Quicken, everytime a bill is paid electronically it is automatically entered into an accounting system as a categorized expense. Then, the Contractor can take a floppy disk backup of these records to the accountant every month. This will allow tax planning and record keeping to occur more easily.

Step 14.3: Convert To Online Banking Now.

Begin Contracting

So how do we begin? Well, all we have to do is find agencies that will hire us as a 1099 employee. Usually the smaller ones will. The bigger nationwide ones tend not to. The large sized ones really want to hire you Corp-to-corp. For that we would have to lay out more cash to start up and have more people involved doing our accounting and taxes.

Theoretically, it is costing the agency 7.5% less in taxes to employ the 1099 Contractor, so they should be open to letting the Contractor charge higher rates. This would make up the difference in these additional costs. Most headhunters don't realize this, or aren't going to admit to this, being the tough negotiators that they are. So, some forceful negotiations will be required on your part to get this. Its simple addition right?

Step 14.4: Search For Contract Jobs Through Agencies Now.

Summary Of Chapter 14

Elevating to Contractor status after Temping for a few years will allow the Temp to save more on taxes, and get used to running a business. Working as a 1099 employee of job agencies is a safer way to do this. An online banking method must be in place before the Temp can try Contracting. Accounting and Taxes are very important parts of running any business.

The Consultant's business skills need to be second nature. When consulting, much more attention and time will have to be devoted to job searching and networking. That's why it is important to become a Contractor and master these business skills, first.

Building up a consulting business is a low-risk, sequential process. After learning the ropes by Temping and Contracting, a solid consulting business can be established, easily. Consulting takes even more know-how, as we shall see in the next few chapters.

Chapter 15:
Advancing Into Consulting

Temping and Contracting through agencies, in and of itself, is very enjoyable and economically great. There are many agencies to help you find work. Becoming independent of the agencies takes many more skills, however. Let's introduce the basic problems of consulting in this chapter.

The Problems Of Consulting

Getting the next job after this, is where the real challenge comes in. When you reach this second point, you will be faced with new problems that come with this new situation:

- A Consultant must handle the negotiations alone.
- A Consultant must be more careful when choosing who to work for.
- A Consultant must get his own jobs.

Sounds simple enough doesn't it. Well, it really isn't all that simple. Millions of words have been written about these subjects. These problems are what the rest of this book is about.

Negotiating As A Consultant

Problem #1, negotiating as a Consultant is easy if you have practiced negotiating for a few years as a Temp and a Contractor. There are a few differences, however. First, is that the negotiation will be done in person. Second, getting your normal rate, with no strings attached, could be a challenge. Finally, getting the agreement put in writing, and witnessed, will be sometimes challenging. These subjects are covered in the next few chapters.

Choosing Who To Work For

Problem #2, carefully choosing who to work for will take new skills. If you have been Temping or Contracting for a while, the agencies were carefully screening companies and clients, making sure they had the ability to pay. Now the Consultant has to choose those companies. Following some general guidelines, it will also be easy to spot a client that will try to trick you out of your pay.

Getting Your Own Jobs

Problem #3 is the big one. Getting your own jobs as a Consultant is the real challenge. You must know where to find work, and work must know where to find you.

Overcoming these three problems requires preparation, studying, and analyzing. This will take a while. But that's okay. We are comfortable, right now, working as a Contractor while we figure this out. Right?

Step 15.1: Memorize These Basic Problems Of Consulting.

Chapter 16:
Financial Principles Of Consulting

This chapter exposes five important money concepts used throughout consulting.

Financial Principle #1:

The first principle is demonstrated in a story that took me several years to fully understand:

An Electronic Engineer moved from Southern California to Northern California to begin his consulting career in "Silicon Valley," the heart of the electronics industry. After searching for work, for several weeks, he met with a friend of his who was a very successful Electronic Consultant in the area. He told his friend that he wasn't getting any job offers. His friend looked over his resume and said it was very impressive. They studied how the Engineer interviewed and decided that was good, also. They analyzed virtually everything related to finding work, and his friend could not find anything wrong. As they were about to give up, his friend asked, "How much do you charge your clients, anyway?" The Engineer responded, "$55 an hour." "Oh, no wonder!" his friend said surprised. "Raise your rates to $80 an hour."

He took his friend's advice and soon got more job offers than he could keep up with.

The moral of that story is twofold:

1. Anyone familiar with consulting and the financial analysis we have done in an earlier chapter knows that if you are only charging only $55 an hour, you are not going to make enough money to pay your taxes and stay alive. Clients feel that they are doing you a big favor by not hiring you (i.e. they think you are stupid).

2. If everyone else is charging $80 an hour, and you are not, then you must not know what you are doing. You are a bad businessperson because you aren't charging enough to make a profit. Even clients know this.

These facts lead us to the following principle:

FP #1:
Consultants need to charge about what their competition is charging, and appear to be making a profit and paying their taxes, or no one will hire them.

Financial Principle #2:

A second basic business practice needs to be understood by Consultants. It is introduced, here, in the form of this question:

Question:

From a financial stability standpoint, who would be better to work for: a large, older corporation, or a small, young, high-tech, startup company?

Answer:

1. Younger companies do not always have enough money in the bank. Younger companies do not always have experience in estimating project costs or managing money. They are, also, more

inclined to try to get something for nothing. They sometimes plan, on purpose, to be shrewd businessmen, at first. They try to cheat others because of their low operating budgets. Sometimes they don't realize that they are under-funded. So, they run out of money by mistake. They, typically, only have one product to market. If they misjudge that market, they may go out of business rapidly.

2. Older companies are usually more stable, financially. They also feel they have a responsibility to the public to adhere to good ethical practices. They never try to cheat anyone, especially their vendors, employees, and customers. They are also compelled to produce higher quality products. Although an older company can get bogged down, stagnate, and loose large amounts of market share, they tend to be much safer companies to work for.

Here is an example of what happened to me. Once I decided to work for a company to head up their new hardware design department. Now the company had been doing software for 20 years. So, I felt it was relatively safe to go into a new area for them, hardware. Technically, they weren't a startup company, right?

As I began working there as a Consultant, I started to notice that they were getting upset with how much I was charging. Each person in upper-management, one at a time, tried to convince me to come on full-time and get some stock options. Sound familiar?

Anyway, it dawned on me that, not only did these people not know what they were doing in this new field, but they also had no idea how much it was going to cost to develop this new hardware. For starters, it would cost $70K for a lab full of equipment. Needless to say, they were highly underfunded! This reinforces the following principle:

FP #2:
Consultants can't afford to work for startup companies or small companies going into a new field, because they are not financially and/or morally stable.

This principle is difficult to get used to, because a lot of Consultants want to help startup companies, and a lot of startup companies need Consultants. It can be done later, when the Consultant has a lot of money in the bank. There is too much additional risk for a Beginning Consultant. If necessary, there are ways to insure that you will be paid by using retainer fees, which will be discussed later.

Financial Principle #3:

Most Accounts Payable (AP) departments have a slight problem when it comes to paying the Consultant's invoices. Possibly it is due to the fact that they know the Consultant is making 3 times more than the average worker is. This means they can pay the Consultants invoices 3 times less frequent, right? Wrong! They forget that taxes haven't been taken out yet. They forget that the Consultant has more bills to pay. The Consultant has more activities to fund.

Another possibility is that the AP department is on a power trip. Turns out these people are pretty much rewarded for stringing out an invoice payment or paying the corporate bills as late as possible. It's not their fault. Their supervisors expect them to do this. They think, somehow, that they are doing the company a favor! They don't realize that they are really making the Consultants and suppliers super angry.

Here is a common scenario. Let's say your boss wants to approve your invoices, weekly, by signing them. Let's also say that the company pays the employees every two weeks. So you figure, hey, I will just invoice every two weeks, and they will probably pay me one week later. So, on your invoice you put a payment due notice of "Net 15" (payment due in 15 days). Well to the AP department, this means at least Net 30! So, 30 days later they write a check. Then it moves out of their department into other departments where it takes about a week to get the treasurer of the company to sign it. It then takes a few more days to go through the company mail system. The Post Office then takes 3 days, or so, to deliver it. So adding this up: 5 to 6 weeks later, you get your first check. That's 7 to 8 weeks after you started the job!

Another common practice in the AP department is to leave everything in the inbox for one week. On Monday, the following week, at 12:00 noon, the invoices and bills are taken out and processing starts, for the previous week. If a new invoice comes in at 12:01, it is not even looked at until 12:00 noon the following Monday! So, when called and asked why they didn't pay the invoice turned in on Monday, the AP people will say, "What invoice, we didn't get one this week!" Slick aren't they :~(

When you start to ask how you can improve the pay cycle, everyone will give you this blank stare, like a deer staring at on-coming headlights. Then they reply, "You can ask to be paid anytime you want! We have to pay other people and suppliers every week," they reply. After screaming at them for a few weeks, someone from the AP department will say, "We can pay you weekly if you like."

Here is the proper procedure for turning in the invoices at the client's site:

1. Find out when the AP department begins processing their in-basket every week.
2. Make sure each invoice says "Due On Receipt" in the "Payment Terms" box on it.
3. Get the invoices signed by your supervisor.
4. Make a Xerox copy of the signed invoice and keep it.
5. Fold the invoice into thirds or put it into an envelope, so it won't stick to something else.
6. Turn in the invoice before the magic "in-basket processing time," weekly.
7. Forget about having them "call you when it's ready." Tell them to mail it to you.

Although it says "Due On Receipt" it will still take 7 days to receive payment in the mail. If payments still don't come weekly, start calling them 2 or 3 times a week. If payments still don't come weekly, talk to their supervisor. If payments still don't come weekly, talk to their supervisor 2 or 3 times a week. If payments still don't come weekly, talk your supervisor. If payments still don't come weekly, tell everyone all work is stopped until you are paid in full. This usually gets some attention. The point is Consultant's may have to fight to get paid on time like everybody else. This all leads us to the following principle:

FP #3:
Consultant's invoices are rarely paid in a timely manner. Invoice properly, and be ready to train the AP department.

Financial Principle #4:

When you finally get paid for your invoice be sure it is taken to the bank that day. Pick a bank near where the work is being done and go there at lunchtime. Be sure to deposit the entire amount and get a receipt. Don't get cash back. It will drive your accountant nuts trying to figure out how much the company paid you. You may also go crazy trying to figure out who paid, especially when you are doing multiple jobs. Your income receivables must be traceable back to each invoice you submit.

FP #4:
Deposit You Entire Paycheck Into The Bank.

Use the ATM machine to get cash afterwards, if you need to get petty cash.

Financial Principle #5:

We've covered this subject throughout the book. Here it is again. No matter how good we are or how many contacts we have, outside forces, beyond our control, will make us unemployed, from time to time. Sometimes it is because of a good reason, like the marketing department found out they wouldn't be able to sell the product you are working on. Other times it may be purely political. For example, the company may change ownership and the new management will come in and lay off all of the Consultants on the first day. Whatever the reason, a Consultant must be prepared for this to happen.

FP #5:
!Downtime Warning! Consultants need a reserve of cash, to survive a certain amount of unemployment, or downtime.

In order to prepare for our downtime, we must have a special savings account set up for that. The size of the account is somewhat difficult to figure out. I would say about 3 months worth of bills and taxes would be adequate. That's a lot of money! Usually, though, you will have an invoice payment arriving weeks after you've been laid off. And 3 months of downtime is really pretty rare. The only time that will occur is when you are getting a bad reference, or you got laid off, by surprise, just before the Thanksgiving/Christmas/New Year's season.

Most of us would never get off the ground as Consultants if this amount were required to begin consulting. Yet, most other books on consulting insist that you've got to have this amount before you start.

This book differs in that subject. If you started as a Temp and progresses to a Contractor first, then you know that these jobs are readily available. So, you don't have to worry about it! You have a fallback plan! You just have to be willing to seek out Temp or Contracting jobs again when your downtime account starts to dry up. It's a built in safety net! This is taboo in most other consulting books. They consider going back to Temping to be a cop-out. Not me. I view it as a fall back plan. Likewise, going back to captive work is equally as good of a fallback plan, if Temp work can't be found in time.

How much does a surprise layoff cost? Well, if you're in electronics, and you are laid off just before the November Comdex Trade Show, you're looking at a long layoff. Almost every company in electronics is racing to get to that show. This is followed by the Thanksgiving/Christmas/New Years season. During this time, the board of directors has all of the managers and directors proposing a new budget for next year. No one is thinking about hiring someone during these two months. Let's say for example that you are charging $75/hour and are working the national average of 49 hours a week. The loss for the layoff during these two months would be:

$75/hour * 49 hours/week * 4.33 weeks/month * 2 months = $31,825

!Youch! That's a pretty good loss of income!

It is not good to think of your downtime this way, however. The best way to view downtime is a combination resting period and learning period. If you save for your downtime, then you can turn your down-times into mini-vacations. This will clear your mind better, shake off the old job, and help you think clearer about the next endeavor. Maybe you can pick up a book or two and read about new subjects related to your field.

Step 16.1: Memorize The Five Financial Principles Now.

Summary Of Chapter 16

Remember these five financial principles of consulting:

- You must charge the right amount.
- You must work for well-established companies.
- You must use the invoicing system properly to get paid regularly.
- You must deposit the full amount of the paycheck into the bank for traceability.
- You must have a cash reserve ready for downtime events or be willing to take on Temp jobs again as a backup plan.

If you remember and practice these five Financial Principles, you will avoid most of the financial pitfalls of consulting.

Chapter 17:
Billing Methods For Consulting

There are only a couple of standard ways to charge for consulting services rendered:

1. Fixed-Price Bidding.
2. Charging By The Hour.
3. Using Up-Front Retainer Fees.

Fixed-Price Bidding

Fixed-price, or piecework, is where the Consultant bids on the whole project for one single amount of money. The amount agreed upon will not change during the course of the project. The amount, however, can be given in pieces, as the project's milestones are reached. Usually, the project is paid for, all in one payment, upon delivery of the project.

Fixed-price is the most dangerous way to Consult. Quite often, payment ends up in dispute. Verbally, and or even in writing, the client will tend to change his mind about the features required in the project. As the project progresses, it is virtually impossible to complete it, since it is a "moving target." These changes in the scope of the project are very costly to the Consultant, both money-wise and time-wise. Not only were these changes not accounted for in the original bid, but they also cause scheduling conflicts for future work.

I've seen a lot of Consultants fail at fixed-price jobs. Fixed-price has the added danger that usually you are only paid at the end of the project. Remember, there are a few dishonest clients out there that get Consultants to work fixed-price for them, and never pay, after the product is delivered.

Fixed Price is the kind of pricing that dishonest clients want you to use, because they can say, in court, that you never completed the work to their satisfaction. They usually have the excuse that it was supposed to have that one extra feature! They take the product from you, wait to see if you will take them to court, then get in front of a judge and say, "If only Mr. Moore would have put in one more _____ that we wanted, we would have paid him." Then the judge rules that if you put the _____ in, they will have to pay you.

So there you are, working for the people that never intended on paying you, again. So, you complete the project once more. Now will they pay you? Who knows? Wait another 30 days and see if a check comes. If not, take them to court again. Does this sound like a good way to get paid? What if they pay, then cancel the check, but you don't go to the bank for two weeks?

I should point out that, personally, I never do fixed-price work, as you can probably tell. It is much safer to work on an hourly basis, than a fixed-price basis, mainly because clients change their minds, too often. Other people can also "help" to mess up the project. Even if they have a written specification, someone inexperienced may have prepared it. The spec may have too many "bells and whistles" in it, instead of focusing on the core project. Marketing can come back from a trade show and say, "All of our competitor's products have the new XYZ feature." Remember, it is easy enough for you to make your own mistakes. Why let all of these other people make mistakes that will directly affect your grocery money, and not theirs?

Proponents of fixed-price payments claim that you can make much more money charging this way. The Consultant, in the right circumstance, can get paid to do something for a second client, just as he did for the first. In this case, he stands a chance of making more money on a similar design. Fixed-Price bidding would work well in that case. However, it is agreed by all that the risk being taken is much higher by doing fixed-price bidding.

The second time you work for a client, on the same type of project, almost identical to the first project, fixed-price bidding would be okay. You would stand a better chance of approximating the time it would take to do the project. This tends to work out better in the computer software fields.

When bidding fixed price, Consultants also need a Profit Factor to multiply their estimates by. You can't do the work to just break even. You have to make a profit! You also can't assume that nothing will go wrong during the execution of the project.

After several years of measuring myself, I have found that the factor Pi = 3.14, is a good number to multiply everything by, when giving estimates. First, I figure out how long I think it will take, then, I multiply by Pi. The Egyptians found this out when they first estimated how long it would take to build the pyramids (not really).

Your profit factor may be a different value than mine, because of the differences in the fields we are in. Maybe yours needs to be 2Pi! Estimate each task item, multiply it by a profit factor, and you will have a realistic fixed-price estimate, hopefully with some profit included, in most cases.

Charging By The Hour

Since Clients change their minds too often, about what they want you to do, working by the hour makes more sense. It is the way we are used to thinking about pay. It is much less work. We don't have to spend "free" time putting together bids for jobs. It also fits the client's mode of operation better. The client pays all of the captive employees this way. The infrastructure is already in place for this. We can also start on the project sooner. Proposals and bidding take too long.

Charging by the hour is the best way to consult. You will get paid for every second that you work. The client is free to change his mind at any time, something they do often. The client can change his mind without causing contractual problems. Why wouldn't a client want to pay this way?

Clients get scared paying this way. They see the clock ticking in dollars when they pay the consultant this way. When a mistake has been made by a previous consultant, then the see that they are paying a second time for something that should have been done, a long time ago. There are many reasons that they will try not to pay you this way. But, to a good consultant, someone with high moral standards and good communication skills, the client has nothing to worry about. Consultants should insist that they be paid this way.

During the negotiation process, it may be comforting to the client to reassure him of the things you will not be charging him for. For example you may mention that you will not charge him for travel time, even if he sends you across town to have a meeting with a potential customer. You should also mention that you will not charge him for lunch or coffee breaks, and you will be subtracting this 1.5 hours from your time card everyday.

One technique used in getting paid hourly is to never let the client owe you more money than you can sue for, for free, in Small Claims Court. In many counties, the Small Claims suing limit has been raised to $10,000, in recent years. These cases are easy to win if you have a written contract. It is always a good idea to find out how much the Small Claims Limit is, in the region you will be working in.

To keep yourself within the Small Claim Court Limit, you have to get the client to agree to frequent invoicing terms. Adjust your billing dates so they are more frequent. Invoice every 7 days instead of every two weeks. Have the client pay you "Due On Receipt" which actually takes 7-14 days. This will keep the client from getting too far ahead of your work.

If the client is stubborn, requiring Net 30, and if your hourly rate is fairly high, then maybe you should consider using retainer fees.

Using Up-Front Retainer Fees

A retainer is a cash advance on work the Consultant is about to perform. The Consultant collects this money before work begins, up-front. The Consultant puts the money in his bank account, and invoices against the amount. Each invoice shows a subtraction from the amount, and a credit that is left over. This is done until the credit remaining reaches a low level. At that point, the client is obligated to refill the retainer amount back up.

Retainers are great for the Consultant to insure pay, because he has already received it. However, if the work is not performed, a general fear of many clients, then the client would be obligated to take the case to court. So, requiring retainers can scare off many clients. On the other hand, if you are charging a fairly high hourly rate, and the client insists on paying you Net 30, on a monthly basis, you will be floating a lot of money, perhaps way more than you would care to. So, haggle with the client. See if he will back down on his Net 30 requirement if you insist on using a retainer fee. If not, require the retainer. Most highly paid Consultants require retainer fees regularly.

Estimating the amount of retainer can be an extra hassle. If the client insists on Net 30, and monthly invoices charge him the amount you will be floating on your first check is 8-weeks of pay. If the client thinks the amount is too high, reassure the client that the remaining credit value of the retainer, not used up by the end of the project, will be returned to him promptly. Put this fact into your contract.

Personally, I only use the retainer fee concept to haggle with shrewd or delinquent payment clients. If you start on an hourly-basis job, and thepaychecks stop coming, stop all work. Then, require a retainer fee to re-start the project back up, and re-write the contract.

Retainer fees are a must when working for small, startup companies, or companies entering a new field of endeavor. It is also recommended that you require two weeks worth of warning before you get laid-off, in writing, also. Many startup companies are notorious for spending money that they don't have. Avoid them as much as possible. They can barely afford to hire college students to do their work, much less, highly paid Consultants.

Mixing And Matching Billing Methods

Your billing methods need not be fixed. You can mix and match. The best way is to charge hourly, especially when it is the first time you are working for this client. Then, after you learn how well they plan and manage projects, you can charge fixed-price the second time. The retainer fee can be used as a huge threat or re-start penalty fee if they stop paying on time.

If you will loose a client, by not bidding fixed-price the first time, then maybe you should walk away. Tell the client he should get a bid on it, from someone else. Call him back in a few days and see if he got one. If not, tell him that you could still do it hourly, and it would probably save him a lot of money, because of your experience in this field. If he did get a quote, ask him how much it was for, and tell him to keep you in mind if something goes wrong.

Step 17.1: Decide On Your Billing Method Now.

Summary Of Chapter 17

In this chapter, we studied the three main ways to bill the client. Charging by the hour is known to be the best way for the Consultant. We've practiced negotiating and charging by the hour, for years, as Captive and Temp employees. Shouldn't Consultants get paid like the rest of the world? Avoid billing any other way, but hourly.

Chapter 18:
Negotiating As A Consultant

Since you are representing yourself as a Consultant, negotiating can be a little more challenging than it is for a Temp, or a Contractor. Of course, the general rules established for negotiating still apply.

Consulting Differences

There are some new dangers encountered, when negotiating as a Consultant, not encountered in Temping or Contracting:

1. **Groups of people will interview you simultaneously**. This can be bit nerve-racking.

2. **The negotiation of pay will be intermingled with the interviewing process**. This makes interviewing and negotiating a little more tricky.

3. **You must negotiate face-to-face with the client, and not through an agent**.

4. **You will be asking for much more money**. Remember it is costing you more money to be a Consultant. This will make the client very tense.

5. **There may not be any witnesses to your agreements with the client**. It's your word against his, in court. Who is the judge going to believe: a successful, tax-paying, businessman with 100 employees or one measly Consultant?

If we are cautious, none of these differences will be a real threat.

Step 18.1: Memorize The Differences Between Consulting And Contracting Through Agencies.

Interviewing As A Consultant

As a Temp or a Contractor, you probably will be interviewed occasionally by a group of people. A Consultant will be interviewed by groups of people, most of the time. There is nothing new to learn here, though. The interviewing principles we discussed in a previous chapter still hold. Focus on presenting your skills first. Do this with plenty of pictures and samples of work. To satisfy large groups, bring more samples and more pictures. Postpone haggling until they have accepted your qualifications and you are satisfied with the goals they want to reach.

Presenting Your Hourly Pay Rate

Many times your rate will be discussed on the phone before you arrive. When doing so, it is best not to scare off the client. Act like you normally charge different ballpark amounts depending on the situation. Then hopefully they will want you to visit the company and talk to them in person. After you decide the project has some interest for you, you can nail them with your astronomical fee. While determining your hourly rates, be sure to include a haggle factor in your price. They're still going to negosh you down a tad.

When the time comes, present your rate with a casual lead-in and a blazing ending.

Explain it like this:

"Well, it seems like a useful project to be working on, the people are friendly, the company seems like a productive atmosphere, and everyone seems honest. So, since you agree to pay me on an hourly basis and you agree to pay me weekly and since you are going to let me do half of the work off-site at my office, I can give you a great deal. Then state in a definite way, "I can work for you for _____ dollars an hour."

Be sure NOT TO STATE this last sentence in the form of a question like, "How does _____ dollars an hour sound?" This will surely lead to them saying something negative. Be definite in your statement. Don't flinch while you say it.

Of course, they may still want to haggle and bump you down a notch. But act surprised if they do. Try not to let them. Say, "Gee, I really thought I was giving you a good deal since I normally charge $10 an hour more than that." The project sounded like it was something interesting to work on, so I was giving you a discount already." Then, hopefully, they will haggle you down just a bit and everyone will be happy, especially since you factored it all in.

If they really start sounding disappointed about how much you charge, hold your ground. Hit them with your standard Squeeze-Factors. Say things like:

1. "This is a long drive for me, in rush-hour traffic."
2. "You can't pay my invoices on a weekly basis, like you do your regular employees."
3. "There will be a lot of overtime required to catch the project back up to schedule."
4. "You have already haggled me down to an amount lower than I really wanted to go."

For a real show, get out a calculator and pretend you are calculating something. Then respond with, "Sorry, but that is the lowest I can go."

A good client only haggles you down once. A bad client, who is ruthless, dishonest, or strapped for cash, will always try to haggle you down more than once. We will discuss this more in the next chapter.

Inexperienced clients may even try to get you to commit to coming on as a captive later! If they do this, then they may be honest but they surely don't know anything about paying consulting wages. Watch out.

So, if they seem to be way out of line, prepare for battle. You have probably already lost the job, anyway. You may have just discovered a dead-beat client. Hit them now with one or two good lines of reality. Here are some of my favorite comebacks:

1. "A car mechanic charges $75 an hour, surely Electronic Engineering is a bit more difficult!"
2. "I have 30 years of experience working at more than 37 companies in this industry, on very successful products. {Pause} Check my references if you don't believe me. {Pause} How long would it take you to find someone else like me?
3. "Think of all the profit you have been loosing because you didn't have someone that knew what they are doing, like me!"
4. "Sorry gentlemen, but I can't work for that little and stay in business. I have to pay taxes, buy computers and software, go to seminars, and pay for my own benefits, just like your company does. I have to make a profit too, so I can take the kids to Disneyland once in a while." Then slowly get up and walk away.

Appealing to their business sense will usually work to your advantage. Everyone understands that we are all in business to make a profit. As you are leaving, all the business-wise people in the room will be thinking of your last words. "What does he mean he has to make a profit to?" Then it will hit them, "Oh yeah, that is why all of us are in business." And suddenly, half of the room will want to hire you.

After you gain some years of experience in consulting, you can just say, "I've been charging $100 an hour for the last five years." They then assume you won't go any lower and they just pay you that.

GOOD NEWS: Very little haggling actually occurs in the later years of consulting.

By the way, for all of the Engineers out there, the IEEE reported that in 1998 the national average hourly pay for engineering consultants was about $98 an hour. The survey is good reading for all interested in consulting. It can be seen at *http://www.ieeeusa.org/BUSINESS/98feesurvey.html*.

Get Your Rate In Writing

If they give you your rate, you will need to close the deal in the next 24 hours. Take their contract and read it overnight, or have them sign yours this day. If they give you one of theirs to sign, make sure it has all of the items on it that yours has. Contracts are nothing magic. They are mainly used to clarify the agreement by both parties, in case, one of the parties forgets who is supposed to do what.

Be sure to include everything you have agreed upon, and a general description of what the project is including:

1. Who is making the agreement: an actual person's name and a company name.
2. Pay Rate.
3. Work locations.
4. Amount of travel, hotels, food (per diam pay if any).
5. Payment schedule for invoices.
6. Payment penalty for late payments.
7. Client can lay off Consultant anytime without notice.

8. Consultant can quit anytime without notice.
9. The name of the project.
10. General description of the tasks to be performed.
11. Equipment to be supplied by either party.
12. All disputes will go to an arbitration hearing.
13. If it goes to court the looser will pay all lawyers and court costs.

Step 18.2: Study The Elements Of A Standard Contract.

Now get that contract signed.

One thing to watch out for in contracts is in the "terms for terminating" the contract. You do not want to force the client to give you advance notice in writing, oddly enough. Whenever you require something in writing, the client will never give it to you. Most clients tell you not to come back to work on Monday, but your contract is still intact because they didn't give termination notice in writing. You need to be able to re-negotiate with a client that lays you off by surprise. You don't want the old contract to be involved with an old project starting back up.

Never get involved with contracts that have other stipulations or strings attached. Here is an example: Once a client didn't like paying agency fees. So, they called the agency and asked to buy them out. The agency demanded $25,000, which they paid. So, I converted from a Temp to a Contractor and got my write-offs back. The client then had me sign a contract that said if I ever quit in less than a year's time, then I would owe the company $450 a week for all of the weeks left in that year. That way he could recover some of the $25K if I quit. That sounded good to me at the time. I never had a hard time working non-captive jobs before. I thought it was a mistake on their part making it harder for them to get rid of me. Instead, it worked out the opposite.

Ten weeks later I found out it was a terrible place to work with lots of hostilities and inexperienced people. Japanese companies owned part of this company and they were also angry because all of the projects were 6 to 10 months late. If I quit and found other work I would owe them $20,000 dollars. I had to wait there miserably, until they fired me. Then they said I was on call, meaning they weren't going to give me anything in writing that said the contract was terminated. I should have never signed that contract. They really needed my help anyway and would have had no choice but to keep me working there. It wasn't my fault they didn't like paying agency fees. So remember, don't sign contracts with "Strings Attached."

Get It Witnessed

You Are Not Done Yet—In a court of law, it will be your word against the client's, unless you GET A WITNESS from their company to sign that contract, too. Insist that you meet the Accounts Payable Person in person. Introduce yourself. Now, they will know who is sending them invoices, and you will know who may not be paying you on time. Exchange business cards with this person. Ask Accounts Payable, stupidly, where you should send your invoices. Discuss the contract with them by showing them the part about paying invoices "Due On Receipt." Ask what time and day they process their in-basket, as we discussed before. Ask them if they wouldn't mind initialing the part about the "Due On Receipt" method of payment.

A complication to all of this comes up when you agree to work for someone that is a long distance away. Once I worked for a company out of state. A friend had recommended me for the job. He had worked for them before, and they paid him. So, they faxed me a contract containing our agreement. I signed it, and had my friend witness it, and faxed it back to them. They signed it, and mailed it back to me. Once I had the version that they signed in my hands, I started working for them.

Anyway, however you do it, get it in writing and get it witnessed.

Getting Raises

Asking for a raise is a very controversial subject in the consulting world. Some consultants think it damages your relationship with the client. It could if it is done in the middle of a project. If done at the right time, however, nothing bad happens.

The right time to ask for a raise is at the completion of one project and during the assignment of an additional project. By waiting for this moment, the client has already done his manpower allocation study for this next project and realizes that your services are definitely still needed.

The method for getting a raise is best sent as an email to your immediate supervisor. This email will state in no uncertain terms that you are raising your rates. The technique is not to ask for a raise but to state as a fact that you are raising your rates. It is recommended that you give them about 1 month before the raise begins because that's how long it takes the corporate system to respond to it. Here is the text of the typical email:

"Please be informed that effective one month from now I will be raising my hourly rate to _____ dollars an hour. I will be using the money to go to more seminars and upgrade to a new computer running the latest software.

Thank you for retaining me for this new project. I look forward to making it as successful as the last project." That's about it.

To decide how much to ask for will take a little research. It may do some good to ask a few of your other consulting buddies at the same company what they think of the new rate you will be asking for. Sometimes it will make them ask for a raise ahead of you, so be careful.

The in-basket in the Accounts Payable department is also a good source of rate information. As you casually drop in your weekly invoice, you may notice another consultant's invoice already in there. Read it and memorize his rate for future reference. I usually make a database of all the consultant's rates at the company. Besides, most consultants discuss their rates openly if you take them to lunch. By having data, you can make a much wiser decision come raise-time.

Raise amounts are relative to your capabilities to get things done. At big lethargic corporations, you may not appear to management as someone that can get a job done quickly. In these situations, the corporate system has slowed you down to a crawl. You may not be able to gauge your performance in the eyes of management. So, it may be difficult to justify the advanced guru rate. On the other hand, who knows what the corporation thinks. Maybe they think they are a finely honed company that adapts rapidly to market change. Either way, you have to weigh all aspects in determining your new rate. Having some data to go by helps a great deal. Go for it.

Summary Of Chapter 18

Most clients at well-established companies have the money. It's just hard to get money commitments out of them.

Hold your ground during these negotiations. Remember how much it is costing you to Consult. Don't forget how many bills and taxes you are paying to Consult. Don't forget about all the benefits you are paying for. Remember, you are in business to make a profit. Don't give away the farm. Don't forget about your Dream Rate Goals either.

In the next chapter we will discuss how to avoid working for rip-off clients.

Chapter 19:
Recognizing Dead-Beat Clients

During job interviews, a few potential clients will try to convince you to work for less money. That's fine and we expect some of that. But, if they start getting a little extreme, watch out!

Does The Client Have Enough Money?

The first general warning sign is when the client tells you that you are not really the person that they are looking for, but they want to hire you anyway. After they decide you probably can do the job, they will complain about how much you charge…especially since you are still not the best person for the job.

The second general warning sign is when the client tries to get you to accept other things in lieu of money. The will start promising you things like things like "more work after this job", "at a higher pay", as well as stocks, royalties, cars, per-diam, and virtually anything else, EXCEPT MONEY. Meanwhile, they will try to keep you confused about not being the right person for the job.

The harder the client tries to get you to take less money, the less money he has. As you run into these conniving con-artists, keep in the very front of your forehead:

- Your taxes and your bills.
- How much it is costing you to recover your benefits.
- How much your competition is getting paid.
- Your downtime savings account.
- Your Dream-Rate Goals.

Don't take less money than you are worth. We've done the math. There is no way we can be in business and not make a profit.

I don't want to give you the impression that there are a lot of bad clients out there. I'm not trying to scare you. Many safeguards are built in to the techniques used in this book. These are summarized in the next chapter. You should not have to worry about meeting these types of people because I've already met them. By learning from my experiences, and by studying the "Indicators Of Dead-Beat Clients" in this chapter, you will be immune to their cut-throat practices. Here are three example stories of actual run-ins with flakey clients. I hope you will view these stories as comical.

Dead-Beat Client Story 1

One fellow wanted me to start on $25,000 design project for him. Our first meeting was at his house, not his company. I, inadvertently, mentioned that I liked his bass guitar when I saw it sitting in his living room. I told him I used to play bass, in the late 60's. He offered to give me his guitar if I started on this project right away. He swore he had the money to pay me, over and over. But, starting a business deal with a guitar didn't make any sense to me, so I hesitated, for about two weeks. I told him I had to complete some previous commitments (which I always seem to have lying around). Three weeks later, he called me, and I told him I was still wrapping things up on the old project. This fellow was flat broke by the end of the fourth week. But, he recovered and is still in business today.

Dead-Beat Client Story 2

Another potential client, seemed to own a good-sized company. He wanted me to design something for him that he couldn't seem to describe very well, over the phone (first clue, right?). So, I asked him to call me when he had more of a definition. Although he said he needed this product done in a hurry, he didn't return my call for three weeks. Finally, he called me to set up a meeting. I reminded him that three weeks had gone by, and therefore, I had already taken on other work. He asked if I could recommend someone else.

I asked around, and found some friends of mine who were willing to do it. These friends reported to me the following story: The client set up a meeting, at a restaurant half way between their work and his place of work. The potential client didn't show for a whole hour so my friends ordered lunch. The potential client finally arrived another hour later, right when they were done eating. He ordered a glass of water and then went to the restroom. The waitress told my friends that this fellow always has these "glass-of-water" meetings there.

When he finally sat down, he told them that he was sorry for being late, but his lawyer needed to talk to him about the people that were suing him! He then proceeded to describe an $10,000 project, which would have taken my friends about a month to complete. He was surprised by their estimate, however, and said he figured it would only cost $500 and would take a few days. He promised them though, that if they did this project for him for $500, he would give all of us many more projects at higher rates than our standard rates. Then, he left and did not offer to pay for lunch. This fellow is still in business, somehow.

Dead-Beat Client Story 3

A third guy tried to get me to work, at his office, after I told him on the phone that I could only do the work at my office because I already had another project going. He then offered to pay me $10 per hour less than my standard fee, whenever I worked at my office (did he say less?). Why did he want to punish me for working at my own place where I am far more productive? So, I hesitated to work for him. I told him I would call him back in a few days. I didn't.

About 2 weeks later, after he couldn't find anyone else, he agreed to pay me my standard fee and let me work off-site. This guy complained, during the whole project, about how little was getting done and how much I was charging. At one point, I really worked hard on his project. Two of the days, I worked 15 hours per day. Then, he told me that he didn't believe these hours I was reporting and never to work more than 8 hours in one day again. On the day I had completed his project, he was amazed that it came up working the first time (hey, so was I). He started telling me how much they would need my services in the future, and then he rushed me out the front door (pushed is more like it). I didn't even get a chance to say goodbye to the other Engineers I worked with. I later decided that he really didn't have enough money to hire someone like me, even though the project was a complete success. My last invoice was mysteriously lost for three weeks, but was eventually paid.

The three stories above are rare incidences of the types of weird clients you can possibly run into, while consulting. ***Once you establish a rock-solid framework in your head about what it costs for you to pay your expenses and reach your basic dreams, nobody will be able to cheat you.*** These con-artist types of clients won't even be able to make you flinch. Here is a list I've compiled, after several years, that can be used as an indication that there is something fishy about the particular client you are being interviewed by.

Indicators Of Dead-Beat Clients:

- The client tells you that you are not really the person they are looking for, but wants to hire you anyway.
- The client offers you other things instead of money. No matter how tempting, never except anything for pay other than money.
- If the client actually takes out the money and shows it to you, it won't be there when it is time to get paid.
- The client will start promising you things like "more work later at a higher rate of pay."
- The client keeps switching, back and forth, from talking about your pay rate, to defining the project, like he is trying to confuse you on purpose. He is trying to con you! He may have money, but will complain about it all the time if you work for him.
- The client only wants you to bid on the project as fixed-price, with one payment on delivery, paying invoices Net 30, and is not open to consider other alternatives.
- Somehow you find out that the company doesn't pay its invoices on time.
- If you tell the client that you need one more week to finish off a previous project, and then, you wait another two weeks to see if he calls you, and he "forgets" to call, then most likely, he doesn't have money.
- The client doesn't want you to see his company on an interview.
- The client let's you see his company and it is in his garage at his house.
- The client has a bonified business location and it is no bigger than a garage.
- The client talks about lawyers, divorces, car wrecks, or getting sued in the first few minutes of your interview.

- The client directly insults your field of expertise, in the first few meetings.
- The client takes you to lunch and does not offer to pay for your lunch.
- The client insists that you do all of the work, at their office.
- The client tells you how long the project will take before asking you first.
- The client complains, day-to-day, about how much you charge.
- The client says they don't believe the hours you are reporting.
- The client complains, day-to-day, about how little progress you are making.

Some Poor Clients Mean Well

When you are first starting out, many people will want to help you by sending you "clients," from all corners of the globe. Usually, every starving inventor, for a 50 mile radius, will come over to your office, "giving you work." Of course, they think you can do miracles with their life savings, of $1000. I have, frequently, come very close to feeling sorry for these inventor-types that need help starting a new product. Their product ideas are innovative and their projects sound interesting. Sure they don't have much money, but if it goes...

Nevermind, I can't afford to help them. I have my own profit-sucking experiments to conduct. My own personal projects are far more valuable for me to work on. Most of us would rather work on our own ideas for free.

Going To Court

The greater majority of clients out there are on the up-and-up. However, there are a few that like to get something for nothing. We also can goof up and think that we have found a great startup company to work for, only to find out that they ran out of money. When these types of things happen, we have to accept the fact that we are going to drag them into court.

Out of 37 clients, I've only taken two cases to court.

Case 1: Immoral Founder

The first case was a startup company (well, I was a greenhorn). The original founder of the company got some venture capital by letting the investor become president, and the he became vice-president. I was to get 5% of the royalties, if I was done in 4 months, plus my normal consulting wage. Near the end of the project, the founder broke the circuit board I was working on, in an attempt to push me past the due date. Plus, he reported to the investor that I wasn't making any progress. I took them to court. I subpoenaed the other 5 engineers I worked with! They testified that they saw the board working and it was fully documented. I won. The founder of the startup, the guy that tried to cheat me, was fired over this, a few weeks later. He was the original founder of this company! Imagine being fired from your own company! They decided not to produce the product, so I never got any royalties though (see).

Case 2: Immoral President

The second case was a 10-year-old company. It had a very shrewd, immoral president. The president was my direct boss. My case was settled out of court, on the day before the trial, in my favor, after I subpoenaed about 5 people, and the accounting records.

Subpoena With A Purpose

In these cases, I try to subpoena everyone that witnessed the work, the accountant, and all of the accounting records. I subpoena the person that writes the paychecks, to prove they have given me one in the past. I also subpoena all of the accounting records for the year, to prove my pay cycle was regular. This creates an extra hassle for the accounting department, which makes them furious.

It costs about $75 each, for the sheriff to deliver each subpoena. When you do this, you get to tell the sheriff what time to deliver them! A good time is at lunchtime, when all of the employees are out in front of the company, at the lunch truck. This can cause a lot of ruckus at the company that day. It is fun to watch from across the street, too!

Small Claims Court doesn't pay you for time lost while going to court. Of course, neither will anyone else get paid that you subpoenaed! The looser of the case does have to pay for the Sheriff to deliver the subpoenas, and the mileage driven to court by the people subpoenaed. The people subpoenaed also loose most of a day's worth of wages! So, they get mad at their boss, the client, for not paying you. Usually, the client settles out of court due to these internal pressures. Just the delivery of the subpoenas, particularly if done by the sheriff, is good enough to scare a company into paying you.

If the sheriff can't get a hold of the person, he will call you and ask for suggestions. Then you can send him to the client's house, if you know his address. A fun thing to do is to send the sheriff to the clients house at around 5:30 PM when all of the neighbors are coming home from work. He may not be home then, but the sheriff will attempt the delivery 3 times! It's very embarrassing trying to explain to the neighbors why the sheriff came over three times. The client doesn't really need to be subpoenaed anyway since he has to show up to court because the claim is against him. But, it is fun to do anyway since he has to reimburse you for it.

The subpocna process alone usually will cause the client to break-down and just pay you. You have caused about five of his employees to complain to him, internally. His spouse and neighbors have probably asked him questions at home. He has to take a day off to go to court, too. He knows you are serious because you sent the sheriff. He knows it is not a game anymore. So, usually he cracks under pressure.

The client will usually call the day before court to pay you. When he does, tell him you want what he originally owed, plus the cost of the subpoena's, plus the cost of the time lost for doing all of this court stuff. If he refuses to pay you for this time, tell him you will see him in court tomorrow then. Usually it works. Make sure you get paid with a money order and not a check. Don't cancel the court date until the money is in your bank.

Anyway, if you follow the guidelines in this book, you probably will never have to take a client to court.

Summary Of Chapter 19

Hopefully, you've noticed how easy it can be to recognize dead-beat clients that are out to rip you off. The dishonest ones usually give them-selves away in their first meeting.

If one slips by you, he will owe you an amount small enough to go to Small Claims Court. There, you will subpoena him and all the people that you worked with. You will do this in an embarrassing way by hav-ing the sheriff drop them off at an inconvenient time. Most likely they will crack and pay you.

In the next chapter, we will summarize all of the safeguards we have in place to insure a prosperous consulting career.

Chapter 20:
Safeguards For Consulting Prosperity

Many safeguards have been put into this book to prevent bad things from ever happening to you while consulting. This chapter lists them, so that you will feel more comfortable about going into this field. Here is our list of safeguards, thus far:

- We are experienced at working for more than one company.
- We know that we do good work because other workers tell us.
- We charge a fair-market price, the same as our competition, so that clients will feel comfortable giving us work on a regular basis.
- We are located in a geographical area that has enough demand for our services.
- We are willing to travel many miles a day for work.
- We charge enough money to save up for some downtime.
- We charge enough money to make a profit, after accounting for our living and business expenses, like all legitimate businesses.
- We work for only for medium and larger, well-established companies.
- We work only on written contracts.
- We work only when our contracts are signed.

- We work only when are contracts are also, witnessed, usually by the person that writes paychecks, in the Accounts Payable department.
- We refuse to sign, and walk away from, all contracts that have "strings attached."
- We work only for cash money.
- We bill the client on an hourly basis.
- We invoice weekly with "Due On Receipt" invoices.
- We require the client to pay the invoices, weekly.
- We stop all work if the client owes us more than the Small Claims Court limit.
- We require interest be paid on late invoices, as part of the contract.
- We are not afraid to take dead-beat clients to Small Claims Court.
- We require large retainer fees (advanced pay) to start a project back up, after delinquent payments or project postponement.
- We can be terminated by the client anytime, without a written notice (better for us).
- We can quit working for the client anytime without notice.
- We refuse to work for start-up companies.
- We refuse to work for small companies going into a new field.
- We refuse to help small inventors, as our primary source of income.
- We will not take jobs with Dead-beat clients, especially clients that don't want us to see their company, insult the field that we work in, or will not pay for lunch.
- If, for some reason, we can't find our own work as Consultants, we will call the job agencies and Temp or Contract again, for a while.

Step 20.1: Memorize this list. Become this list.

If you will adhere to these concepts and principles, your consulting experience will be a pleasurable one.

Chapter 21:
Getting Consulting Work

Hundreds of books have been written on the subject of getting consulting work. There is really an unlimited number of ways to do it. Some ways require very little work. Some ways require a lot of work. Many new ways of finding consulting work have popped up recently, thanks to the Internet. This chapter is an introduction to the ways to find consulting work, or more importantly, having it find you.

Ways Of Getting Consulting Work

These are the main categories for getting work offered to you:
1. Getting referrals from industry friends.
2. Finding jobs on your own.
3. Helping others find you.
4. All of the above.

Getting Referrals From Industry Friends

Word Of Mouth Referrals

There is a major misunderstanding that consulting work is found by referrals. Rarely is that the case. Not only are the referrals scarce, the timing of them is usually bad. Most of them come when you are up to your elbows in alligators. So, referrals are not all that frequent nor do they occur at the right time.

In addition, referrals come in for companies and situations that you are trying to avoid, such as startups, small private corporations, and inventors. So, referrals, many times, are not the right ones for you, either.

Usually, when you run out of work, the world is quiet. So, you have to rattle the trees until something falls out. You have to put your ear to the ground. You have to try to pry your way into a new job. You have to beg for a referral. You need to find someone that knows someone on the inside. You have to take the initiative to get things going. So "word of mouth" referrals usually starts with "words of your own mouth."

Networking

Since you will be the instigator of your own future, Networking is a requirement, not an option.

There is a saying these days:

If ya ain't workin' then ya ain't networkin'.

Networking is the most crucial element of consulting. If you are anti-social then you might as well stay working for job agencies.

Definition of Networking:

Purposeful and continuous communication with all of your industrial contacts.

Networking means calling people back even if they don't call you!

Remember that 30% to 50% markup that the agencies used to get for placing you? Well, now you get to keep it if you keep in constant contact with your industry friends. What could be an easier way to make money than calling all of your friends and fellow mercenaries in the industry and talking shop? Does this sound like something you can handle socially?

Networking is the second best way to find job leads. Keeping in touch with your past ramrods can certainly lead to jobs. Usually, about one out of five people called will give you a definite job lead and a manger's name.

If you want your friends to give you referrals, you have to schmooze. They are usually too busy working to really push for you. So, meet with them off-hours. In other words:

Spend Quality Time With Your Industry Friends.

Take them to lunch. Invite them over for dinner. Go to your industry trade shows together. Join some industry-related organizations and go their events together. Organize your own events. Have a party at the local beer joint with just your industry friends. Laugh about old jobs. Brainstorm your industry. Call them often. Then, when you need their help, they will be looking out for you. Don't forget to return the favor when they are in need. In actuality, networking is one of the most fun aspects of consulting!

Step 21.1: Make A List Of All Of Your Industry Friends And Contacts And Call Them For One Hour Per Week.

Networking Must Target Managers

Unfortunately, our friends and acquaintances don't do the hiring. Managers do the hiring. *Networking must surely lead us to managers with job openings, if it is going to work!* Our networking friends and contacts need only to lead us to manager's names. We need to contact managers, any way we can, to get work. We can also make it easy for managers to stumble across our name. This is usually done by way of Internet websites and Email.

Establish A Networking Database

Networking skills have to be organized to be successful. This is best done on the computer of course. A database of fellow mercenaries, past clients, reps, vendors, FAE's, and distributors is required. The database must include managers, to accomplish our networking goal. The database should be organized by Company so we can remember all of the contacts more easily. Constructing this database will take some time. It should also be expanded weekly.

> **Step 21.2: Begin The Networking Database And Update It For One Hour Per Week.**

In order to get a foot in the door, managers names and emails will be required. It doesn't matter if you've heard of them or worked for them before. A Consultant can never have too many hiring manager's names in his database. Here are some ways to get managers names.

Past Managers And Past Jobs

First, put in all of your past clients (managers) and all of your past contacts into the database. Now call as many of those past acquaintances and ask them what happened to all of those managers. Then call these managers directly. If you've been Temping and

Contracting for a few years, you should already have quite a few manager's home phone numbers.

> **Step 21.3: Put Past Manager's Names Into The Database And Call Them All.**

Getting More Manager's Names

Ask for and collect your friend's and fellow mercenaries' resumes. Now call each friend back and ask them who their bosses were at each company listed on their resume. Ask them if they think that manager still works there, or where they think they are now. Be sure to ask them for their email addresses! Now, if 10 of your friends worked at 10 companies each, using this technique, you would now have the names of 100 more hiring managers. If your friends are Temps, Contractors, or Consultants, then you already know these particular managers have hired non-captives in the past!

> **Step 21.4: Collect The Names And Emails Of 100 More Managers From Friends.**

Searching For More Managers

More research can also lead to a larger database of manager's names. Industry directories, City Chamber Of Commerce, Stock Market Reports, City Newspapers, Commerce Business Daily, Trade Magazines, and so on, could contain a manager's name. Engineering Managers, for example, usually give new product announcements to get free advertising in trade journals. Since many of these items are on the Internet, you can read past magazine articles about companies online, to get more names. Of course, you can also try the receptionist at the company.

Government Announcements Of Manager's Names

Commerce Business Daily (CBD) is particularly interesting as a manager contact resource. It reports daily, all government contracts that were awarded, how much they are worth, and the manager's name that received the award. It also has many government requests for Consultant's services. If you run across an award announcement for a local company, an ad in next Sunday's Newspaper usually accompanies it. The difference is that now you know the hiring manager's name. CBD's website is at *http://cbdnet.gpo.gov*.

Research The Company's Background

Once you have the managers to call, it is best to do a little research on their company. Search for the company website using Altavista™ or one of the more robust search engines. Get on their website and down-load data on products or services related to your work. Call some of your parts and software reps, and see if they know what tools are being used at the company. Get whatever information you can on the manager, the company, the software, and the tools they are using. Type all of this information into the database so that you can refer to it for years to come.

Step 21.5: Update The Networking Database With More Managers Names.

Networking With Professionals

A Consultant not only has to be well connected with friends and industry acquaintances, but also with fellow Consultants. To be a professional, a consultant must hang around with other professionals.

Sometimes it seems like these pros are competing with us. But they are not. On the contrary, their work spillover is our next job. Likewise, some of our work spillover can be their next job. A professional has hundreds of industry contacts, especially with other professionals in the same field. You must belong to the inner social circles of fellow Pro's. In other words:

Spend Quality Time With Other Industry Professionals.

There are good, friendly people everywhere in your industry. The Professionals doing the same thing as you, are the friendliest. To meet them you must join the same professional organizations that they belong to. To get and maintain these contacts you must schmooze. This means you must go to the meetings. At these meetings, you must contribute something. Don't worry about saying the wrong thing. Speak your mind. The industry needs opinions and practical ideas. You will gain respect from your peers. Later, of course, they will become your friends.

Professional Organizations that have websites are the best ones to join. Go to the Orange County Consultant's Network at *www.occn.org*. Click on members. My name appears there. A link to my website and email also shows up. This particular club has members that have been doing business in the county for many years. They get overflowed with job offers, so they broadcast them out to the members.

Step 21.6: Join One Professional Organization.

Finding Jobs On Your Own

Now that you have a networking database, you can find your own jobs. Finding your own jobs takes alot of work and can be very frustrating. It takes practice and persistence.

Call Past Managers And Clients

Concentrate on all of the managers and clients you've worked for in the past. They are your #1 best source of new work. If they don't have a project available when you call them, your call will start an avalanche of ideas in their mind. Find out what they are working on. Ask them about their bosses. Get their email addresses.

> **Step 21.7: Call All Of Your Past Managers And Clients.**

Cold-Call New Managers

It's always better to get your resume to a project manager than to a Human Resources (HR) person. Sometimes managers hire people, on a consulting basis, to get around the red tape caused by the HR department! After you identify a company that has openings, it is best to try to get the name of the manager there. Then call him. This is referred to as a "cold-call" because the manager doesn't know you.

To sell yourself to such a manager, you are going to have to prepare a carefully put together speech. Type the speech out, in your word-processing program so that you can rearrange it, so it sounds good. Make sure you ask the manager some questions so that he feels that he is a valuable part of your conversation. Usually, these cold-calls will result in the person asking for your resume and blurb sheet. It will usually take a few months before this manager can figure out how to employ you. That's why it is so important to market and sell your services weekly.

Cold-Email New Managers

Email is less personal and lasts longer than a conversation. No conversation takes place until after the resume is presented. This is a more relaxing way to present yourself. Some beginning Consultant's voices get too shaky on the phone. Other Consultants sound like they are begging for a job, over the phone. With email, the Consultant's reputation precedes him. The manager has more time to study how best to use the Consultants skills. If the manager has an immediate need, you will get called. If the manager has a future need, he may save your resume on his computer. If he doesn't need you at all, he may file your resume in the bit bucket (the electronic garbage can). That's why it is imperative to follow-up the cold-email with a cold-call, about 3 days later. Find out if there is any interest at all. In general, cold-emailing works much better than cold-calling.

The catch is that cold-emailing requires an email address. These are somewhat harder to come by, than just a name. One way to get them is to ask the HR people. Try to get one of them to give you their email address, supposedly so that you can send them your resume. Then, try constructing the email to the manager of interest, in the same manner. Send the manager your portfolio. If it bounces back, then you need to find out why the email address didn't work. Call the receptionist. They may or may not help you.

If you know someone that has worked there or is working there, getting email addresses is much easier. Don't forget to cold-email all of your friend's past managers.

Call And Email Industry Contacts

In the course of Electronic Hardware Design, I influence a lot of purchasing decisions for components. There are people that sell these parts. These people are called vendors, or sales representatives. There are also people trained in helping us to get the parts to work in our circuits. These are called Field Application Engineers or FAE's. We call all of these people "Reps" for short. Many of these reps can recommend you for consulting work. But, again, you have to take the initiative to call them all. They know that, if they can get you in there, they can sell more parts, software, or whatever the case may be. They have all given me their business cards with their email addresses on them.

Reps know which companies use the parts or software that you are an expert in. They also have sales offices in different regions. I stay in touch with both the Los Angeles and the Orange County Offices of people that represent or sell Intel, Motorola, Texas Instrument, and Altera parts in particular. That's the field I'm in. They have given me many leads for companies starting new projects.

There are also software leads, in addition to parts leads. Orcad, Viewlogic, Pspice, Maxplus II, and Quartus, for example, are tools that I use in hardware design everyday. I've used some of these tools for more than 15 years. The companies that sell them know of me. The reps tell me who is using these tools and where they are. They are a great source for information like this.

Step 21.8: Email Some Contacts And Ask What Tools Are Being Used At Some Of Their Client's Companies.

Mass Mailings

This is an older technique that is claimed not to work too good. It did for me, so I thought I would share it. I looked up 200 names of electronic companies, on the net, from one of the Yellow Pages, and imported the data into a database I created. These were all companies in my local telephone area codes. I then used the mail-merge feature of Microsoft Word and printed out mailing labels for envelopes. I stuffed my resume into those envelopes and mailed them out. I received 4 jobs from this. Three of the four jobs were not from the people that I actually mailed my resume to! Instead, they were handed off, from that person to another! Isn't that a coinkydink? For example, one of the four jobs, lead to work at a company in a different county, who was the brother of the party I mailed it to. Companies like knowing there is Consultants available in their local area code. I claim mailings do work, although it took about 20 hours worth of work and $200 of materials to do it.

> **Step 21.9: Mail Your Resume To One Hundred Local Companies That Might Need Your Help.**

Attend Job Fairs

Job Fairs are starting to become popular. Make the time to drop in on these Human Resource (HR) people and introduce yourself. Usually they are accompanied by hiring managers and directors. Make sure to get business cards and email addresses from both the HR and the hiring manager. Put the websites and emails of these contacts into your database.

Go to Job Fairs whenever they come to town. Go to Job Fairs whether you are working or not. Job Fairs do not occur that frequently.

If you are unemployed, you will find that the last Job Fair was one week before you were laid off.

You can look up upcoming Job Fairs in the newspapers that are on the web, in your local area. Local to me are the LA Times site at *www.careerpath.com* and the Orange County Register at *www.ocregister.com*. The classified section in Yahoo also has Job Fair announcements. These ads then link to the website of the Job Fair promoters. There you can usually get a list of the companies that will be at the Job Fair. Once you have the company names, you can try to find their websites and see what kind of job openings they currently have. You can target specific companies looking for people with your skills, this way. Then, you will at least end up with a list of local companies that use people of your particular skills!

To quote a Consultant that commented on the Internet, "Don't come clean with the HR pukes. Only give wind to the project managers that accompany them." You can tell from this that HR people are sometimes viewed as barriers to consulting, can't you?

Step 21.10: Attend The Next Job Fair And Pass Out Your Blurb Sheet.

Apply For All Captive Jobs On The Internet

There are many Job Search Engines on the Internet as we have already mentioned. However, most of the jobs that come up are openings for captive employees. We covered this technique before in an earlier chapter: Play the old bait and switch. Apply for all captive job openings, but make sure your resume says you are a Contractor in the title. Sometime in the future, these potential clients may call you. Resumes can be easily emailed to potential clients. After several days of emailing, several hundred companies, in your area, will have your resume. Some will call you and ask if you want full-time work. Ask them if they have ever used Consultants. If they have, keep their email address in a special database for future reference. Meanwhile, if they can't find anyone, they'll eventually call you.

> **Step 21.11: Apply For Captive Jobs On The Internet Using A Contractor Resume.**

Apply For Old Agency Jobs On The Net

Occasionally, a Job Agency will have a job listed for months or even years. It is not good to trick them into telling you where the job is located. You may someday need their help again. So, go ahead and apply for the job through them. They will ask you your rate, and as a Consultant, it will be too high for the job opening. Tell them that you may go lower if it is the right opportunity. Your resume will get submitted. Perhaps this client is fed-up with waiting and will pay whatever you both want.

Some client companies will only hire through an agency. What if they want to hire you through the agency and pay you your normal rate? Well, that's fine. On a 1099, or Corp-to-Corp basis, you will still be Contracting.

Deja Voodoo

Many times, a potential client will not be thinking about hiring a Consultant. He will be sitting at his desk when this resume pops up, out of the clear blue sky. "Who is this person and how did he get my name and email address?" he will think. Again, the first 20 seconds of your resume are very important. Then it hits him, "Oh, a Hardware Engineer looking for work (or whatever your title is)," he thinks to himself.

"That's right, just the other day I was thinking about how I was going to accomplish that new project." In this case, you have created your own opening, somewhat by accident. You have reminded the client of something that they forgot to plan for. To them, it appears that you have read their mind. You appear to have precognition, or Déjà Vu. This occurs quite frequently. It seems to happen more often than you would think. Unbeknownst to the client, however, you just happened to get your resume to him, at that time, by pure accident. Just get your resume onto several managers' desks and one of them will think of a way to use your talents. So, Déjà vu → Do.

Helping Others Find You

Now you should be able to find your own work, if need be. It takes a tremendous amount of work to find your own jobs. That's why investing in ways to make it easy for people to find you instead, is much wiser. The Internet is the key to this.

How Would You Find A Consultant?

First, look at it from this point of view. Ask yourself, "If I was a client, and I needed to hire a Consultant, how would I find this person?

For ease of explanation, let's choose a particular example. Let's suppose we are looking for an Engineer with experience in Visual Basic (VB) Programming and telecommunications products.

First, I would do a lot of searching on my own. I would go to the Microsoft Visual Basic website, the company that sells VB, and see if they have a Consultant's Referral Program. If not, I would then search the Internet for the words "Visual Basic" and look at some of the websites that show up. I would also look for a Visual Basic Magazine online, and see if there are any ads in the back of it for such services. I would call other contacts in the industry, other engineers and managers, sales representatives, and field application engineers (FAE's) that I've met in the past. I would search the website of the companies that sell the telecommunications parts to us. I may also call these companies directly. I would search the web for other keywords, such as Consultant, Engineer, Software, and so forth. I would also search the online Yellow Pages for Engineers in my area. I would look into Engineering organizations such as the Institute Of Electrical and Electronic Engineers (IEEE). Many professional organizations have an online consultants network, such as the IEEE's Orange County Consultant's Network. I might also contact the Visual Basic professors at the local universities. I would look at some competing company's websites, such as other companies making similar telecomm chips, and see if they have a referral program. I might read some magazine articles in trade magazines about the subject that I needed expertise in. Then, I might try to contact the author of the article and see if he knows where to find a Consultant. Luckily, many of the trade magazines are on the Internet now. Perhaps I could find an article that mentions several companies or individuals that could provide the service I need. I would also search for a Visual Basic users group, and attend one of their club meetings. After the meeting I would go up to the speakers and ask them if they knew of a good Consultant.

Simultaneously, I would ask others to help search for me. I would ask other people working on the project if they knew of anyone that could do the job. I might post job requirements (called job reqs) out on the Internet job boards, if that didn't cost too much. I might put an ad in the newspaper. If I still couldn't find my Consultant, then I would have to ask many job agencies to submit resumes, and settle on a Contractor type.

Is this how you would find a Consultant?

Being Findable

You can see from the reverse perspective above, that there are many places that a Consultant needs to be found at. Vendor's websites, industry directories, professional organizations, phone books, trade magazines, newsgroups, etc. all need to know of you and have a link pointing back to your website, containing your resume and blurb sheet. Your website must also be registered on many web-based search engines. You can tell that the Internet is changing a lot of ways people shop for goods and services. Consultants have got to keep up with this technology. They need to be "Findable" on the Internet.

To be found, a Consultant must have a portfolio on paper and an electronic portfolio on the Internet. The paper items point to the electronic items, and the electronic items point to the Consultant. Being Found is really easy these days. Just get your name all over the Internet.

Establishing A Web Presence

Having your own website is required for consulting these days. Then, the phone book, trade directory listing, articles, and registered-guru listings can point to your website. A website must have a "company" appearance to it. Websites are about $1000 to have designed. Websites cost about $20 a month to reside on a server computer. Other people maintain the server for this fee. All you do is answer email that comes in. It gives you a professional place to hang your Skill Bullet and Blurb. If you use someone else's server, then they can promote your website on some of the other websites they have put up for other customers. In addition to linking to other websites, you can sell or promote things on your website like books, industry surveys, newsletters, and so on.

Step 21.12: Hire Someone To Design Your Website.

Register Your Website

In order for your website to be locatable by the general public, it must be registered with several online search engines and directories. Before doing this however, the website must contain a "title" and a list of "metanames." These metanames are the key words used by search engines to find your site. For example, a search for FPGA will cause a hit to my website at *www.ee-consultants.com.*

There is a free service called WebsiteGarage at *www.WebSite Garage.com.* WebsiteGarage will analyze your site and suggest metanames. WebsiteGarage also has a feature called !Register-It! This feature will register your site semi-automatically with 400 search-engines and directories for about $40. After pushing the Register-It button, the process will take several hours of touching up application forms that come electronically. It begins by asking your site name, title, and a small subset of the metanames. In 4 to 6 weeks after registering the site, each search engine will read your real metanames and store them for future searches.

> **Step 21.13: Register Your Website With Search Engines.**

Link Everything To Your Website

Whenever you publish anything, such as a business card, magazine article, newsletter, book etc., it must have a link to your website. Whenever you answer a newsgroup or email, give a link to your web-site. All of these things will point back to your resume, blurb sheet, and past experiences. When other people see your capabilities, they will try to figure out a way to make use of your services.

Step 21.14: Change Your Business Cards, Resume, and Blurb To Include Your Website.

Get Registered As A Guru On Other Websites

Having just a website doesn't do much good by itself. You've got to get other companies to point their website to yours. Many of the software, component, and tool companies now are on the Internet. If you have used their products for a few years, and have made friends with their local reps, you can get registered on their website, as a guru, in that subject. The local reps may have to sponsor you to get you listed as a guru on the company website. Some companies require that you take additional courses to further qualify you as a guru. Then, anyone needing help near your location can find a link to your website by looking for guru's on their website.

For example, go to the Altera site at *http://www.altera.com/html/programs/alliances.html.* Click on Altera Consultant's Alliance Program (ACAP). Then click on ACAP Consultants. Then Click on my company Explore Electronics Inc. It says a little bit about my company and down at the bottom of the page is a link to my website. So, I am a consulting guru listed on the Altera website.

Step 21.15: Apply For Guru Status On At Least 1 Website.

Get Listed In Directories

Almost every type of industry has directories. The electronics industry has quite a few of them. My company is listed in a few of them. Most listings are free! However, these are usually only published once a year. Luckily, many are being duplicated on the Internet now. We are definitely moving towards a paperless society. Take the time to get your company listed in the directories for your field of expertise.

If you are involved with Engineering, then you must get put into the IEEE directory. It is enormous. Check it out at *www.ieeeusa.org/employment/global*. Also, there is a good survey to read at *http://www.ieeeusa.org/BUSINESS/98feesurvey.html*.

Step 21.16: Get Listed In At Least 3 Trade Directories, Today!

Get Known In The Venture Capital Community

Let's say you are interested in starting up a new product-based company. These companies require funding by venture capitalists, or angel investors. When the VC (Venture Capitalists) are given a business plan they like, they bring in certain key people to put into the management team. They usually bring in the CEO (chief executive officer) and the CFO (chief financial officer). Other Directors, which usually includes the founders of the company (or entrepreneurs), along with the CEO and CFO form what is known as the Board Of Directors. Most Board Members get about a 2% ownership of the corporation. Their value is their past success record and the industry contacts they bring to the table. What is not commonly known is that a Board Member can sit on the boards of several companies.

In addition, most startups these days have what is called a Board Of Advisors. These advisors usually form a technical or scientific knowledge pool that the company can call on to help with the planning of new projects. Advisors work on an on-call basis and usually get about 0.5% ownership of the corporation. A good book on

Startup companies is **"High Tech Start Up,"** by John L. Nesheim. Consultants make good advisors.

The VC community therefore requires many experts. Also, many other industries depend on the VC community to help them drum up new clients. Examples of these are Accounting firms, Legal Firms, Staffing Firms, and so on. So, to couple Entrepreneurs with the VC community, Venture Forums and Trade Shows are put on multiple times a year. There are also seminars taught by VC to help the entrepreneur write better business plans.

If you act interested in writing a business plan for a startup, you can get your first exposure to the VC community in your area. I paid $100 to go to my first seminar put on by LARTA (Los Angeles Regional Technology Alliance), in LA. Their site is at *www.larta.org*. The first thing you notice is that the VC presenters, the sponsors, and all of the "wannabe" Entrepreneurs are all trying to network with each other. Usually, there is a table in the back of the room where anyone can place down their Blurb Sheet or a stack of business cards. By registering early, your email and website are including with the course notes. During the session break, you can drop off your Blurb at everyone's seat. Then Schmooze. Meet people. Many of the presenters are sitting on Boards and are looking to put together new startup companies, management teams, and boards of advisors. It is not unusual for these fellows to be sitting on the Boards of multiple companies. Remember some of these people are the funding sources for huge billion dollar conglomerates such as CMGI, AMGEN, and, these days, many .COM companies (pronounced "dot com" companies). At these seminars, you will learn more about what it takes to start and run businesses, thus giving you very much more insight into the role of consulting and it's importance to business. You will also meet many more industry contacts.

To get some idea of the magnitude of the VC community in the LA area, go to the Direct Stock Market website at *www.dsm.com*. Click on

"Webcasts: Conferences and Events," and you will see a list of all of the latest VC seminars that are going on in area. You can also watch most of these seminars on your computer! Of course, then you won't be able to Schmooze, but knowledge is power.

Step 21.17: Attend The Next Venture Capital Seminar On Startup Companies.

Get Known In The University System

Universities and National Labs, such as JPL and NASA, also have to form alliances with VC's and industry to turn their research products into real products. There is a law that says if you get money from the government for research, then you must turn that new technology into a product and get it out into the public. However, it is also against the law for a university or lab to produce and sell it's own products. These two laws force alliances between VC's, Professors, Ph.D. Students, Entrepreneurs, and many support companies such as Attorney Firms. To break into this group, you have to act interested in licensing one of these new technologies from the university and start a company based on that technology. So, again, you pay your $100 go to a seminar, and drop your Blurb and Card on the back table. Then Schmooze. These alliance seminars will give you much more insight into the importance of the university to the community and how that relates to consulting.

Make sure you also visit the "Incubator" Sites on campus. These are usually tall buildings owned and run by VC's, housing many wannabe startup individuals. They usually don't have the expertise they need to define and build the prototype products that they put into their business plans.

Universities also use many business advisors to prepare business extension courses on various subjects such as Entrepreneurship,

Marketing, E-Commerce, and so forth. Becoming an advisor for one or more courses gives you exposure to the inner workings of the university system. Many university professors are consultants to the local businesses. Since they like academics more than consulting, they are happy to refer jobs your way. Being an advisor also exposes your company name to everyone that reads the course catalog.

Step 21.18: Attend The Next University Seminar On New Technology.

Local Consulting Firms Need You Too

There are usually a few consulting firms in your geographical area. These are founded by two or more consultants and then made into a standard company. They bid on jobs that are found by their industry contacts and past relations. They also advertise their services. Ironically though, most of their employees are captive employees.

Many times they will get overloaded or go into a field they don't have expertise in. So, they will require the aid of consultants. When they bid on jobs, they usually try to charge on the high end of the consulting scale. Then, when they hire a consultant to perform the work, they are able to skim some money off the top.

Going and meeting the founders of these companies is recommended. They may not have the expertise that you can bring. It is better to go meet them now so you can tell them how much you charge ahead of time. Then when they bid on contracts they can adjust their billing rate. They are usually comfortable to work for since they came from the consulting world. But be careful, they are small potatoes. If you work for them, make sure the prime-contractor, their client, is a big company.

Step 21.19: Visit 2 Local Consulting Firms And Introduce Yourself.

Secret Consulting Cliques

Local consulting firms and professional organizations are usually well connected to hidden consulting groups. These are usually older consultants that do multiple jobs out of their house. They may have belonged to some of these organizations in the past and became bored with them. However, they are always searching for more consultants to work with them. They monitor the activities of these organizations and magically find you. If you have some skill that they need, eventually they will pull you into their circle. Once you are "in", the job offers will be endless.

All Of The Above

It should be obvious by now that we need to do all of the things mentioned in this chapter. You need to be able to find your own clients and potential clients need to be able to find you. Investing in ways for them to find you is the most valuable in the long run. Get your website going as soon as possible. You can make it look pretty later.

Here are some more big ideas that can be used to further promote your new business.

Do Multiple Jobs At Once

It is important to pursue employment at multiple places at the same time, at least part of the year. One technique is to get a 40-hour a week consulting job with a large conglomerate. Then, get a 20-hour a week assignment from a smaller firm. That way you are getting a tremendous exposure, and you have a backup in case one of the two companies hiccups. This technique works even better if the second job is through a consulting firm. Eventually, you will meet many other consultants that need you a few hours here and there. Multiple jobs lead to multiple contacts, quicker.

Promote Yourself Through The Media

Getting quoted in the local media is a good way to get your reputation out there in the eyes of the masses. Reece Franklin's book called **"Consultant's Guide To Publicity,"** is the best book on this subject. It comes complete with Press Kits and Media Lists. Reece is an expert in promoting to all areas of media. This is a "must-read" for anyone wishing to really promote his or her consulting business.

Promote Yourself Through Publishing

Consultants must also appear as Pro's on paper. You can start by publishing your own Email-Newsletter about what you and your mercenary friends are working on. Send it to all of your other friends and past clients. Force your consulting and Contracting friends, and past clients, to get to know each other, if not in person, at least on paper. Don't forget to contribute some positive excitement and humor to your industry.

Publishing a book on the latest tools of the trade has also reached a new plateau thanks to the Internet. Look at the site *www.iUniverse.com.* Click on "New Authors." For a small fee, these people turn your WORD document into a hardcopy book and an ebook in a few months! They will design the front and back cover and, best of all, register it with all of the online bookstores! It used to take years to get a book published. Agents and Publishers rejected this book for two years. Luckily iUniverse came into existence. Write about something simple. Most people try to write about subjects that are too large. Make sure your book or article has copious links to your website and email address.

Continuously Keep Networking

Consultants must network, continuously. That is the most important part of consulting! Schedule a time so that every week at that time, you can network. About two hours a week is a good amount of time to spend. Call your contacts and go to lunch, mainly. Spend at least 2 hours a week calling and emailing for work in that situation. Remember, you are getting paid the 30% to 50% extra, the amount an agency would have charged, for finding work on your own. This is how you earn that extra money. If you get too many jobs, hire your friends and contacts to help you.

If the company you are working for, starts complaining about how much you charge, or the hours you are reporting, or that your invoicing is irregular, then change from networking to job searching. The company may be experiencing new financial or political problems.

Keep Your "Toolbox" Up To Date

New opportunities can arise based partially on luck and partially on skill. The skill part we can take care of by constantly learning new things in our field, before a client needs that skill. Having these up-to-date skills is referred to as "having your tool-box ready." Then, it's just a matter of time before an opportunity comes along where that new skill will be required.

Consultant's can actually find work by taking classes and going to seminars on the latest techniques and tools. Some of the teachers for these courses have captive jobs during the day. They may need Consultants. The people taking the courses with you, obviously, are also going to use these new skills, at their companies. Find out where they work.

The main thing is to keep moving around, stay active, go to unusual seminars, keep learning, read strange books, keep collecting names, attend club meetings, keep schmoozing, and keep networking.

You can stumble across new jobs and managers' names everywhere. Have your notepad ready to write down names, have handfuls of business cards ready to give out, and have your tool box ready full of the latest skills. Then, when a new opportunity comes, you will be able to recognize it and grab it.

Many Other Ways

Don't forget to read the other masterpieces on ways to find consulting work. With the Internet, the techniques are evolving rapidly, but the old fashioned ways still work too. You are now finally able to comprehend what the heck all of those other books on consulting are talking about. Their story begins right about here.

The Advanced Techniques used in finding consulting work are listed meticulously in these other books. For example, you could write a newsletter about your industry and email it to a chosen sector of the market. Write magazine articles and get them published in a trade magazine. Give a seminar on some new skills you've learned. Make appearances and speeches at the local universities and trade shows.

The difficulty with these Advanced Techniques is making them exciting. Being ho-hum or negative about your industry will surely ruin a professional attitude.

Summary Of Chapter 21

Getting consulting work can happen several ways. Networking is the key to consulting. Our past clients, friends, industry contacts, and other professionals are our best sources for information leading to work. Consultants have to network regularly with professionals in their own field. This takes a lot of work, but it can be made fun.

Unfortunately, our friends and acquaintances don't do the hiring! They can only lead us to manager's names. We need to contact managers, any way we can, to get work.

We can also make it easy for managers to stumble across our name. This is usually done by way of the Internet.

The Internet is a required tool for finding jobs and for jobs to find us. Becoming a part of the Internet movement is essential to successful consulting. A Consultant's name must appear in several places on the Internet. These sites must point to the Consultant's website.

Consulting requires a professional looking website. On this website will be found the Skill Bullet Resume and Blurb Sheet. It may also include any items the consultant is selling or promoting, such as his latest newsletter or book.

A Consultant must market himself weekly. Suffering too much downtime can be avoided by doing so. Downtime can be enjoyable, but it also subtracts money from the Dream Rate Goal. Marketing your skills at least two hours a week is important for limiting downtime losses.

The number of ways for getting consulting work is unlimited. It is essential to keep studying the subject to see how others are doing it. It is continuously evolving. Keep your toolbox up-to-date. Read other books on consulting.

Remember above all, "Knowledge Is Power."

Step21.20: Enjoy Your New, Self-Made Title: *Consultant*

May you be blessed with the peace that comes from not being tied down to working for one company. May you achieve self-satisfaction from being self-employed. Take care of yourselves so you can live long enough to enjoy your hard work. Take the time to be happy and enjoy life with your families.

If any of this did any good please send me an email. I look forward to hearing from you.

Good Luck to you, in all of your noble endeavors.

So long for now,

     Jimmy Moore
     Electronic Engineering Consultant
     Explore Electronics Inc.
     www.ee-consultants.com
     info@ee-consultants.com

Appendix A:
Recommended Reading

"**The Consultants Guide To Publicity**," by Reece A. Franklin.

"**Imagineering—How To Profit From Your Creative Powers**," by Michael Le Beouf.

"**The Seven Spiritual Laws Of Success**," by Deepak Chopra.

"**How To Become A Successful Consultant In Your Own Field**," by Hubert Bermont.

"**How To Succeed As An Independent Consultant**," by Herman Holtz.

"**The Computer Consultant's Guide**," by Janet Ruhl.

"**The Secrets Of Consulting**," by Gerald M. Weinberg.

"**Computer Money**," by Alan N. Canton.

"**How To Manage Your Boss**," by Christopher Hegarty.

"**Directory of Contract Service Firms**," by Contract Engineering Weekly.

"**High Tech Start Up**," by John L. Nesheim.

"**Think And Grow Rich**," by Napoleon Hill.

"**The Power Of Positive Thinking**," by Norman Vincent Peale

"The Complete Idiot's Guide To Making Money In Freelancing," by Christy Heady and Janet Bernstel.

"Consulting For Dummies," by Bob Nelson and Peter Economy.

"Contract Professional, The Magazine For IT Contractors And Consultants," by Skinner-James Publishing (800) 297-6932.

"BLUR—The Speed Of Change In The Connected Economy," by Stan Davis and Christopher Meyer.

Appendix B:
General Self-Advancement

By consulting, we get a chance to reach a much higher potential, than most people do. But, we need to be able to keep improving ourselves, first. This chapter is about subjects that are not necessarily related to consulting, alone. It is a chapter of some unique things that can make a person better. Some of these items were learned by experience and upbringing. Some were learned out of books. Recognizing the fullest of potentials, and turning them into reality requires the mastering of several topics. Here are some of my favorite topics that can help you towards self-advancement.

Creative Problem Solving

Using your imagination to solve problems is a definite skill needed in consulting. Our brains are capable of visualizing problems and their solutions much faster than working with words and equations. The best book on this subject is **"Imagineering—How To Profit From Your Creative Powers,"** by Michael Le Beouf. We have discussed Michael's treatment of "Fear Of The Unknown" in an earlier chapter. Being able to get new ideas by recombining old ones and visualizing them is very useful.

Effective Time Management

Managing time is one of the greatest challenges facing successful people. It is based on the principle that **there is not enough time to do everything that you want to do.** The first step is to set some goals for yourself. Then, based on importance, we can choose what to do, as well as, what not to do. This is accomplished by making lists of things to do, and then ranking them in order of importance. We work on the most important ones first. If one of the important ones takes more than one day, we cut the task up and spread it out over several days. Everyday, we must update our to-do list. We can reach long term goals, as well as, short term goals using this technique.

Variety Time Management

The brain thrives on variety. After setting your goals for one day, it is not good to work on your to-do list one task at a time, until each item is complete. I have found that working on each task for about a half an hour, putting it aside, and then rotating to the next task for a while, works much better. It eliminates fatigue and boredom. Try it for a day. Usually you will find that all of the tasks are completed earlier this way. Note that it does take a very large desk to hold all of these partially finished tasks.

Speed Learning

Consultants (and everyone else) should learn something new everyday. This is done by reading part of a new book and all the usual trade magazines, daily. A special time must be set aside, every-day, for reading and studying. Do the reading at the desk so you can take notes in a notebook.

Some time*there is not enough time to read everything you want to read.* So, choose carefully what to read, as well as, what not to read.

The Speed Learning course has the following procedure for speed-reading. Prioritize your reading by making a list, and a schedule, of the things you are going to read. Before reading, ask yourself what you are looking for. Rank that question as a Who, What, When, Where, How, or Why, type of question. If an answer to a Who, What, When, or Where question is sought, then skimming the text will be sufficient. For the answer to a How or Why question, reading every word may be necessary. Before reading anything, make sure you really, really need the answer to that question.

Stay Well Rounded

Learn about things you are interested in. Don't just concentrate on your field of expertise. Someday that field might not be important anymore. Stay well informed about many subjects. This is really easy to do, these days, with the Internet. Spend a few hours a week cruising the Internet, reading the articles and news there. Stay well rounded but don't gain weight.

Start Writing About Something

In the life of a Consultant, writing will eventually become a necessary function. Start writing little paragraphs in a goof-off-sort-of-a notebook. Write about your industry. Write about your life. Write about your spouse and children. Write about anything you want. Keep practicing your writing. Try to make the writing humorous. Put a date on each thing that you write about.

Practice Predicting The Future

As already mentioned in the text, an amazing feat of consultants is the ability to predict the outcome of a project. Practice predicting the outcome of everything. Predict if the NASDAQ will go up or down tomorrow. Predict who will win the Monday Night Football. Predict presidential elections. Predict the outcome of the new recipe you are going to try on your spouse. Predict what your teenager will say when you lay down new rules. Predict what your boss will ask you tomorrow. Try to make at least one prediction a day. Write the predictions down. Assign dates to when those predictions will come true. Measure the results. See if you were right. Leave a space underneath each prediction to write down the results, and why the results were different than expected. You'll be surprised at how handy this talent will become. I would not tell others your predictions until you are good at it.

Make Better Decisions

To make better decisions, we can tap into the universal knowledge used by every cell in our body. Each cell in us is in tune with the universe, or all-knowledge, or God. Because of this, each cell knows its purpose in the universe. For example, every cell in our body knows how to heal itself, if left alone. So too, the whole body is in tune with all-knowledge. Here is a technique from Depak Choprah's Book called, **"The Seven Spiritual Laws Of Success."** First, meditate and relax. Then ask yourself a question requiring a Yes/No Decision. Usually these questions start with the phrase, "Should I..." In about 10 to 20 seconds, you should get a sensation in your stomach or heart area. If you get a bad feeling in that area, then the answer from the universe is a definite "No."

Balancing The Mind, Body, And Soul

Most people believe that the Self is made of three equally important pieces: the mind, the body, and the soul. Neglecting any of the three causes an imbalance in the Self that leads to weaknesses. The most important of these, and frequently the most neglected, is the soul.

Caring For The Mind

The mind is very real to us, during the day. It brings in all of our senses and feelings and learning's and combines them into a thought or an action. It is also a fact that the mind is three-fourths water. So is the earth. To care for the mind, the body must supply it with large amounts of water. Drinking large amounts of water, especially when first waking up in the morning is very beneficial to both the mind and the body. Water can be more powerful than coffee for waking up.

Meditating

At night, or during meditation, it is now believed that the mind becomes a link to the source of all—knowledge in the universe (frequently referred to as God). Our "subconscious mind" is all knowing because it is connected directly to this universal knowledge. Therefore tapping into the subconscious mind allows us to solve problems and make better decisions, throughout life.

In order to "hear" the subconscious mind, we must shut off all of our senses and thought processes. The technique to do this is called meditating. Meditating allows our subconscious thoughts to spill over into our conscious thoughts, and therefore become reality. Meditating can completely change your life, in one day.

Meditation involves deep breathing, sitting on the ground, relaxing, and closing the eyes. If possible, it should be done in a natural setting, outdoors, in the backyard or at a park. Meditation should be done twice a day for 15 minutes.

To enhance the effectiveness of meditation, the breathing technique used in Yoga is recommended. It is called pranayama. Here is the basic procedure:

1. Exhale slowly, by pulling your chest in then pulling your stomach in.
2. Pause for a few seconds.
3. Inhale slowly, by pulling out your stomach and then expanding your chest.
4. Pause for a few seconds.
5. Repeat steps for 15 minutes.

In about 10 of these breaths, you should start feeling an euphoric feeling as the oxygen rushes into your bloodstream. Make sure you are sitting on the ground when you do this. Visualize all of your thoughts and pains draining out into the earth. Hear only your breathing. Eventually, the sound of the breathing will vanish into the background and a connection to universal knowledge and energy will result.

Caring For The Body

The mind can kill the body by forcing it to get high, get a buzz, or get loaded. Alcohol, drugs and other things, destroys the blood purity and chemical balances in the body. The body in turn retaliates and destroys the mind. The connection to the universal knowledge is numbed. Memory and eyesight are among the second things to go. Healthy blood is essential to a good mind-body-soul balance. The liver must be healthy at all times to keep the blood free of toxins.

Take Herbs, Vitamins, And Minerals

Herbs and vitamins can be helpful for improving the body and mind. Here is a partial list of some popular ones.

> **Warning: Consult your physician before trying any of these Herbs and Vitamins. Don't take herbs if you have a heart condition or are taking any medication on a regular basis, without permission.**

- Gotu Kola and Ginko Biola can accelerate the brain and thinking processes.
- Yarrow Flowers is a very strong "thought clearing" agent.
- Skullcap makes the mind more relaxed and tuned into happiness.
- Vitamin B12 is called, "the vitamin that keeps the mind young." It greatly improves the memory.
- A Multiple-Vitamin-With-Minerals should be taken everyday. It is required for concentration. If you can't keep your attention on your work, or read a whole chapter in a book without becoming tired, then you need a multiple vitamin, daily (and maybe a better book).
- Lecithin increases the ability to learn and should be taken regularly by all students.
- Dandelion Root is a very powerful blood purifier. It can instantly improve the body and mind's health and energy level.
- Vitamin B1 is great for physical vitality as it aids in food digestion and increases metabolism.
- Vitamin E or Raw Wheat Germ Oil can greatly improve the energy level.

There are many other Herbs that are very powerful and good for you. They can be easily researched on the Internet and even purchased there.

Exercise Regularly

Exercise is ultimately the most important thing for body health. As we get older, most of the muscles in the body will turn to fat! We have to stop this ahead of time by making our muscles move weights. The weights can be your own weight or artificial weights.

New blood is formed in our bone marrow. My theory is that we have to rattle our bones, once in a while, to get the chemicals mixed up.

All this jumping and running can cause our organs to pack down inside of our body. According to Yoga theory, this packing down of the organs causes them to decay on one side. To combat this gravity caused problem, we have to stand on our head or hang upside down, once in a while. This can be very stressful on the neck, if the right equipment isn't used. Laying upside down on the stairway works somewhat. Don't break your neck.

We need to exercise twice a day. Once to strengthen our muscles and once to move around. Walks are found to be just as good as running. One amazing benefit of regular exercise is that it causes time to slow down. Living in the here and now, can be improved by exercising. Many times the working class will be asking themselves, "Where did my summer go?" They worked overtime all summer and time flew by. Not when exercising regularly. You will feel more alive everyday! You will be more aware and observant. Your brain will function much better. Time will progress more normally.

Vegetarianism

My wife and I have been Vegetarians since 1978. Our daughter has been one all of her life, and she is perfectly healthy. The reason I decided to became one, was because I found out that I only needed 5.5 hours of sleep a day, instead of 8 hours! My life is much more full because of that. About 70% of the world population is pretty much vegetarian because they can't afford meat. Try it out for a few days. I couldn't imagine being able to fit in meditation, exercise, praying, learning new things, predicting, writing daily, and working 10 hours a day, in the time left over after 8 hours of sleep. There are other arguments in favor of vegetarianism. I cannot go into all of them right now.

Start reading about it. The whole world is starting to take a serious look at this. Wow, do we enjoy being unique!

Caring For The Soul

The soul is our spiritual body. It is the part of us that lives on after we physically die. Having a soul makes us a descendent of the Creator or what most of us in the United States call God or the Supreme Being. Others religions may have a similar term. Not believing in the Supreme Being or the concept of "soul" will cause a great confusion in your life. It is this belief that gives our lives a fundamental purpose, more important than all other purposes. In order to tap into the infinite potential of the universe, we must acknowledge the Supreme Being's existence and the existence of life after death, through the soul. Believe in infinite potential energy. Get some religion. Take care of your soul. By the way, if you still cannot believe in a Supreme Being, I dare to you to ask for proof of His existence. P.S. Make sure I'm not around.

Prayer

Prayer can improve practically everything. Prayer is one of the most powerful concepts in the universe! Prayer comes in two basic varieties. First, there is the act of being grateful to the Supreme Being, for the universe and all that it has provided to you. Second, prayer is used for asking for things that you really need such as guidance, forgiveness, or even a downright miracle. That's something that frequently occurs while consulting! Praying is really powerful when combined with meditation, and a balanced body and mind.

In his book, "**The Power Of Positive Thinking**," by Norman Vincent Peale, prayer is used in powerful ways. His book is based on the Bible and I encourage you to give it a chance. One interesting point that Norman makes is that prayers are answered at the best time. "The universal pace is slow and methodical, but unstoppable," he points out. We must be patient when waiting for our prayers to be answered. It may take days, weeks, or even months. When a prayer is answered, it will be more profound than you ever would have imagined. Norman also says, "When you pray, Pray Big and Powerful Prayers." Most people don't pray for big enough things to happen! He also encourages us to "Trust in the Goodness of God." Put aside the notion that we are only supposed to fear the power of the Almighty. All the animals and plants live on the pure trust in God's goodness. They rely on Him to provide food, water, safety, and companionship, on a daily basis. They seem to be doing well.

Karma

Karma is said to be a fundamental cycle in the universe. If you do good things, then good things will come back to you. If you do bad things then bad things will also happen to you. What goes around will come around. Do good things daily. Plan them before you begin your daily routine.

Forgiveness

Forgiveness is a realization of good Karma. Being able to forgive those who have hurt you, is the best virtue of all! If you forgive, then you will be returned forgiveness.

Humbleness

Remaining mellow, at all costs, is one of the most powerful concepts in the universe. It is a form of forgiveness ahead of time. Christ, Buddha, and many other important philosophers and leaders, throughout all time teach Humbleness.

As mentioned before, Humbleness is so important for success in all things. Don't get involved in clashing your knowledge against other people's knowledge, especially other hired guns (i.e. consultants). It doesn't do any good. You may be right, but then the client will have been proved wrong. So, you're fired anyway. Stay Humble.

Tribal Connections

Tribal energy can be experienced when you are with your family. It is stronger if all of your relatives live close by, too. As we grow older, we need to stay near the tribe and get together with them. Whether or not your relatives know what you do for a living, moving away can be a great disconnection of life's natural resources and energy. In fact, get your relatives jobs at all of the places you consult for, while you are at it! Think long and hard before moving away from your tribe.

Consulting is also an industrial tribal experience. Making and keeping connections in one geographical area greatly enhances your networking power. Consulting is all about networking. After working at many companies and networking with many friends in the area, a very large tribe will develop. Think long and hard before moving away from all of the contacts you've made while consulting.

Being Happy

I have never seen anyone make money, or accomplish anything major, without being happy first. The Consultant must be the happiest of all! They are hired because of their positive good-natured attitude. Positive thinking and staying upbeat when faced with new challenges insures prosperity. If you are on a sinking ship, make sure everyone that is sinking with you is, at least, trying to stay happy. People that are not happy don't make money for long. Realizing why we were all put here on earth, and thinking about it throughout the day, usually gives me a happy feeling. Getting higher pay and having several other jobs to fall back on also makes me happy!

What's left after Consulting?

So, you've been a top notch Consultant in your field for several years. Maybe, you feel that you have to work too hard, to keep up. Maybe, you have reached a plateau in your hourly wage. Maybe, you don't feel as happy as you used to. Well, what should you do?

Consulting is the best way to become an expert in your field. If your field is no longer fun for you, change fields! Keep learning new things. Consulting has made you some money. Now it's time to take and see what else would be fun, to do!

Trading

Oh, by the way, did anyone ever tell you that consulting is not nesscessarily the best way to make a lot of money? Making money trading stocks or commodities, for example, could be a much better way. For one thing, you can do it from home. You work only a few hours a day, Monday through Friday. You get holidays and weekends off. In California time, the stock market opens at 6:30 a.m. and is closed by 1:15 p.m. You could be playing golf by 1:30 p.m. That's 7 hours a day, max. While trading, you are reaping the rewards of other peoples' hard work.

Trading Commodities could be even more financially rewarding than trading stocks. It's about trading food, metal, oil, currencies, etc. These are more necessary for life than stocks. Learn about it. It's not for everyone. Now that you have some extra money saved up, they will let you trade!

Entrepreneurs & Inventors

Entrepreneurship is even more fun than consulting. Americans, in particular, will go out of their way to help an entrepreneur start a new business or an inventor work on a new gismo. We all want to be an inventor or a business owner! Starting up new companies is a great enjoyment for people that already have enough money to live on. It takes a lot of knowledge, as well. After running a consulting business for a few years, you will be well prepared to handle other businesses. Be a new business starter-up-er!

Venture capitalists have millions of dollars to invest in your startup ideas. Right now 80% of all new startups are websites! The main geographical area for website startups is in Southern California. Called the Tech Coast West, the area will be bigger than Silicon Valley in 5 years.

How do you get millions from Venture Capitalists and other Angel millionaires to start your own company? There is only one way. You must write a business plan. To find out how to write the best business plan, you go to courses put on by organizations like LARTA found at *www.larta.org*. In these courses, the VC's are your teachers. They tell you step by step what they expect to see in the plan. Simple Isn't it? If you need a technical advisor, look me up.

Final Thoughts

There are many things that we can do to become a better person. First, we need to take care of our mind, body and soul. To begin with, we should exercise twice a day. We should also take vitamins and herbs, and drink a lot of water. We need to meditate twice a day, preferably outdoors. This will help us reach higher goals without wasting a lot of time. We also need to thank the Supreme Being for all we have gained and ask for all that we will be needing.

During our daily execution of our jobs, we need to apply creative problem solving techniques to visualize solutions. We need to have our goals set and effectively manage our time in reaching them. We realize there isn't enough time to read and learn everything. So choosing carefully what to study is necessary, too. To eliminate boredom, we can work towards our goals in little half-hour pieces.

A consulting career leads to a better lifestyle, than a captive one would. It empowers us to think and act more freely. Yet, we still have to be humble and get along with others. Since our skill level is much higher, others less knowledgeable will be making larger mistakes and hurting our feelings. We have to be good at forgiving others, more so than most.

Consulting ties us to a larger tribe than our natural tribe. When both are located in the local area, a great tribal power and networking influence can be realized. Staying near this tribe can greatly improve the quality of our lives.

Consulting allows us to make more money than a captive job. In our later years, because of this money, we should be able to pursue other avenues of interest. A freelance usually has a more noble cause to work towards. Investing and Entrepreneuring are two interesting avenues to think about.

Most of all, we need to be happy. None of the principles in this book, or any other book, will work if we are not happy. Consciously try to remain happy at all times. Being happy at a job site is usually far more important than the actual progress of the project.

This is just the beginning of the ways to improve yourself. Keep researching these subjects for they will bring great rewards and a better life. I hope this helped you get started.

Take Care, and don't forget to write if you discover something interesting. Have Fun!

Jimmy